SUFFOLK DOWNS

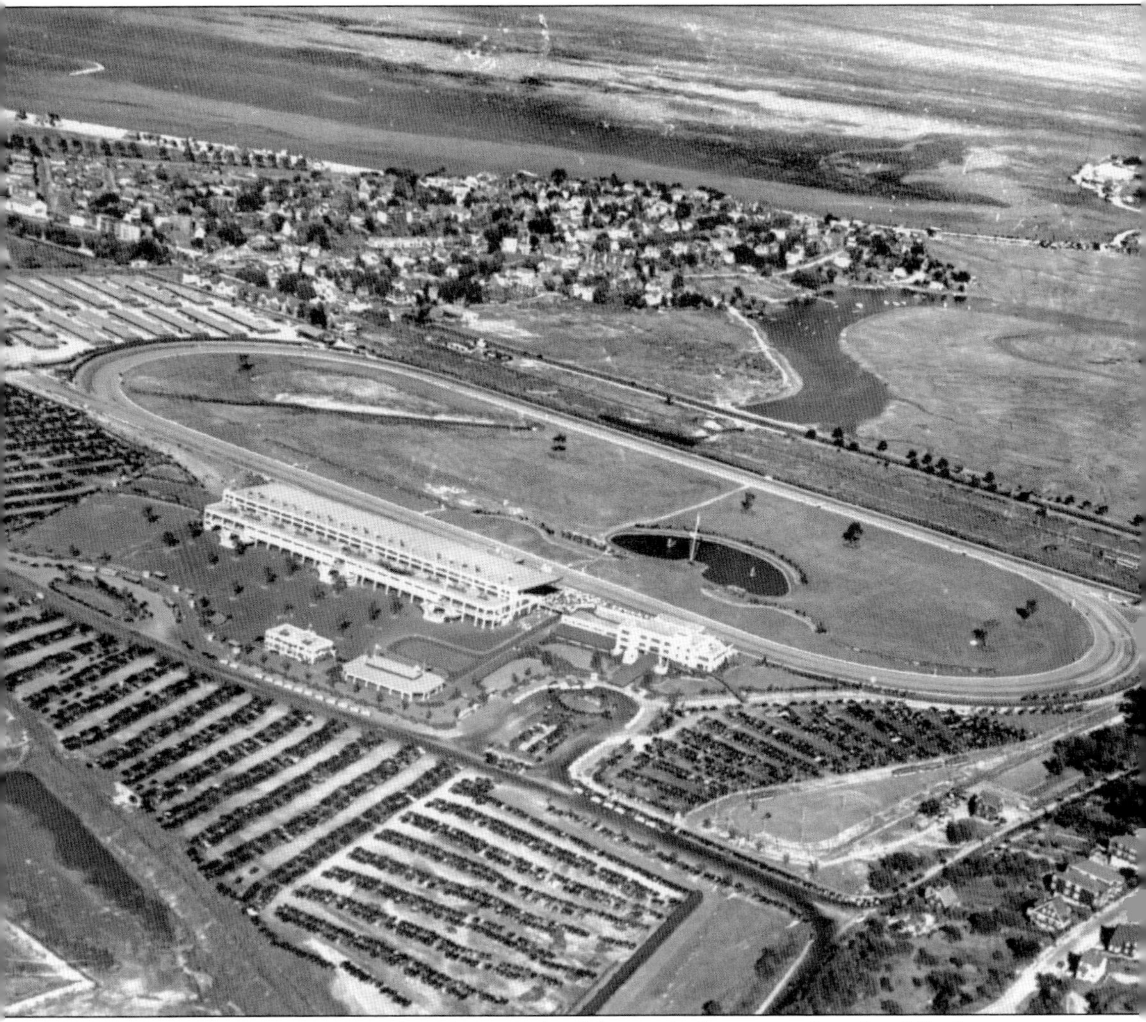

An Aerial View, 1939. This photograph of the track shows a parking lot full of cars on a day of racing in 1939. The track boasted a daily average attendance of 13,767 for the 60-day meet that year, the track's fifth in existence. (Aero Scenic Airviews of Boston photograph, courtesy Boston Public Library Print Department.)

SUFFOLK DOWNS

Christian Teja

ARCADIA
PUBLISHING

ISBN 978-0-7385-3820-4

Published by Arcadia Publishing
Charleston, South Carolina

Printed in the United States of America

Library of Congress Catalog Card Number: 2005923151

For all general information contact Arcadia Publishing at:
Telephone 843-853-2070
Fax 843-853-0044
E-mail sales@arcadiapublishing.com
For customer service and orders:
Toll-Free 1-888-313-2665

Visit us on the Internet at www.arcadiapublishing.com

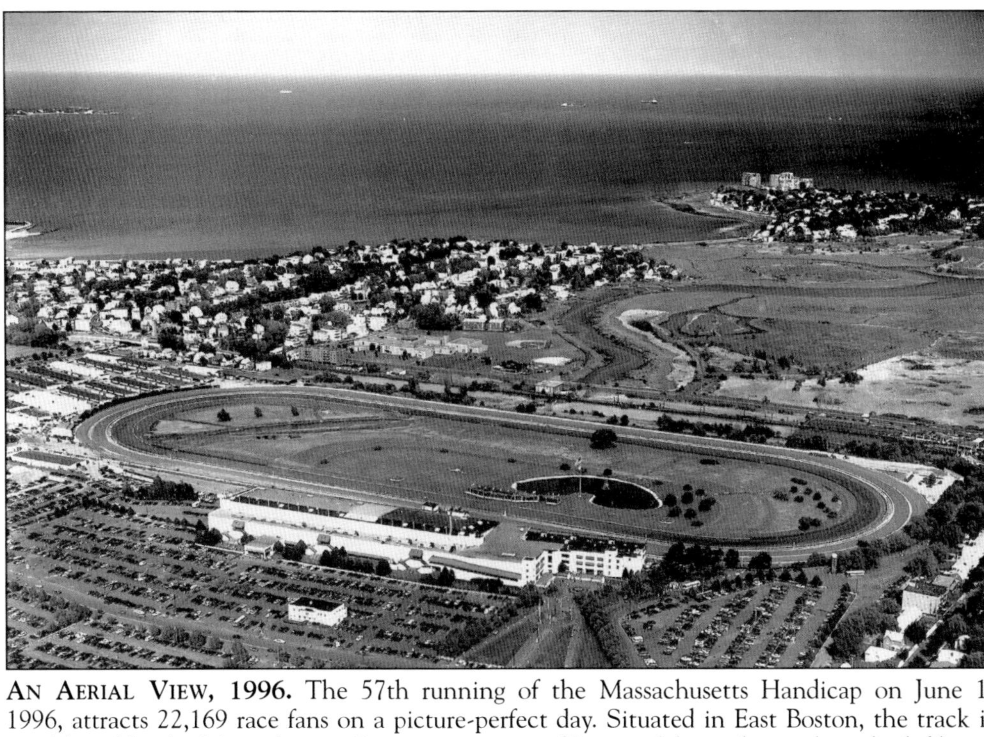

AN AERIAL VIEW, 1996. The 57th running of the Massachusetts Handicap on June 1, 1996, attracts 22,169 race fans on a picture-perfect day. Situated in East Boston, the track is neighbored by the Massachusetts Bay communities of Revere (above the track to the left) and Winthrop (above right). (Aerial Photos International photograph.)

Contents

ACKNOWLEDGMENTS

A project of this scope would not be possible without the help of so many others. I would first like to thank all of my predecessors in the Suffolk Downs publicity office for leaving behind a wealth of resources. They include T. D. Thornton, Chip Tuttle, Fred Conover, Bob Raymond, George Sullivan, Bob Varey, and Nick Del Ninno. Thanks also go to current publicity staff members Jim Bishop, Larry Collmus, and Pat Lamberty.

The images in this book represent the work of many individuals. Tremendous thanks go to current track photographer Chip Bott, former track photographers Bill Denver (of Equi-Photo) and Henry Carfagna, and others who could not be identified.

Special thanks go to Aaron Schmidt of the Boston Public Library Print Department for providing a wealth of images from the track's early years, as well as to John Cronin and Alan Thibeault of the *Boston Herald* for allowing access to their vast library of photographs. Additional images were provided by the Leslie Jones Collection, JoEllen Coen, Bud Morton, Steve Pini, and John Ramsey.

Certain historical facts were gathered from newspapers archived at the Boston Public Library, including the *Boston Globe*, *Boston Herald*, and *Boston Post*. Thanks go to *Daily Racing Form* and Equibase for their racing statistics.

Special thanks go to Richard Johnson of the Sports Museum of New England for his guidance and to Suffolk Downs chief operating officer Bob O'Malley for giving me this opportunity.

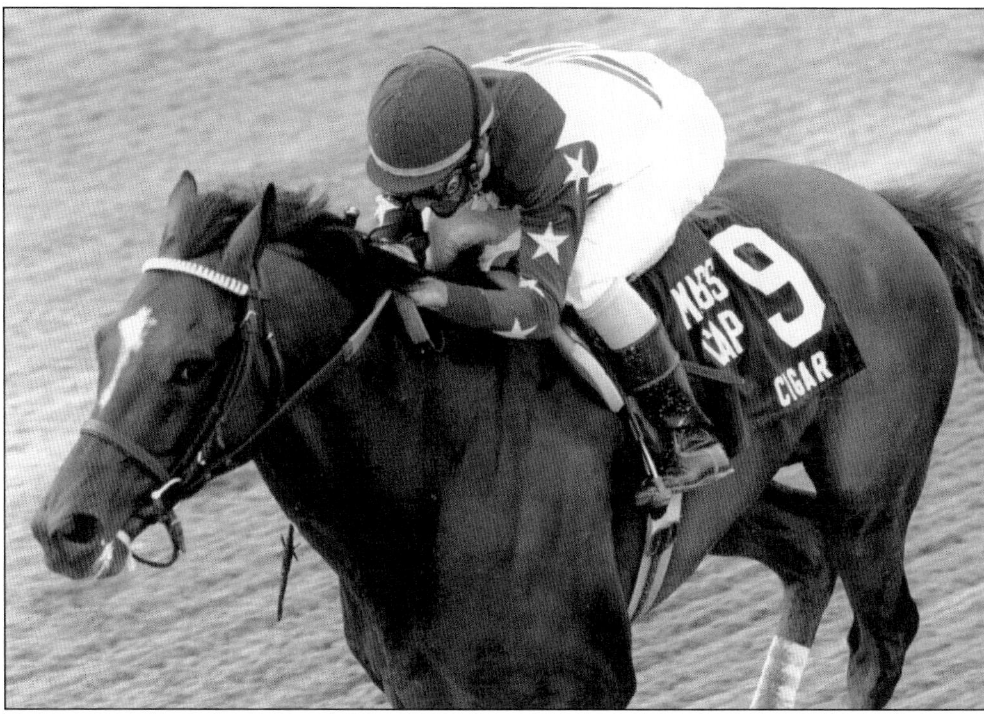

CIGAR. Two-time Horse of the Year Cigar wins the first of his two consecutive MassCaps on June 3, 1995. Jerry Bailey rides Cigar for owner Allen Paulson and trainer William Mott. (Equi-Photo photograph.)

INTRODUCTION

When the Commonwealth of Massachusetts created the State Racing Commission in 1934 and legalized pari-mutuel wagering, the Eastern Racing Association wasted no time constructing the state's first Thoroughbred racetrack, which it named Suffolk Downs. Among the directors of the Eastern Racing Association were Charles F. Adams, founder and president of the Boston Bruins, and his son Weston, who would later succeed his father as team president.

The group secured roughly 200 acres of mud flats in East Boston and Revere and contracted A. G. Tomasello & Son to transform the property into one of the finest racing facilities in the country. Leading the project was Joseph Tomasello, who employed over 3,000 laborers, including 900 carpenters, 200 electricians and plumbers, and 100 plasterers. They were assisted by 638 trucks, 36 bulldozers, and 24 power shovels.

The project was completed in an amazing 62 days at the cost of approximately $2 million. The nation's first concrete grandstand seated 16,000, making it the biggest grandstand in the country. The clubhouse accommodated 5,000 and was reported to be the largest in the world. The grandstand and clubhouse were separated by an area that included a path from the paddock to the track. The original paddock was located on the entrance side of the grandstand.

On July 10, 1935, the track opened its doors, and over 35,000 people walked through them to watch and wager on the eight-race program. Thoroughbred racing in Massachusetts had arrived.

Later in its inaugural year, the track began its greatest tradition, the Massachusetts Handicap. Boasting substantial purse money, the MassCap immediately attracted some of racing's biggest names. Hall of fame jockey George Woolf rode Top Row to victory in the first MassCap. In 1937, the track welcomed the legendary Seabiscuit for the third running of the MassCap. Seabiscuit and jockey Johnny "Red" Pollard did not disappoint the throng of over 40,000 that was present to see them, winning the race in record time. Over the years, the MassCap has continued to be a stage for Thoroughbred racing's top performers as the track has played host to hall of famers both equine and human.

The track immediately wove itself into the city's sporting and social fabric, attracting an average daily attendance of nearly 15,000 in its first year, a figure that peaked at 18,388 in 1945. Interest in racing was so high that the payoff of the daily double was frequently posted in large print across the very top of the front page of the *Boston Globe*. Average attendance remained in the five-figure range until the early 1970s, when the racing schedule was drastically expanded to as many as 200 days a year.

After roughly a quarter-century, the track underwent its first significant renovation in the early 1960s, when the open-air grandstand was enclosed and the appearance of the clubhouse entrance was drastically changed. The grandstand and clubhouse were joined together, and a new paddock and walking ring were constructed between the track and the grandstand.

Further changes, both cosmetic and philosophical, were realized from 1969 to 1970, when the innovative Bill Veeck served as track president. In addition to making physical improvements in the box seating area, Veeck, who is enshrined in the National Baseball Hall of Fame for his accomplishments as a pioneering baseball owner, brought his promotional genius to the racetrack, where he gained publicity with chariot races and livestock giveaways, among other things. Perhaps Veeck's most significant accomplishment during his brief reign was his successful challenge of a Massachusetts law that did not allow children to attend the track.

The track enjoyed one of its finest moments in 1987, when hometown heroes Waquoit and jockey Chris McCarron prevailed in one of the most thrilling finishes in MassCap history, defeating Broad Brush and Angel Cordero. Unfortunately, just two years later, the track suffered one of its darkest times when it closed for two years at the conclusion of the 1989 racing season.

The track was soon brought back to life, reopening in 1992 under the direction of Sterling Suffolk Racecourse, led by chairman James B. Moseley and president John Hall II. Prior to the reopening, a new round of improvements was made, including the restoration of the clubhouse façade to its original form. Just three years later, the track continued its revival, renewing the MassCap, which had not been held since 1989. The MassCap returned in grand style as champion Cigar graced the track for consecutive victories in the signature race in 1995 and 1996 on his way to a record-tying 16-race winning streak.

The track expanded its community reach in 1998, becoming the home of the Hot Dog Safari, a benefit for the Joey Fund and the Cystic Fibrosis Foundation. The end of the 20th century also saw the reintroduction of concerts at the track, a tradition that had included the final Boston appearance by the Beatles in 1966. The 21st century welcomed yet another cultural attraction to the track, the world-renowned Cirque du Soleil.

The publication of *Seabiscuit: An American Legend*, by Laura Hillenbrand, in 2001 and the subsequent release of the movie *Seabiscuit* in 2003 renewed interest in the track's rich history. In 2004, Funny Cide, the horse that many labeled a modern-day Seabiscuit for his improbable success story, thrilled an appreciative crowd with his appearance in the 64th MassCap.

Suffolk Downs has undergone many transformations over the years, but it has continuously been a place where people from all walks of life are welcome. Everyone who has walked through the turnstiles at the track has a story to tell. The images in this book tell many of these stories.

One

THE 1930S

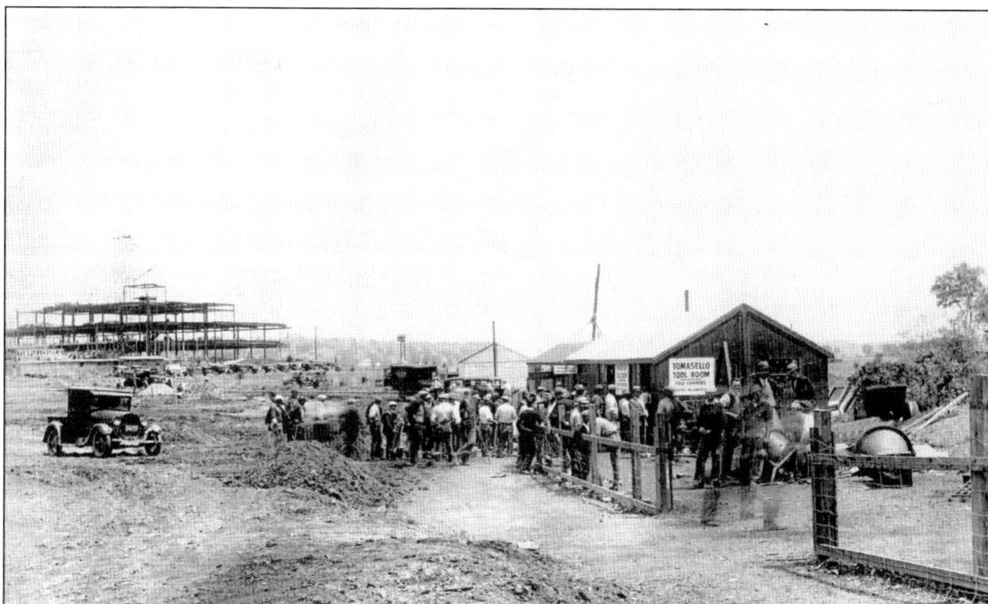

CONSTRUCTION. Over 3,000 laborers, 638 trucks, 36 bulldozers, and 24 power shovels were utilized to construct the facility, which is regarded as one of the most state-of-the-art racetracks in the country. (Courtesy Steve Pini.)

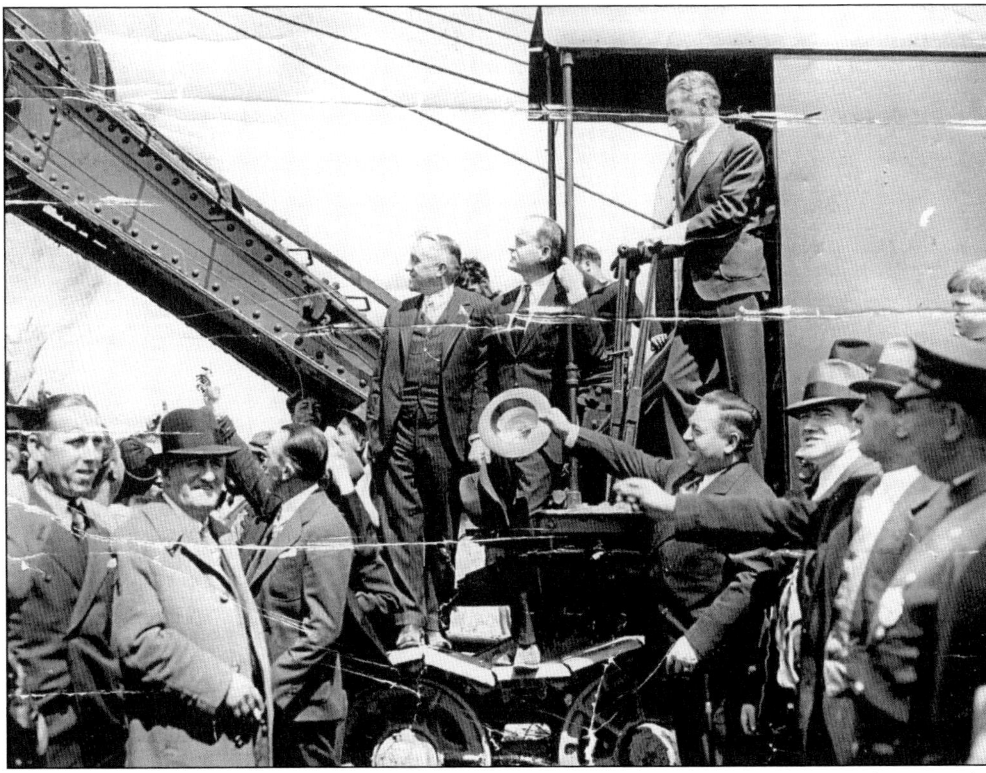

BREAKING GROUND. Upon the legalization of pari-mutuel wagering in Massachusetts, the Eastern Racing Association commissioned A. G. Tomasello & Son to construct the facility, a task that was completed in just 62 days. Unidentified track officials are shown here participating in the groundbreaking festivities. The officers of the Eastern Racing Association are president Bayard Tuckerman Jr., vice presidents Allan J. Wilson and Richard E. Danielson, treasurer C. V. Bruce Wetmore, and assistant treasurer W. H. Stevens. The directors are Charles F. Adams (founder and president of the Boston Bruins), John R. Macomber, W. J. McDonald, Joseph Tomasello, Charles F. Cotter, and Weston Adams (the son of Charles F. Adams), who would later succeed his father as Bruins president. (Courtesy Steve Pini.)

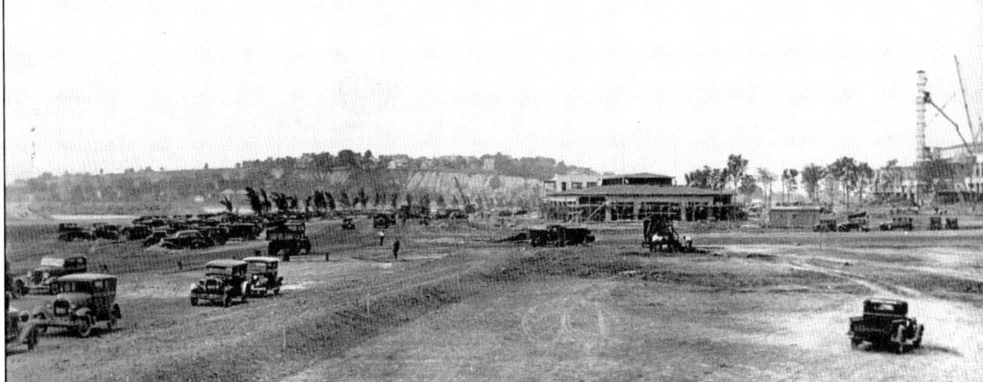

THE PADDOCK. Seen are the original paddock (center) and grandstand (far right). (Courtesy Steve Pini.)

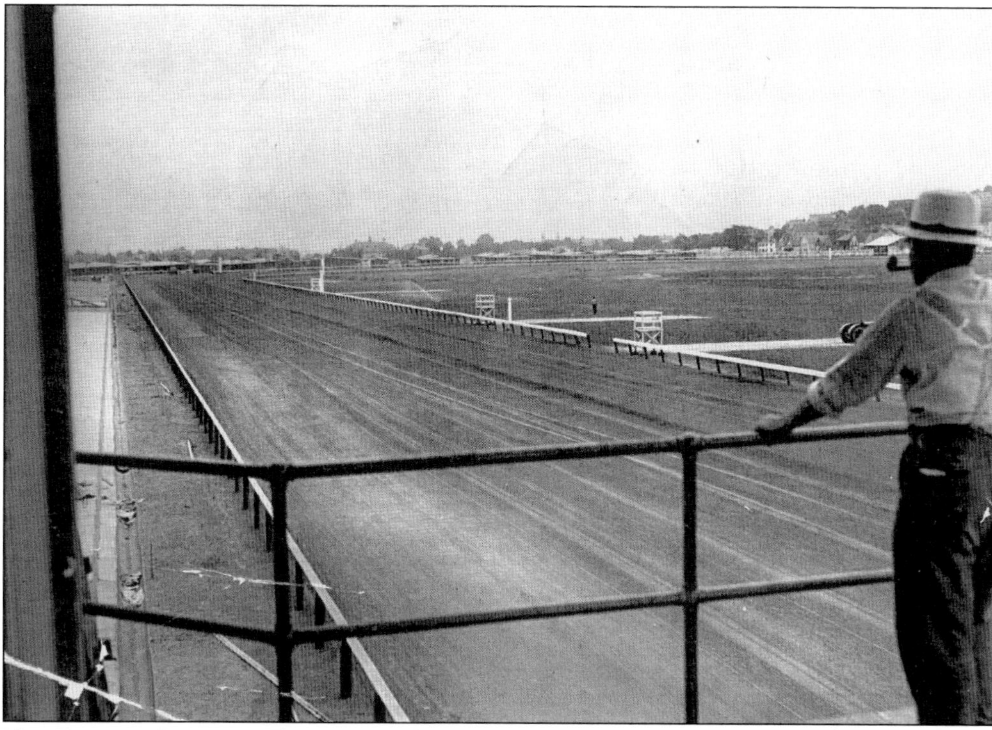

THE RACING SURFACE. The main track nears completion. (Courtesy Steve Pini.)

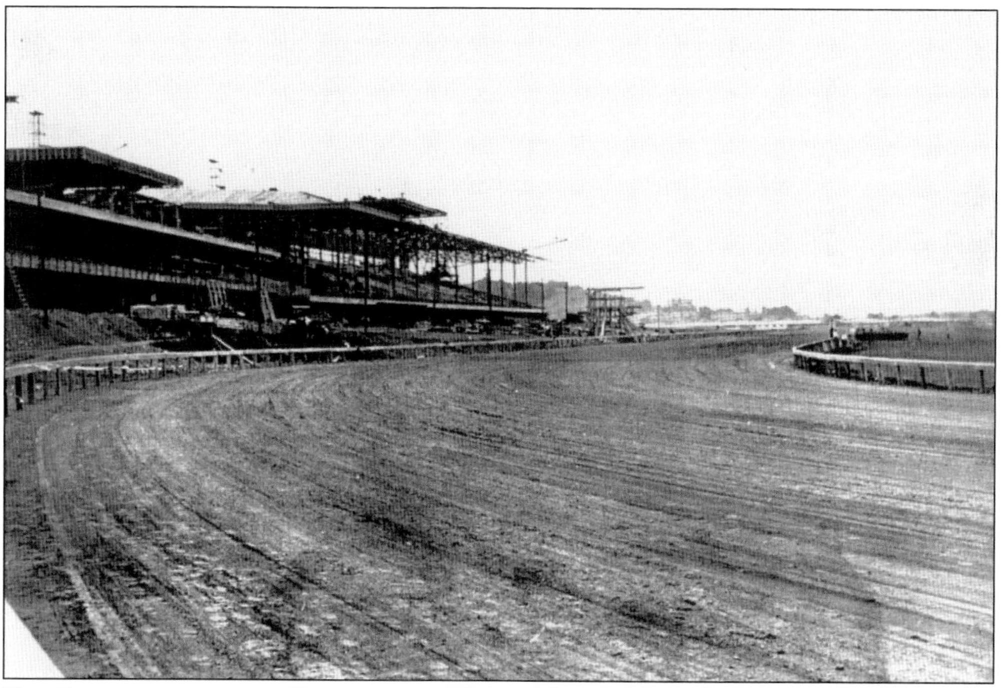

THE CLUBHOUSE AND THE GRANDSTAND. The track boasted the only concrete grandstand in the country at the time. With a capacity of 16,000, it was also the largest. (Courtesy Steve Pini.)

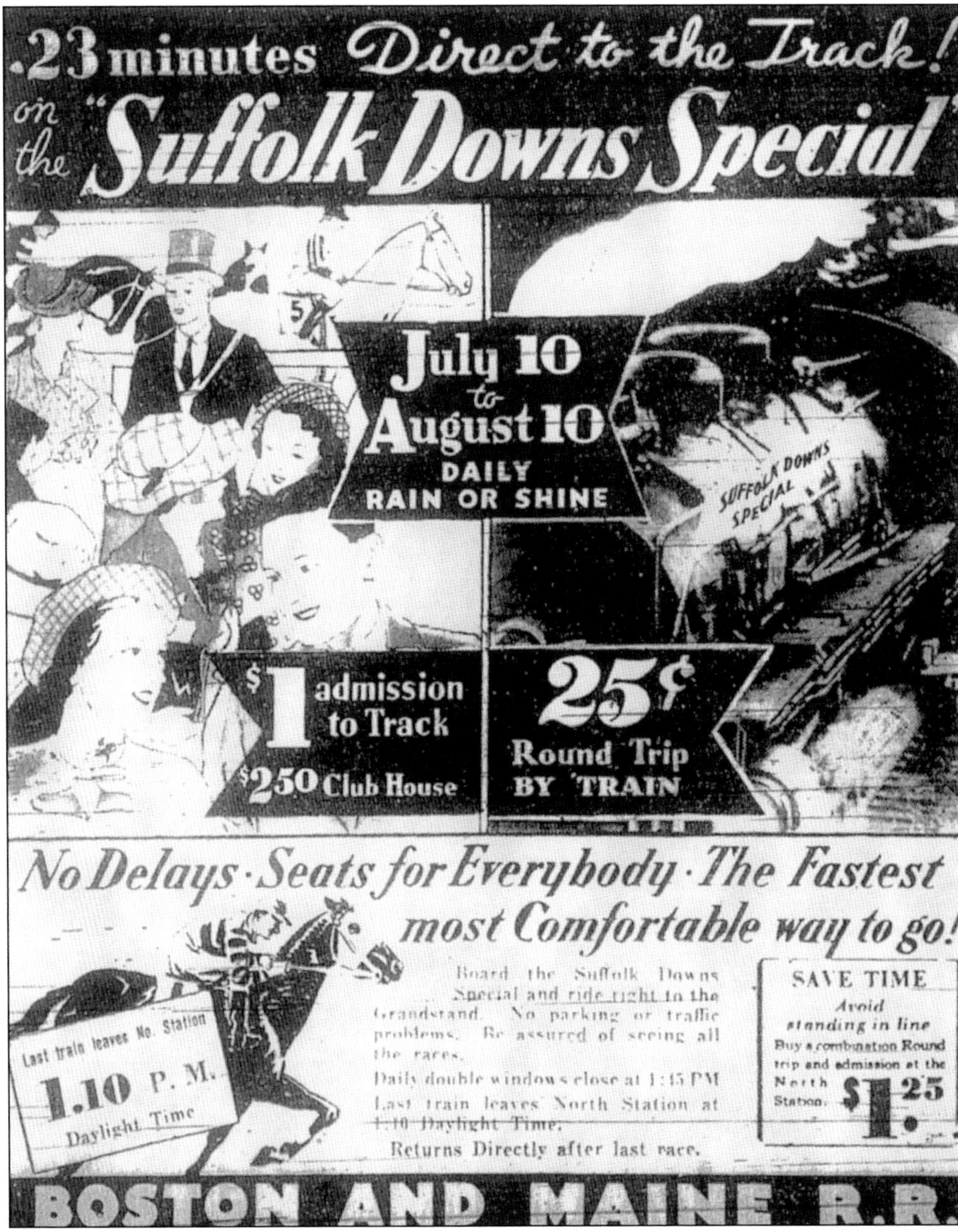

THE SUFFOLK DOWNS SPECIAL. In advance of the track's opening day, this advertisement in the *Boston Post* informs the public that trains will be running to and from the track daily throughout its inaugural season. (*Boston Post* advertisement, courtesy Boston Public Library.)

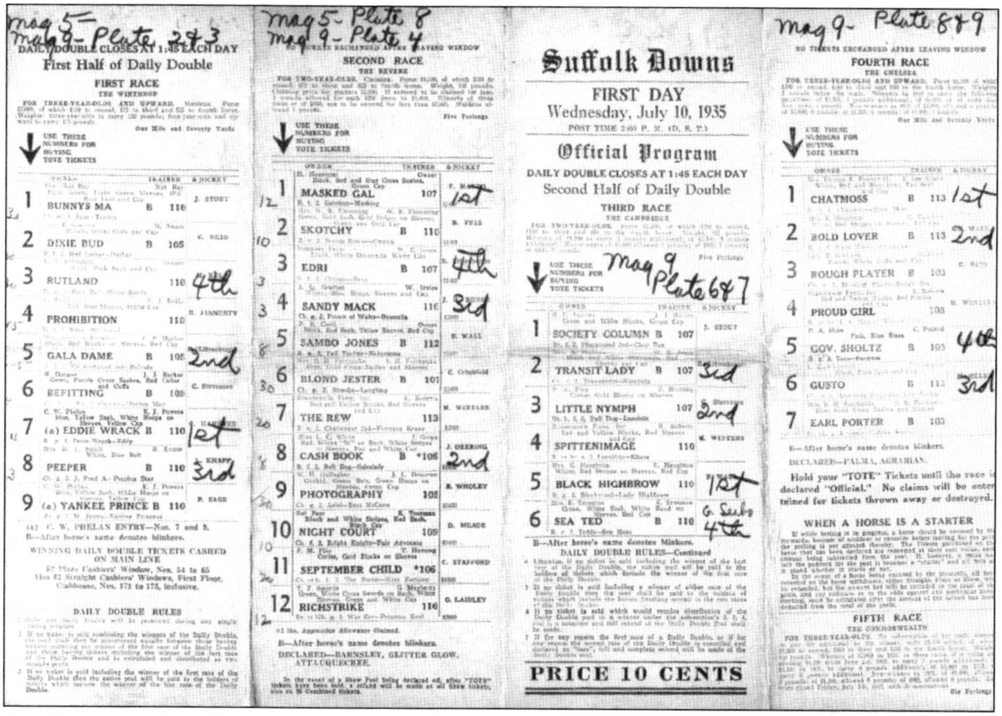

mag 5— mag 9- Plate 2 & 3

DAILY DOUBLE CLOSES AT 1:45 EACH DAY

First Half of Daily Double

FIRST RACE

THE WINTHROP

1	BUNNYS MA	B 116
2	DIXIE BUD	B 105
3	RUTLAND	110 — 4th
4	PROHIBITION	110
5	GALA DAME	B 105 — 2nd
6	BEFITTING	B 105
7	(a) EDDIE WRACK	B 110 — 1st
8	PEEPER	B 110 — 3rd
9	(a) YANKEE PRINCE	B 110

mag 5- Plate 8, mag 9- Plate 4

SECOND RACE

THE REVERE

1	MASKED GAL	107 — 1st
2	SKOTCHY	B 110
3	EDRI	B 107 — 4th
4	SANDY MACK	116 — 3rd
5	SAMBO JONES	B 112
6	BLOND JESTER	B 107
7	THE REW	113
8	CASH BOOK	B *106 — 2nd
9	PHOTOGRAPHY	105
10	NIGHT COURT	109
11	SEPTEMBER CHILD	*106
12	RICHSTRIKE	116

Suffolk Downs

FIRST DAY

Wednesday, July 10, 1935

Official Program

DAILY DOUBLE CLOSES AT 1:45 EACH DAY

Second Half of Daily Double

THIRD RACE

THE CAMBRIDGE

mag 9 Plate 6 & 7

1	SOCIETY COLUMN	B 107
2	TRANSIT LADY	B 107 — 3rd
3	LITTLE NYMPH	107 — 2nd
4	SPITTENIMAGE	110
5	BLACK HIGHBROW	110 — 1st
6	SEA TED	B 110 — 4th

PRICE 10 CENTS

mag 9- Plate 8 & 9

FOURTH RACE

THE CHELSEA

1	CHATMOSS	B 113 — 1st
2	BOLD LOVER	B 113 — 2nd
3	ROUGH PLAYER	B 103
4	PROUD GIRL	108
5	GOV. SHOLTZ	B 105 — 4th
6	GUSTO	B 113 — 3rd
7	EARL PORTER	B 103

Hold your "TOTE" Tickets until the race is declared "Official." No claims will be entertained for tickets thrown away or destroyed.

WHEN A HORSE IS A STARTER

FIFTH RACE

THE COMMONWEALTH

AN OPENING DAY PROGRAM. A marked-up program from the track's first day of racing, July 10, 1935, shows that Eddie Wrack (No. 7), with jockey Carl Hanford aboard, won the first race. An estimated crowd of 35,000 was present to witness the eight-race card. (Leslie Jones program, courtesy Boston Public Library Print Department.)

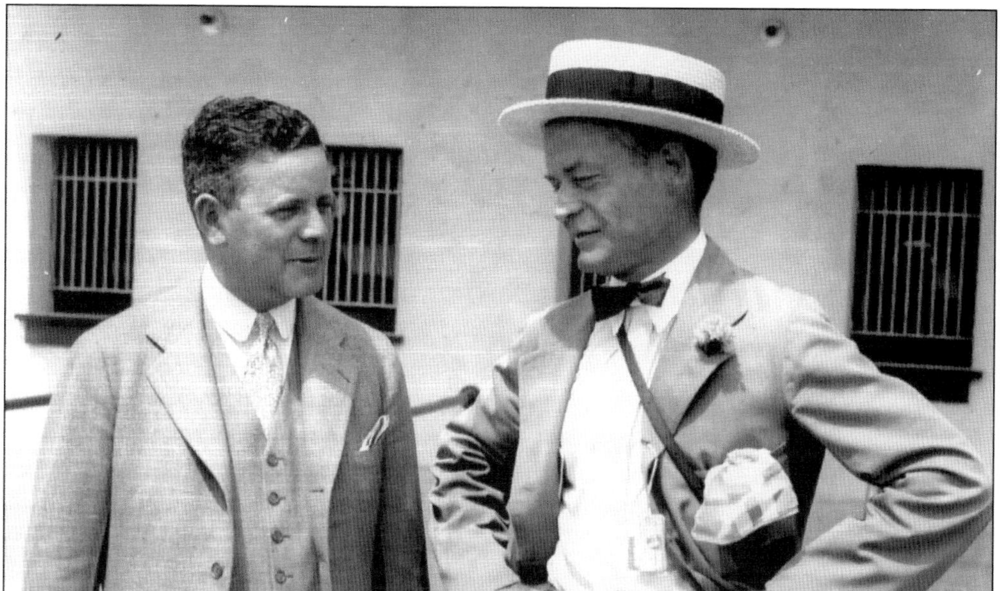

BAYARD TUCKERMAN JR. Publicity director Gus Rooney (left) converses with track president Bayard Tuckerman Jr. on opening day, July 10, 1935. (*Boston Herald* photograph, courtesy Boston Public Library Print Department.)

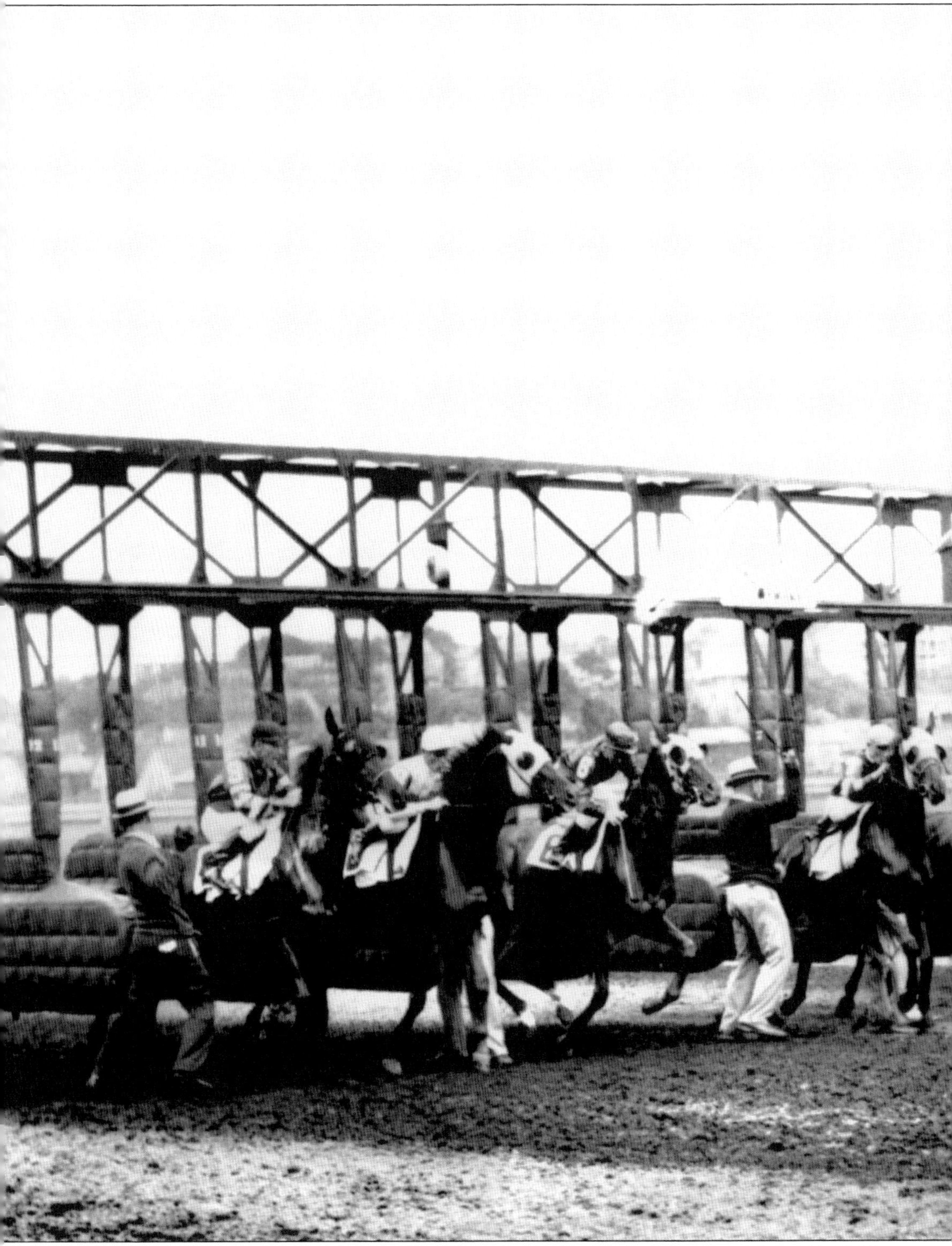

THEY'RE OFF! A field of nine breaks from the horse-drawn starting gate on July 17, 1935, one week after the track opened. The inaugural racing season consisted of 44 days split between

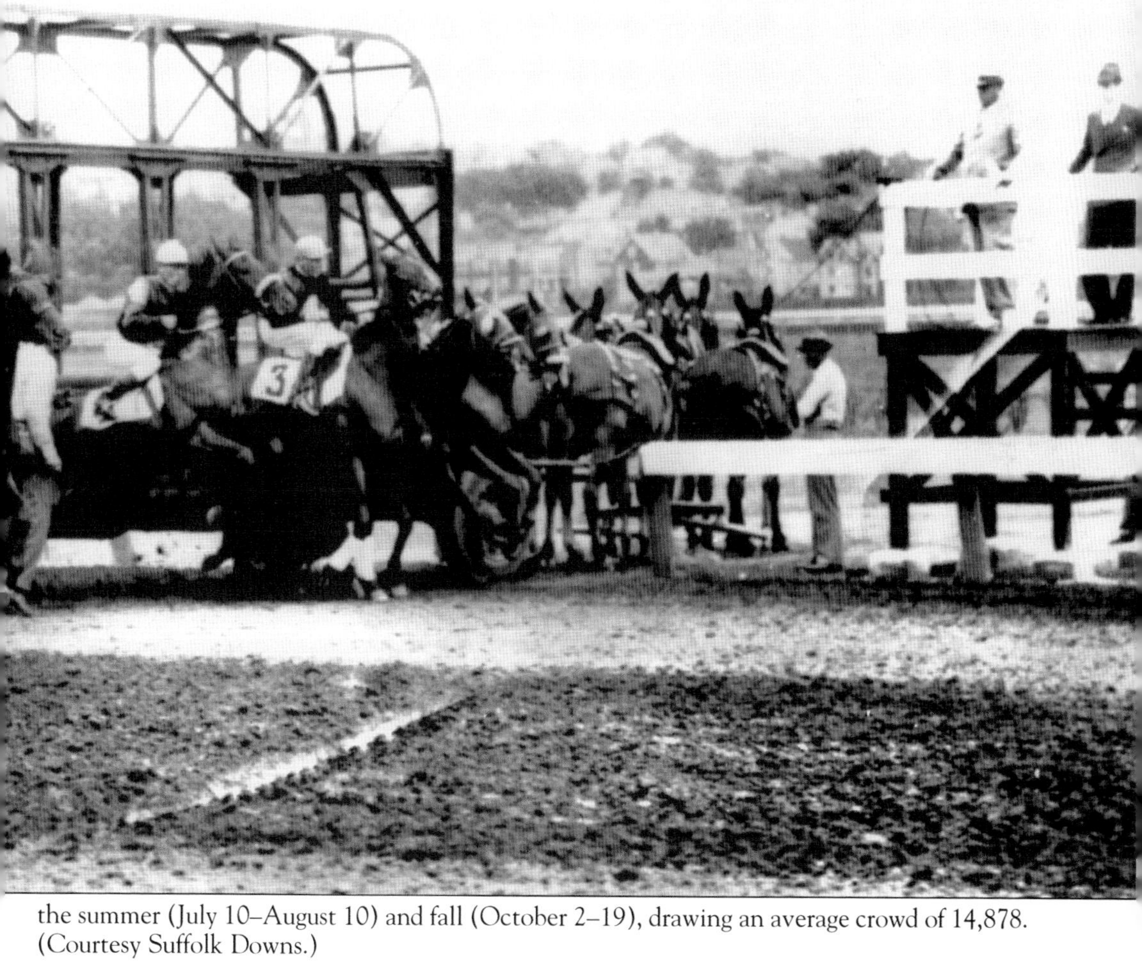

the summer (July 10–August 10) and fall (October 2–19), drawing an average crowd of 14,878. (Courtesy Suffolk Downs.)

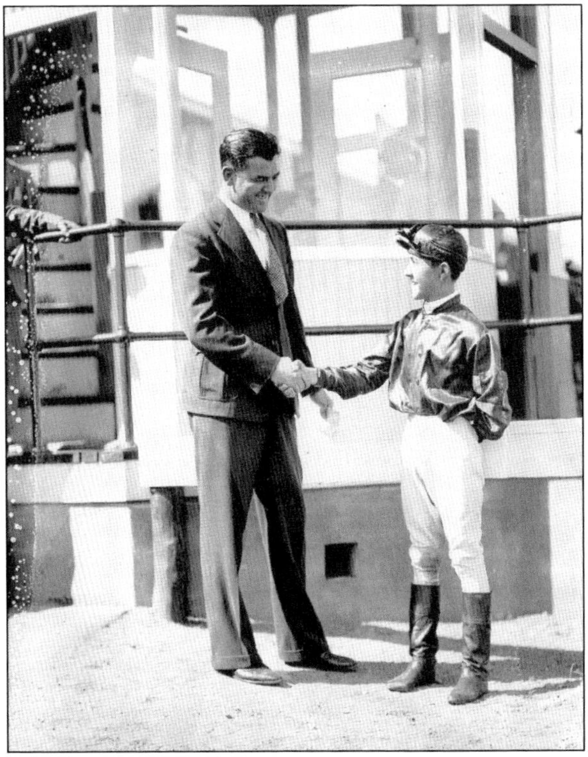

JIM BRADDOCK AND IRA HANFORD. Reigning world heavyweight boxing champion Jim "Cinderella Man" Braddock shakes hands with jockey Ira Hanford in 1935. Braddock defeated Max Baer for the title on June 13 of that year. He served as the referee for a world championship wrestling match at Braves Field on July 30. (Leslie Jones photograph, courtesy Boston Public Library Print Department.)

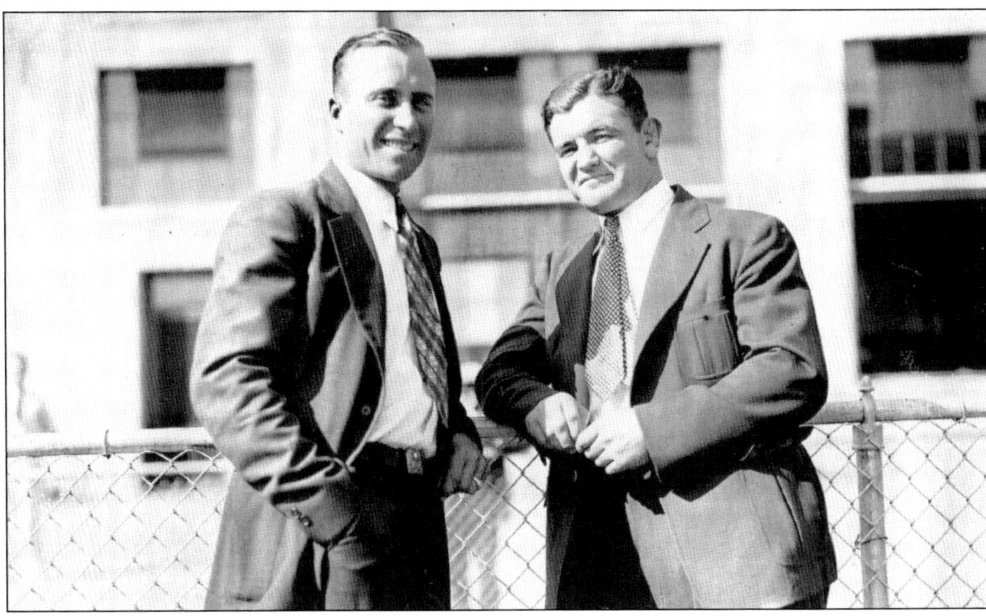

WALLY BERGER AND JIM BRADDOCK. Wally Berger (left) of the Boston Braves and world heavyweight boxing champion Jim Braddock pose in front of the clubhouse. Berger was in the middle of the 1935 season, in which he hit .295 and led the National League with 34 home runs and 130 runs batted in. Berger was overshadowed earlier in the year by the presence of Babe Ruth, who left the New York Yankees and joined the Braves for the 1935 season before retiring on May 30. (Leslie Jones photograph, courtesy Boston Public Library Print Department.)

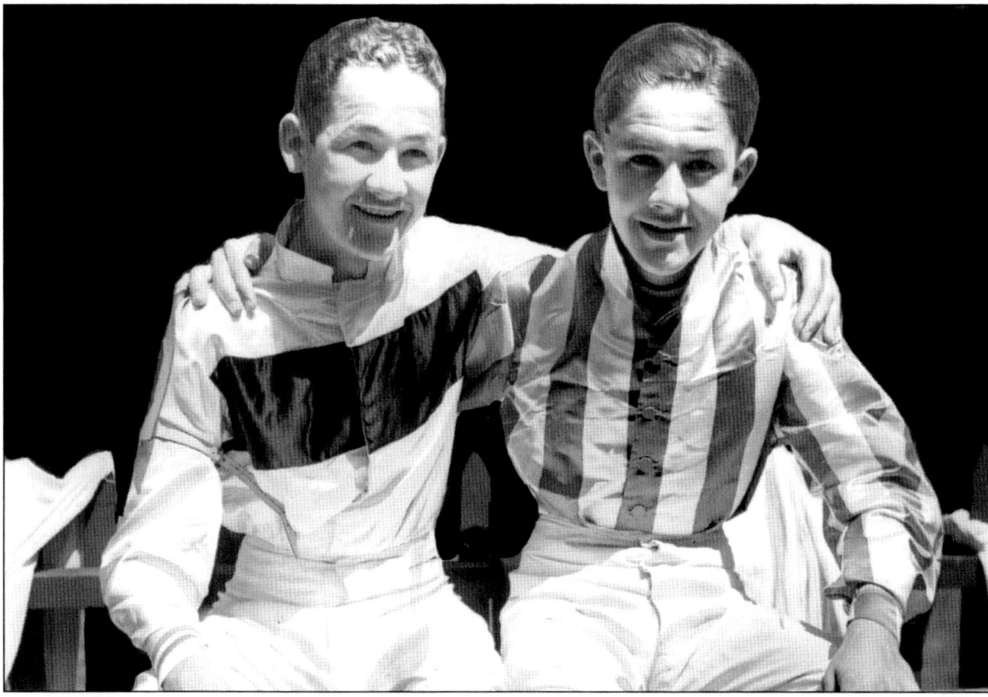

The Hanford Brothers. Brothers Carl (left) and Ira Hanford, shown here at Saratoga Race Course in New York, both rode at the inaugural Suffolk Downs meet. Carl won the first race ever run at the track aboard Eddie Wrack. Ira piloted Seabiscuit three times before the horse emerged as a national hero. (International News photograph, courtesy *Boston Herald.*)

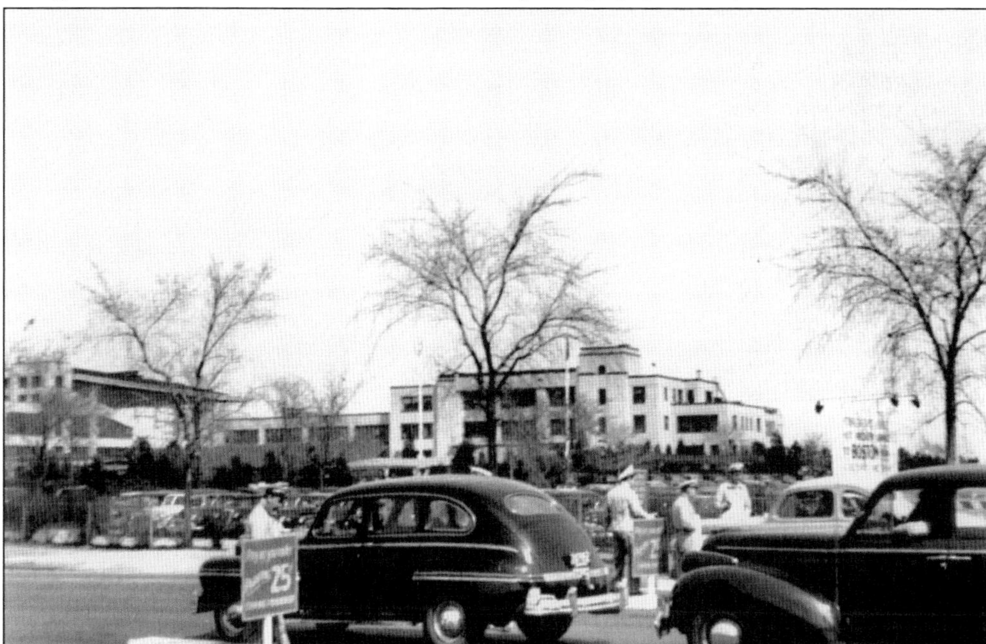

Parking for 25¢. Patrons make their way into a crowded parking lot for an afternoon of racing. (Courtesy Suffolk Downs.)

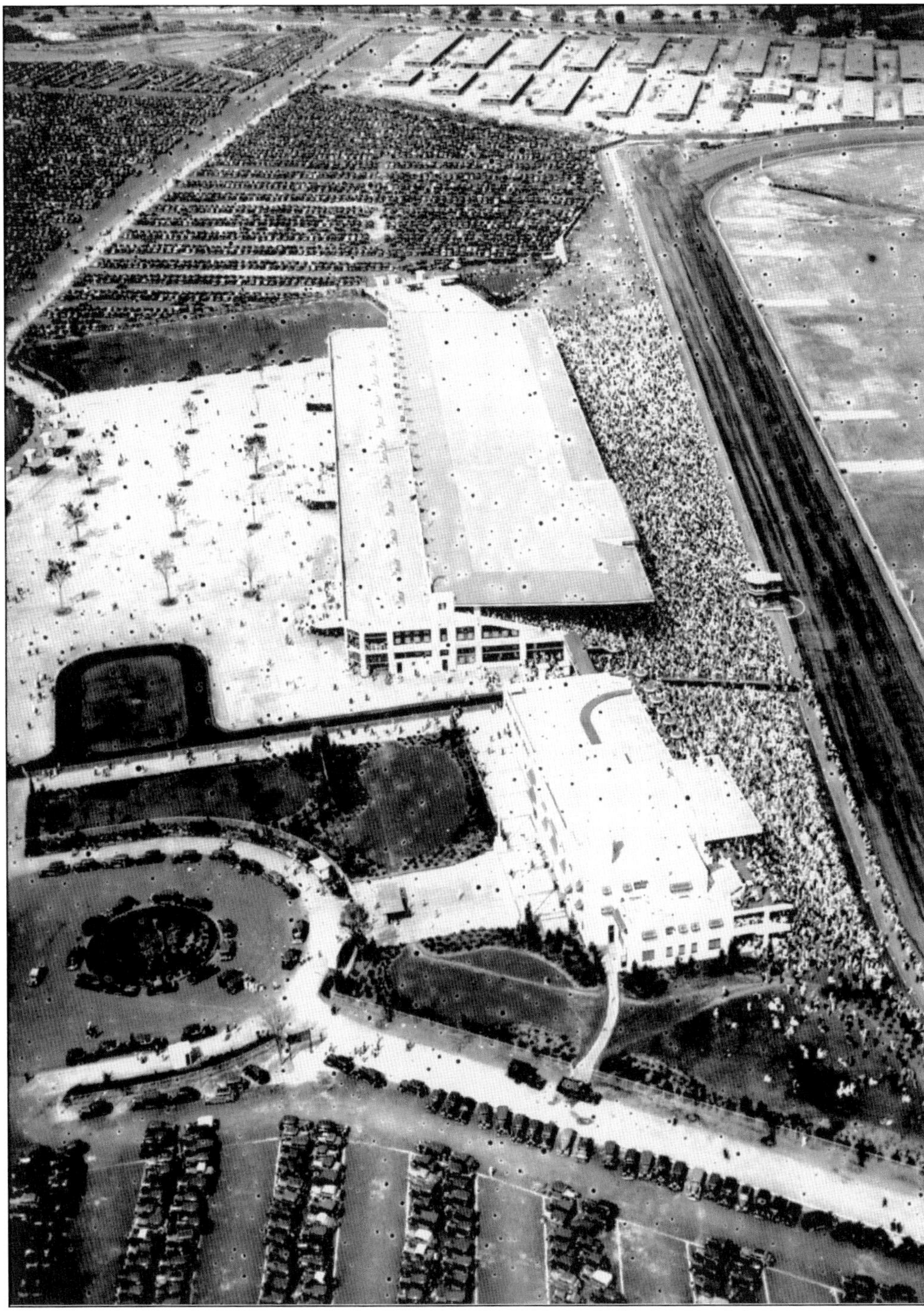

CLOSING DAY OF THE OPENING MEET. The final day of the inaugural meet, August 10, 1935, attracted an overflow crowd of 52,726, a record that stood until June 29, 1938, when Seabiscuit and War Admiral were scheduled to square off in the MassCap before Seabiscuit was scratched due to injury. (Courtesy the Bostonian Society/Old State House, Arthur Hansen Photograph Collection.)

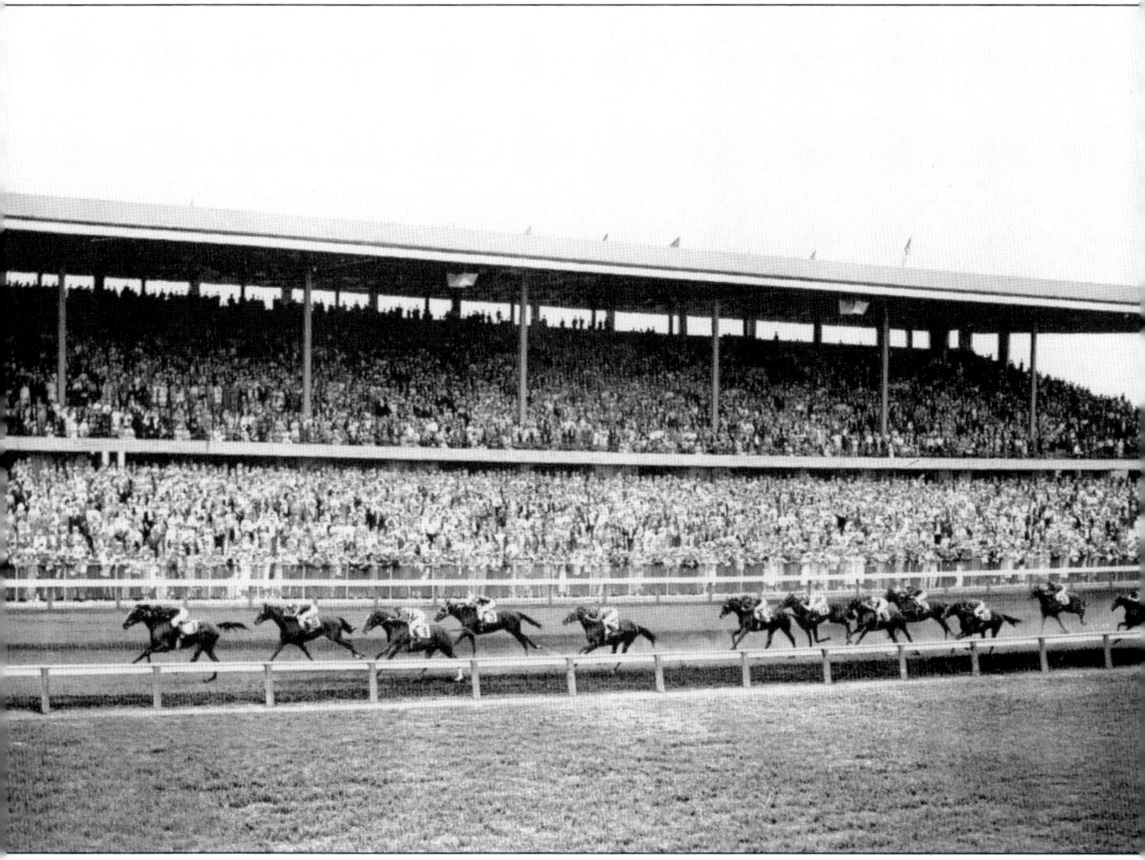

IN THE STRETCH. The field is strung out as horses make their way down the stretch in front of a crowded grandstand in 1935. (Leslie Jones photograph, courtesy Boston Public Library Print Department.)

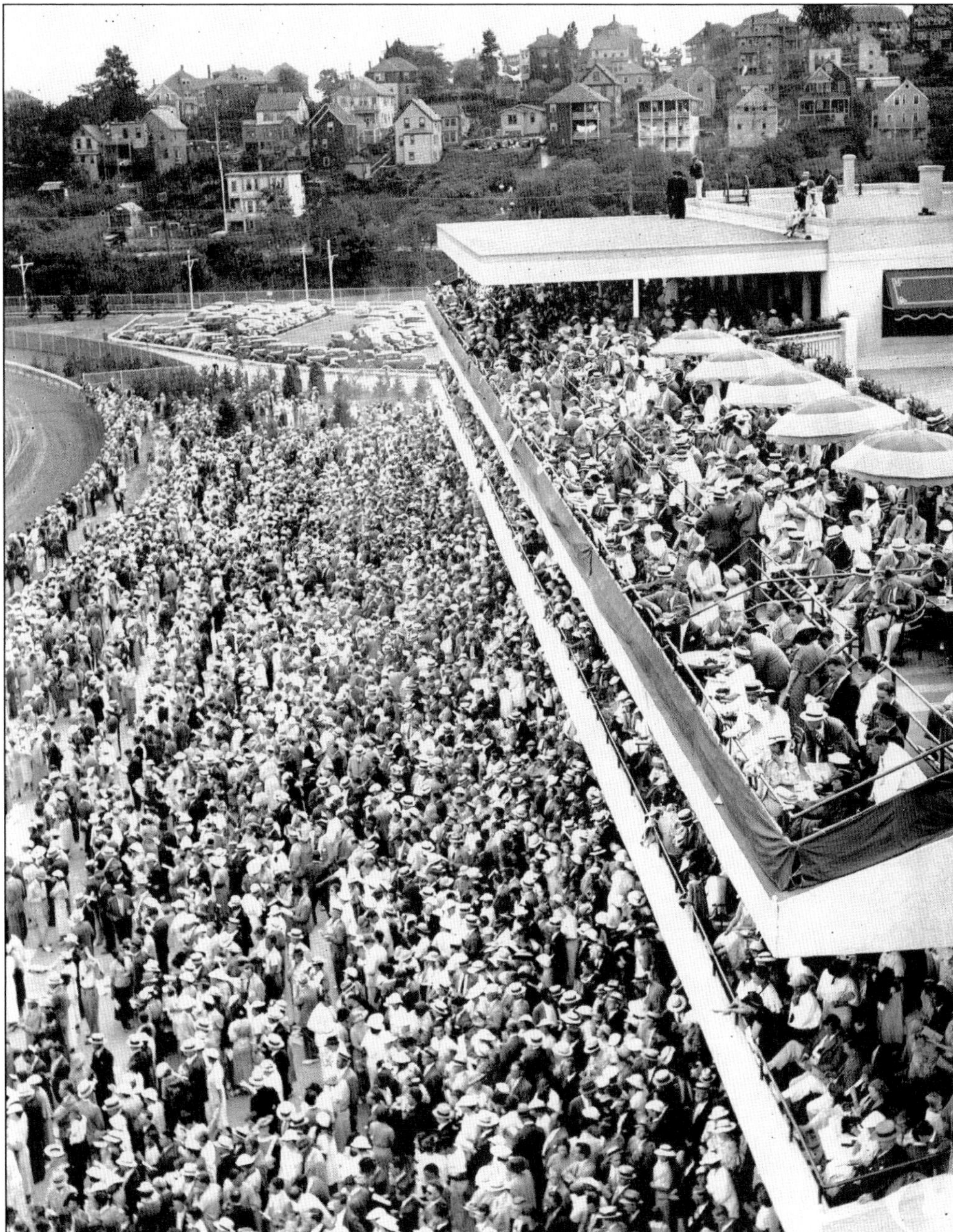

A Packed House. Crowds flocked to the track in its first year. Here, well-dressed patrons fill the clubhouse apron and rooftop balcony. (Leslie Jones photograph, courtesy Boston Public Library Print Department.)

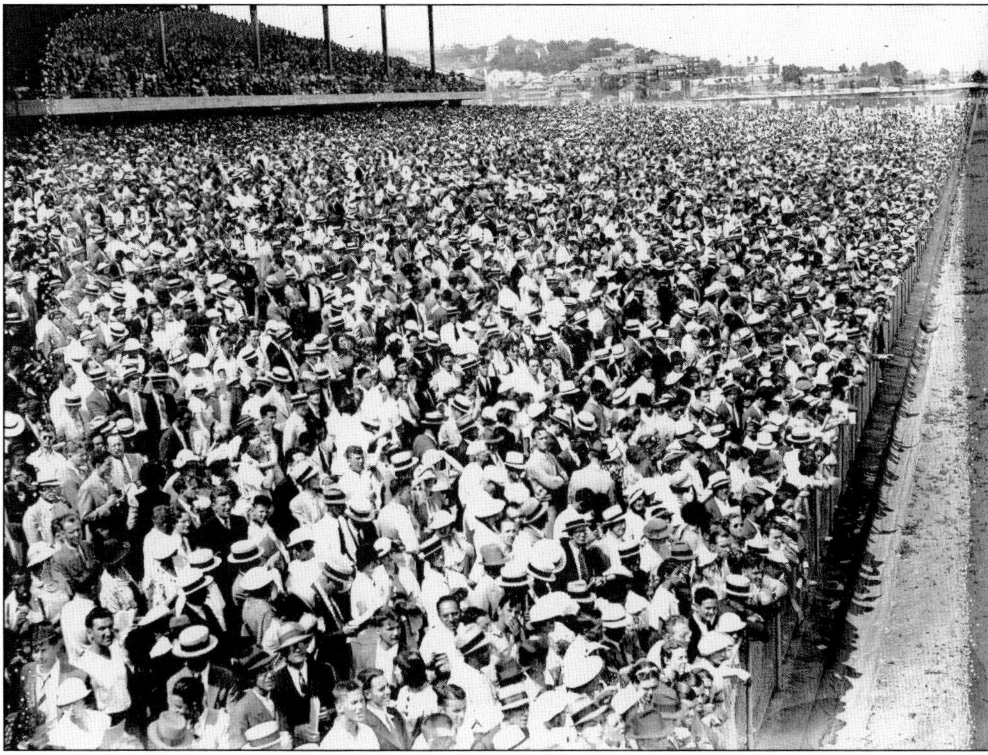

Standing Room Only. Spectators swarm the apron in front of a full grandstand in the track's first year. (Leslie Jones photograph, courtesy Boston Public Library Print Department.)

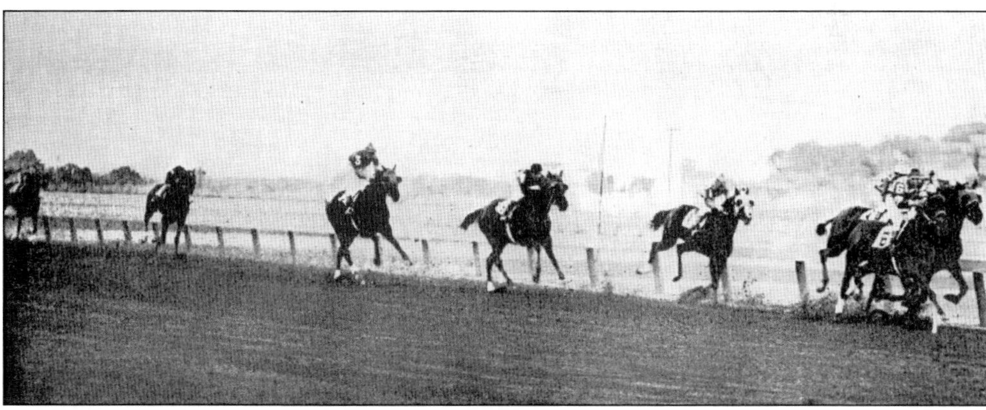

The First Massachusetts Handicap, 1935. Top Row and hall of fame jockey George "Iceman" Woolf scored a neck victory over Whopper in the inaugural Massachusetts Handicap on October 16, 1935. Favorite Discovery, who finished third, was assigned to carry 138 pounds, spotting Top Row 22 pounds and Whopper 30 pounds. (Courtesy Suffolk Downs.)

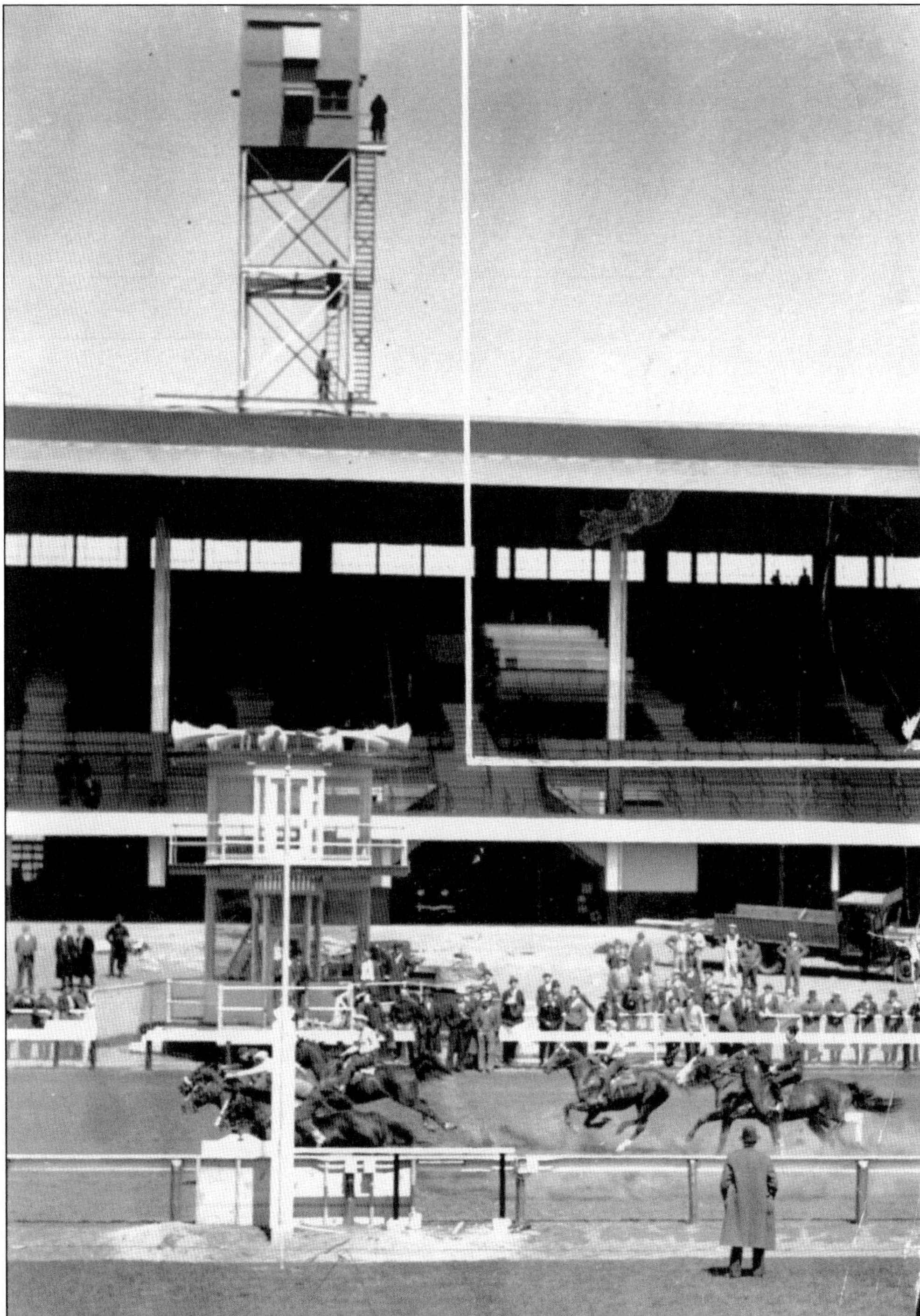

A Photo Finish. Prior to the start of the 1936 racing meet, photo finish technology was added atop the grandstand. Stable ponies gallop across the finish line as part of a demonstration to reporters. The racing stewards used the photographs to determine the order of finish in tightly contested races. (*Boston Herald-Traveler* photograph, courtesy Boston Public Library Print Department.)

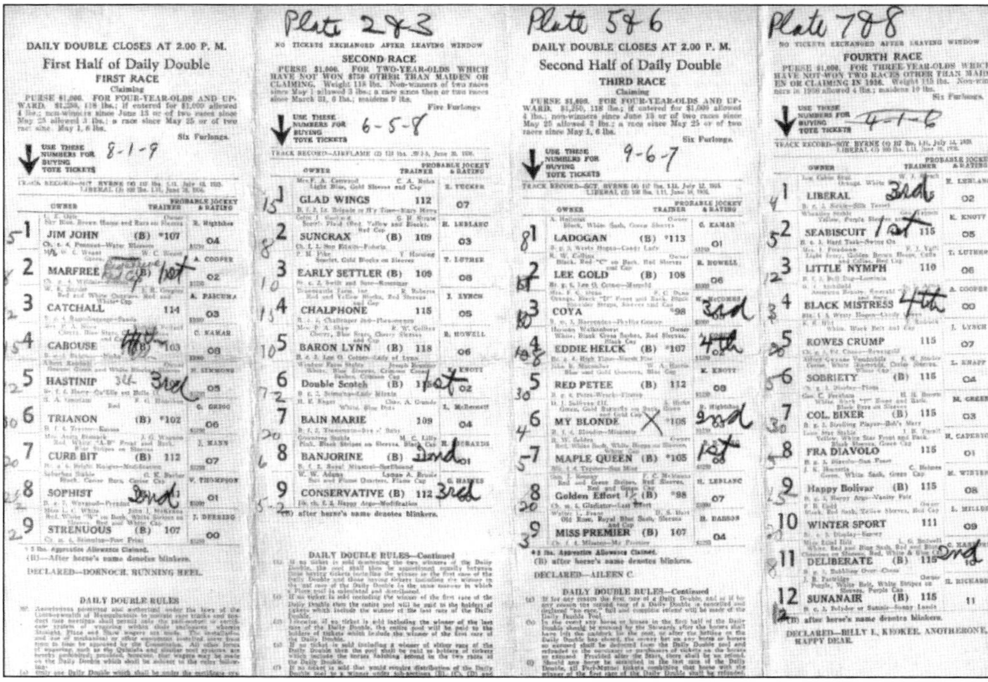

DAILY DOUBLE CLOSES AT 2.00 P. M.

First Half of Daily Double

FIRST RACE

Claiming

Six Furlongs.

USE THESE NUMBERS FOR BUYING TOTE TICKETS 8-1-9

1 JIM JOHN (B) *107 04
2 MARFREE 02
3 CATCHALL 114 03
4 CABOOSE 103 08
5 HASTINIP 3rd 05
6 TRIANON (B) *102 06
7 CURB BIT (B) 112 07
8 SOPHIST 2nd 01
9 STRENUOUS (B) 107 00

DECLARED—DORNOCH, RUNNING HEEL.

DAILY DOUBLE RULES

Plate 2 & 3

NO TICKETS EXCHANGED AFTER LEAVING WINDOW

SECOND RACE

Five Furlongs.

USE THESE NUMBERS FOR BUYING TOTE TICKETS 6-5-8

1 GLAD WINGS 112 07
2 SUNCRAX (B) 109 03
3 EARLY SETTLER (B) 109 08
4 CHALPHONE 115 05
5 BARON LYNN (B) 118 06
6 Double Scotch (B) 1st 02
7 BAIN MARIE 109 04
8 BANJORINE (B) 2nd 01
9 CONSERVATIVE (B) 112 3rd

DAILY DOUBLE RULES—Continued

Plate 5 & 6

DAILY DOUBLE CLOSES AT 2.00 P. M.

Second Half of Daily Double

THIRD RACE

Claiming

Six Furlongs.

USE THESE NUMBERS FOR BUYING TOTE TICKETS 9-6-7

1 LADOGAN (B) *113 01
2 LEE GOLD (B) 108 06
3 COYA *98 3rd
4 EDDIE HELCK (B) *107 4th
5 RED PETEE (B) 112 08
6 MY BLONDE *105 2nd
7 MAPLE QUEEN (B) *105 1st
8 Golden Effort (B) *98 07
9 MISS PREMIER (B) 107 04

DECLARED—AILEEN C.

DAILY DOUBLE RULES—Continued

Plate 7 & 8

NO TICKETS EXCHANGED AFTER LEAVING WINDOW

FOURTH RACE

Six Furlongs.

USE THESE NUMBERS FOR BUYING TOTE TICKETS 4-1-6

1 LIBERAL 3rd 02
2 SEABISCUIT 1st 115 05
3 LITTLE NYMPH 110 06
4 BLACK MISTRESS 4th 00
5 ROWES CRUMP 115 07
6 SOBRIETY (B) 115 04
7 COL. BIXER (B) 115 03
8 FRA DIAVOLO 115 01
9 Happy Bolivar (B) 115 08
10 WINTER SPORT 111 09
11 DELIBERATE (B) 115 2nd
12 SUNANAIR (B) 115 11

DECLARED—BILLY L, KIOKEE, ANOTHERONE, HAPPY DEAR.

SEABISCUIT IN THE FOURTH. Seabiscuit is horse number two in the program for race four on June 29, 1936. He went off at 12-1 and won by one and a half lengths. (Leslie Jones photograph, courtesy Boston Public Library Print Department.)

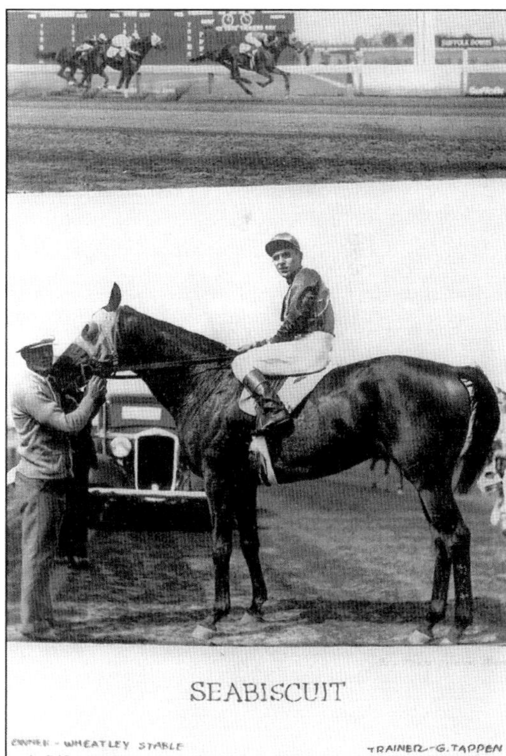

A SEABISCUIT WIN PHOTOGRAPH. This win photograph from June 29, 1936, marks Seabiscuit's first victory in six Suffolk starts. It was on this day that his eventual trainer, Tom Smith, first discovered him, as described by Laura Hillenbrand in her award-winning book *Seabiscuit: An American Legend.* Smith later recommended that Charles Howard purchase the horse, which he did in August in Saratoga Springs, New York. Smith and Howard then transformed Seabiscuit into a national hero. Seabiscuit was a regular on the New England racing circuit prior to Howard's purchase, having also competed at Agawam Park (Massachusetts), Narragansett Park (Rhode Island), and Rockingham Park (New Hampshire). (Courtesy James L. Boucher.)

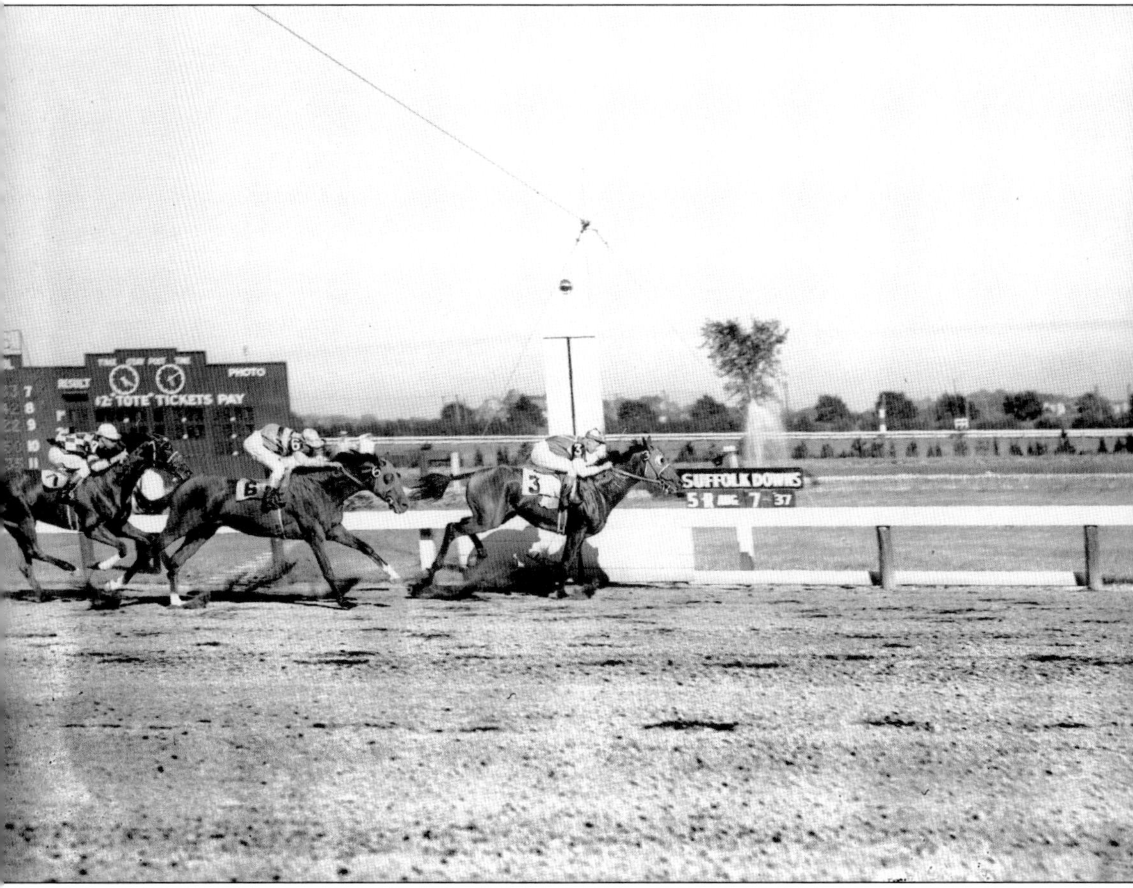

SEABISCUIT WINS THE 1937 MASSCAP. The legendary Seabiscuit won the 1937 MassCap, capping off his career-best seven-race winning streak and defeating 12 rivals as the even-money favorite before an exuberant crowd of 40,000. Seabiscuit, under jockey Johnny "Red" Pollard, broke the track record for $1^{1}/_{8}$ miles, stopping the clock in 1:49. His winning purse of $51,780 was the largest of his career at the time, and it was only surpassed in his final race, a victory in the 1940 Santa Anita Handicap. (AP/Wide World Photos photograph.)

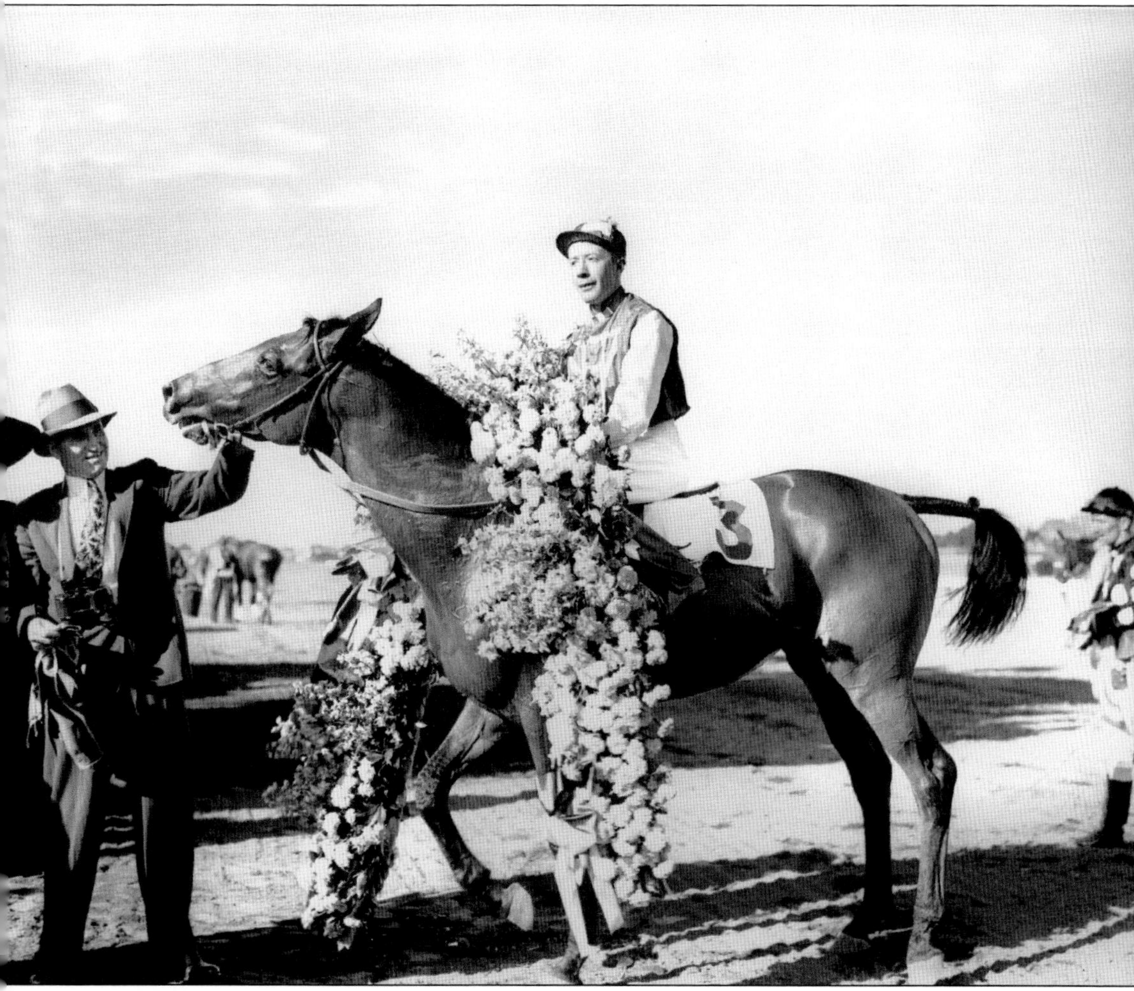

AN AMERICAN LEGEND. Seabiscuit, with jockey Red Pollard, makes his way to the winner's circle after his MassCap victory. To the left are Marcela Howard, wife of Charles S. Howard (Seabiscuit's owner), and trainer Tom Smith. (AP/Wide World Photos photograph.)

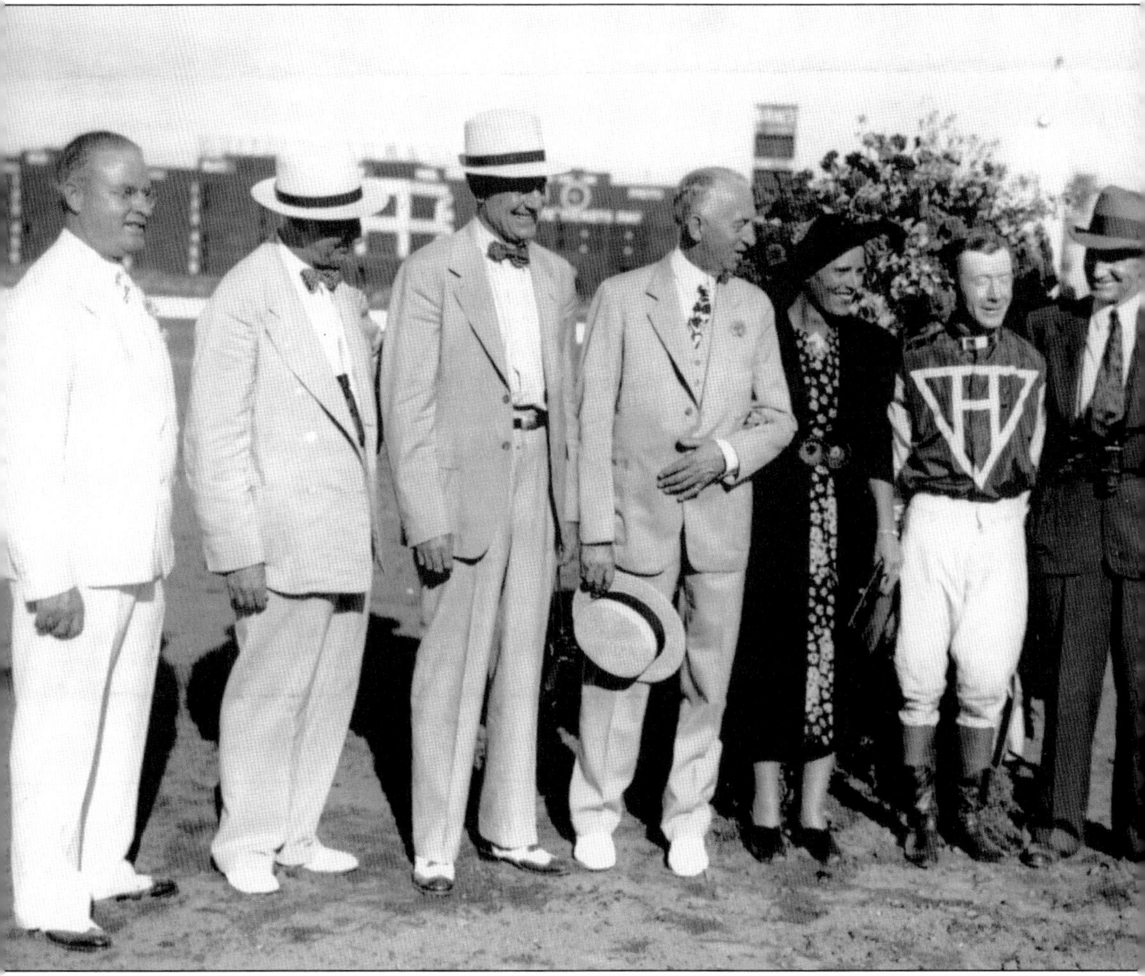

In the Winner's Circle. Seen here from left to right, track vice president James H. Connors, president Charles F. Adams, Seabiscuit's owner Charles S. Howard, track treasurer C. V. Bruce Wetmore, Marcela Howard, jockey Red Pollard, and trainer Tom Smith pose in the winner's circle after Seabiscuit's MassCap win. (*Boston Herald* photograph, courtesy Boston Public Library Print Department.)

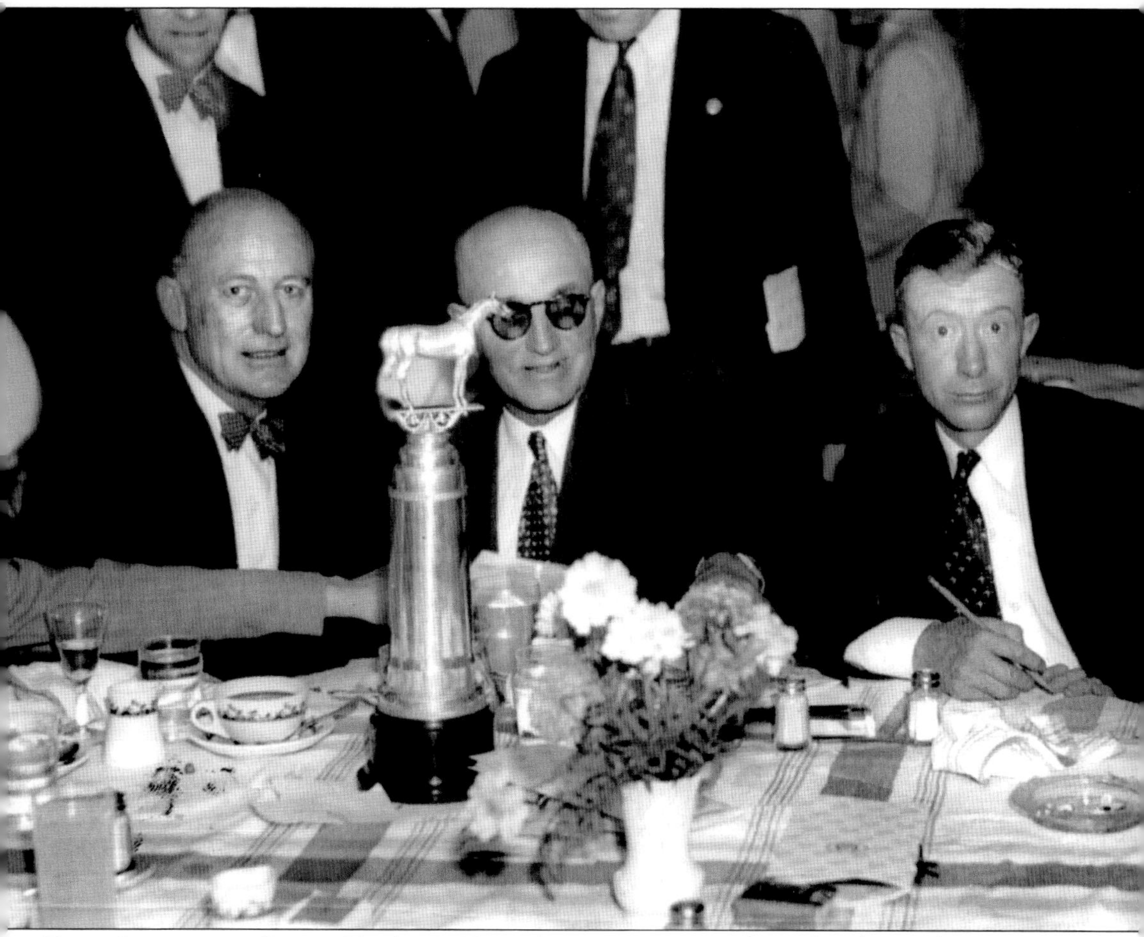

TEAM SEABISCUIT. Owner Charles S. Howard, trainer Tom Smith, and jockey Red Pollard, seen here from left to right, are the honored guests at the 1937 New England Turf Writers' Association's dinner, held at the track after the MassCap. (*Boston Herald-Traveler* photograph, courtesy Boston Public Library Print Department.)

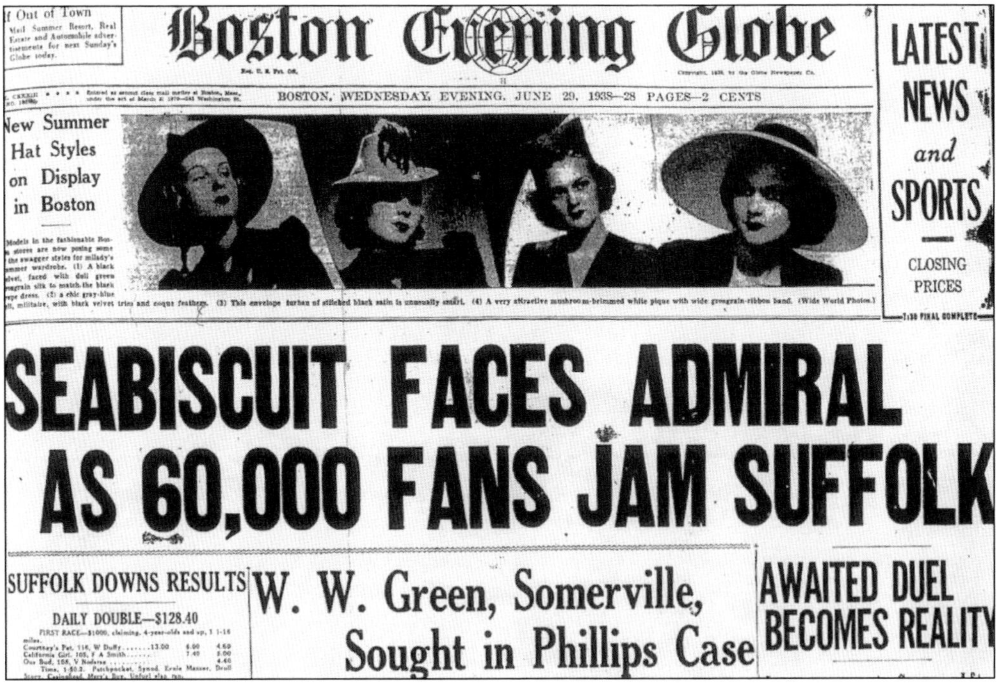

Boston Evening Globe

BOSTON, WEDNESDAY EVENING, JUNE 29, 1938—28 PAGES—2 CENTS

LATEST NEWS and SPORTS

CLOSING PRICES

New Summer Hat Styles on Display in Boston

SEABISCUIT FACES ADMIRAL AS 60,000 FANS JAM SUFFOLK

SUFFOLK DOWNS RESULTS

DAILY DOUBLE—$128.40

W. W. Green, Somerville, Sought in Phillips Case

AWAITED DUEL BECOMES REALITY

THE 1938 MASSACHUSETTS HANDICAP. The much anticipated meeting between defending MassCap champion Seabiscuit and War Admiral, the 1937 Triple Crown winner, appears to be a reality in this *Boston Evening Globe* headline on June 29, 1938. However, Seabiscuit was scratched due to an injury just minutes before the race was scheduled to take place, upsetting the record crowd that had gathered. This helped set the stage for the famed match race between the two champions that was ultimately held at Pimlico in Baltimore and was immortalized in the 2003 motion picture *Seabiscuit*. (*Boston Evening Globe*, courtesy Boston Public Library.)

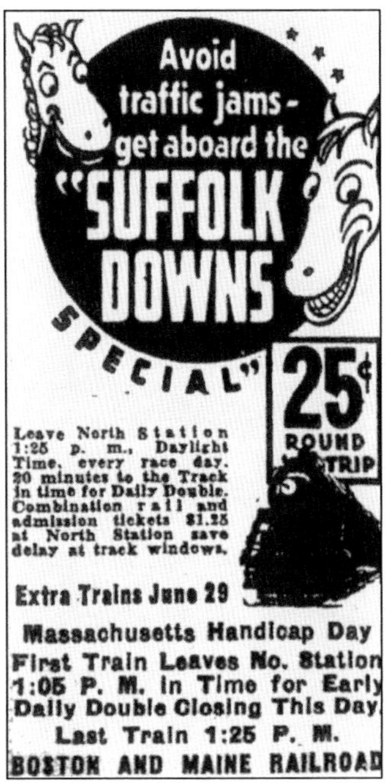

TAKE THE TRAIN. In anticipation of the enormous crowd expected for the 1938 MassCap, race fans are encouraged to take the train to the track in this advertisement. (*Boston Evening Globe*, courtesy Boston Public Library.)

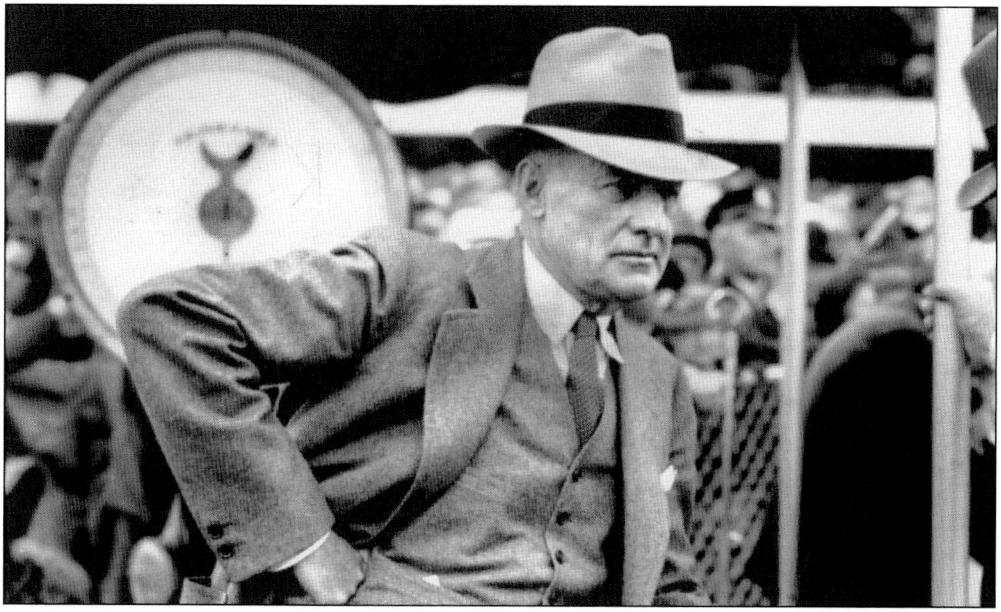

CHARLES S. HOWARD. Seabiscuit's owner, Charles S. Howard, was left to ponder what might have been after his horse was scratched from the 1938 MassCap. The race was won by longshot Menow, with War Admiral finishing fourth. It was the only time War Admiral ever finished out of the money in his 26-race career. (*Boston Herald-Traveler* photograph, courtesy Boston Public Library Print Department.)

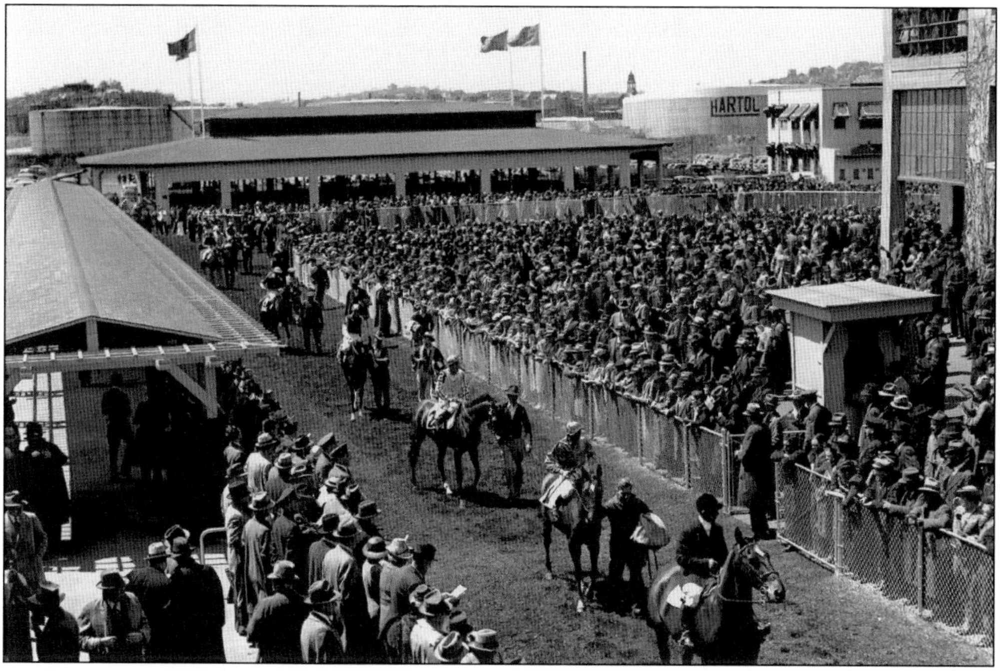

THE ORIGINAL PADDOCK. Horses make their way from the paddock toward the track for a post parade on May 15, 1939. The paddock was located behind the clubhouse until the early 1960s, when the track underwent major renovations. (Leslie Jones photograph, courtesy Boston Public Library Print Department.)

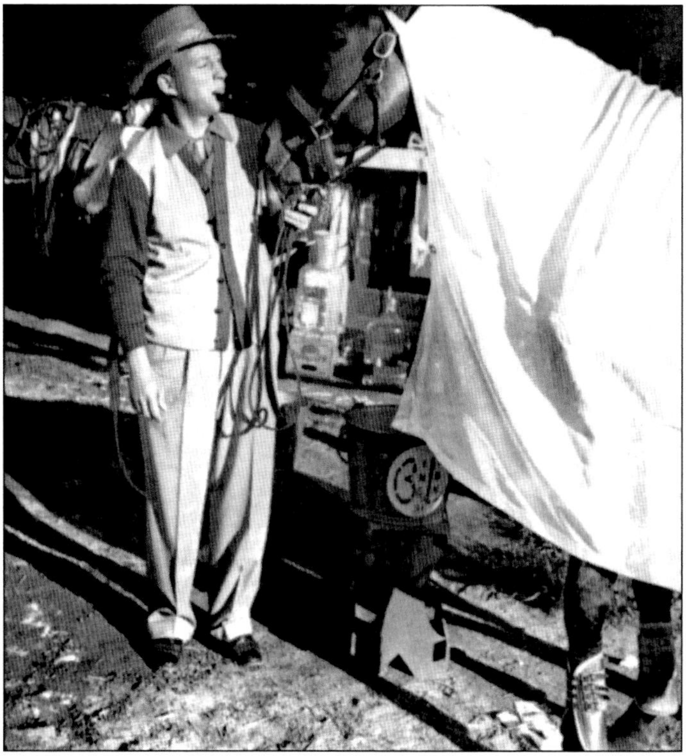

Bing Crosby. Actor and entertainer Bing Crosby visits the stable area in 1938. A horseman himself, Crosby helped found the Del Mar Thoroughbred Club in Southern California in 1937. Below, Crosby (center) watches a race intently from the box seating area. (Brearley Collection photographs.)

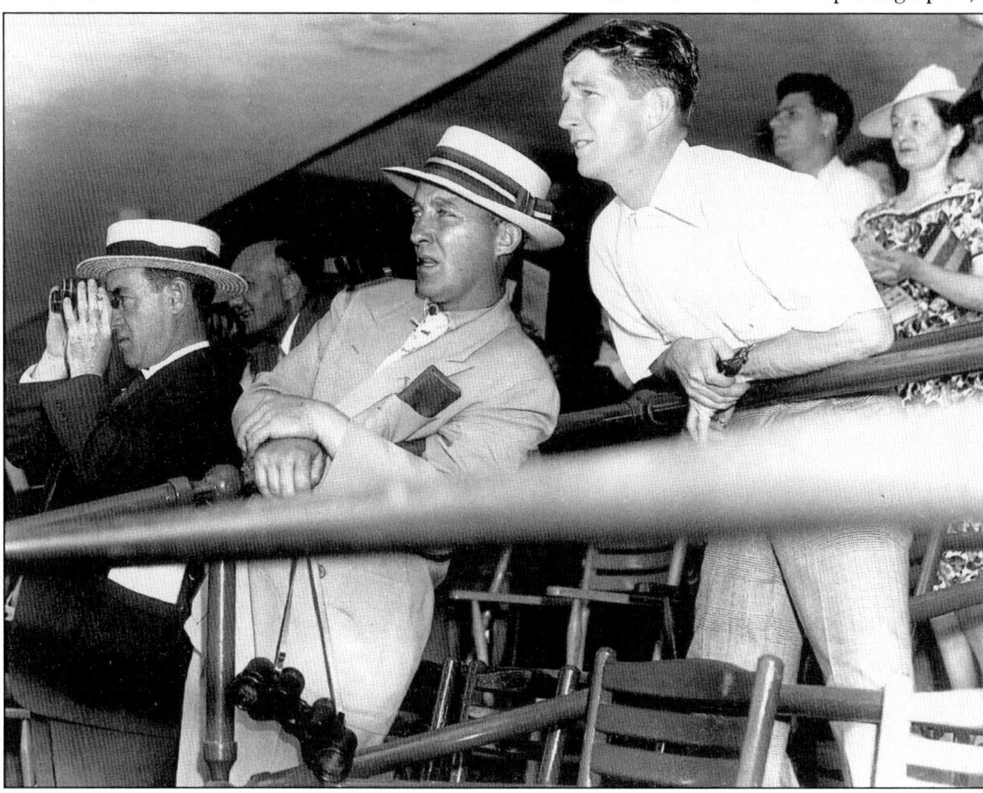

Two

THE 1940S

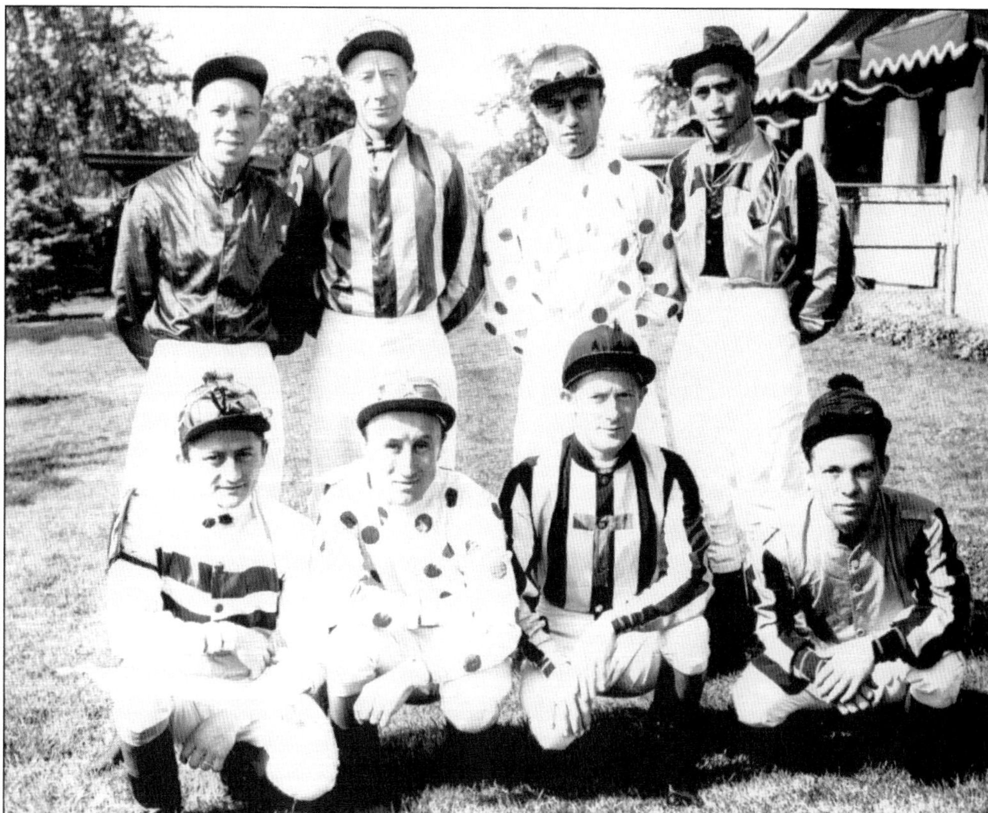

THE 1941 MASSACHUSETTS HANDICAP. Jockeys for the 1941 MassCap include, from left to right, the following: (first row) Donald Meade Sr., James Stout, Nick Wall, and Conn McCreary; (second row) Carroll Bierman, Red Pollard, Johnny Gilbert, and Ruperto Donoso. Ted Atkinson (not pictured) won the race aboard War Relic. (Courtesy Suffolk Downs.)

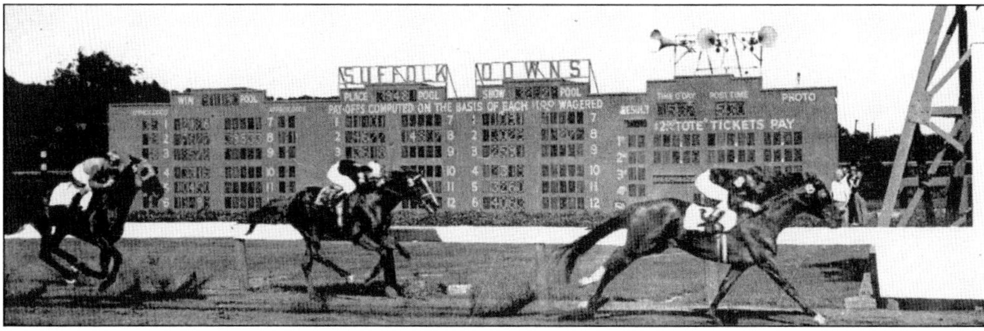

WHIRLAWAY WINS THE 1942 MASSCAP. A year after winning the Triple Crown, Whirlaway became the first and only Triple Crown champion to win the MassCap, setting a track record of $1{:}48^{1}/_{5}$ for $1^{1}/_{8}$ miles in the process. Whirlaway was ridden in the MassCap by hall of fame jockey George Woolf for prominent owner Calumet Farm. (Courtesy Suffolk Downs.)

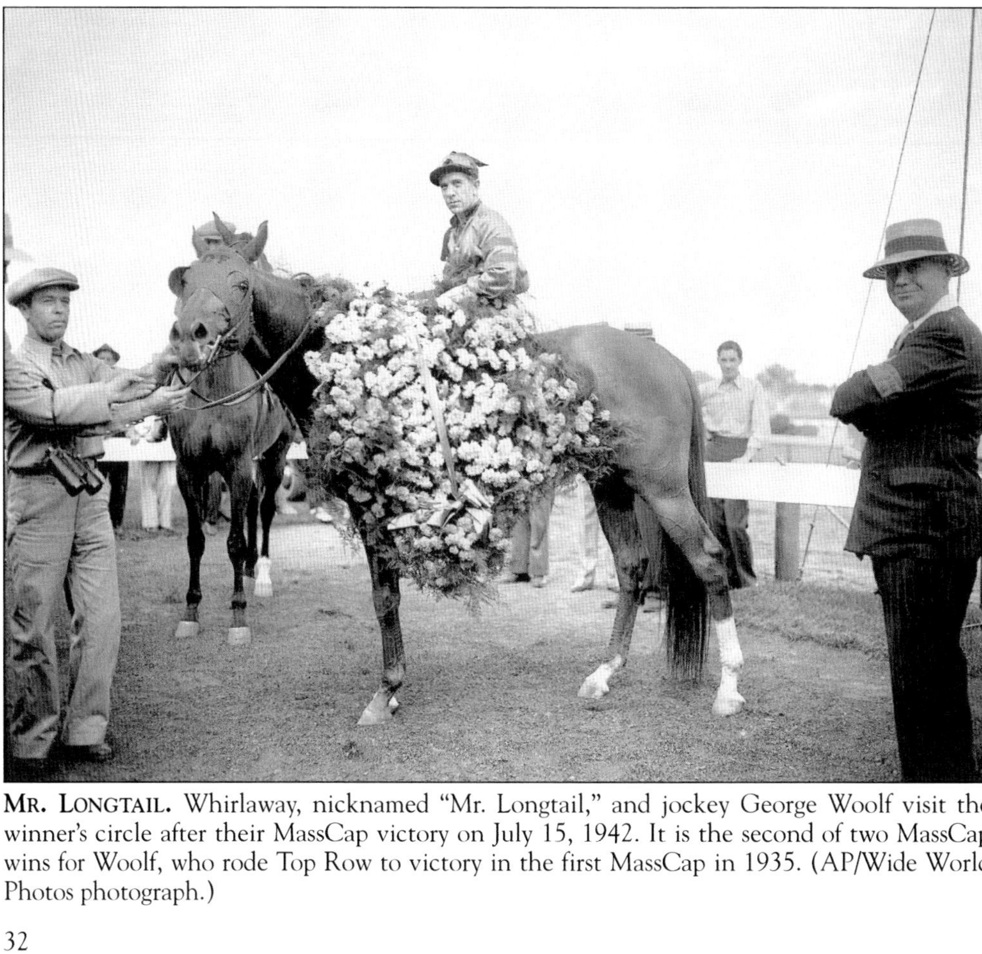

MR. LONGTAIL. Whirlaway, nicknamed "Mr. Longtail," and jockey George Woolf visit the winner's circle after their MassCap victory on July 15, 1942. It is the second of two MassCap wins for Woolf, who rode Top Row to victory in the first MassCap in 1935. (AP/Wide World Photos photograph.)

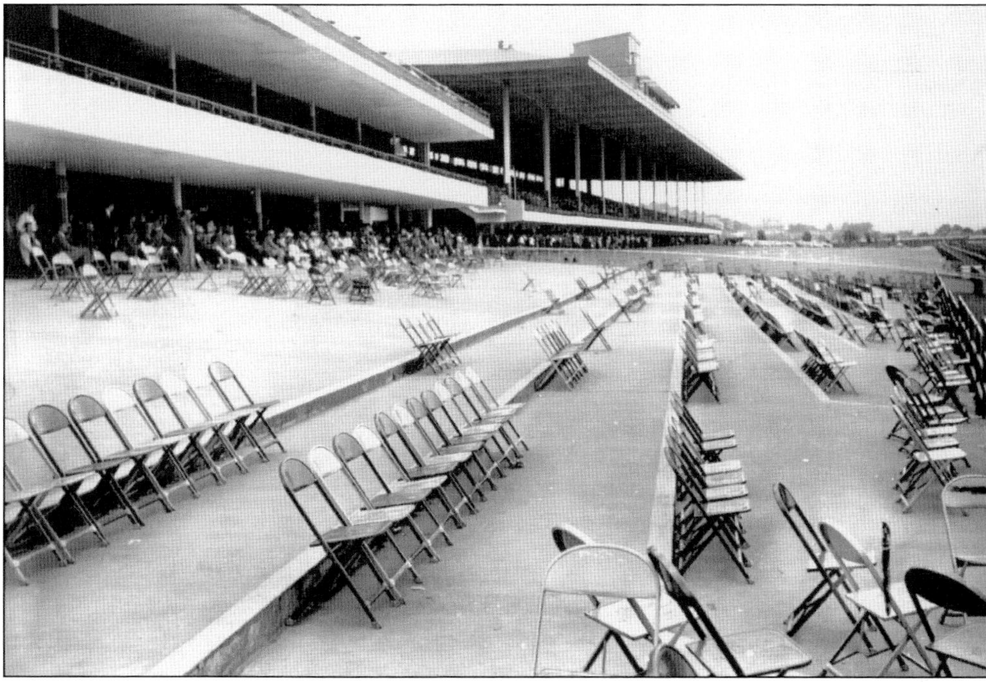

AN AIR-RAID SIREN TEST. Racing fans demonstrate complete cooperation during this air-raid siren test in July 1942, quickly leaving their seats for cover under the overhanging ceilings. (*Boston Herald-Traveler* photograph, courtesy Boston Public Library Print Department.)

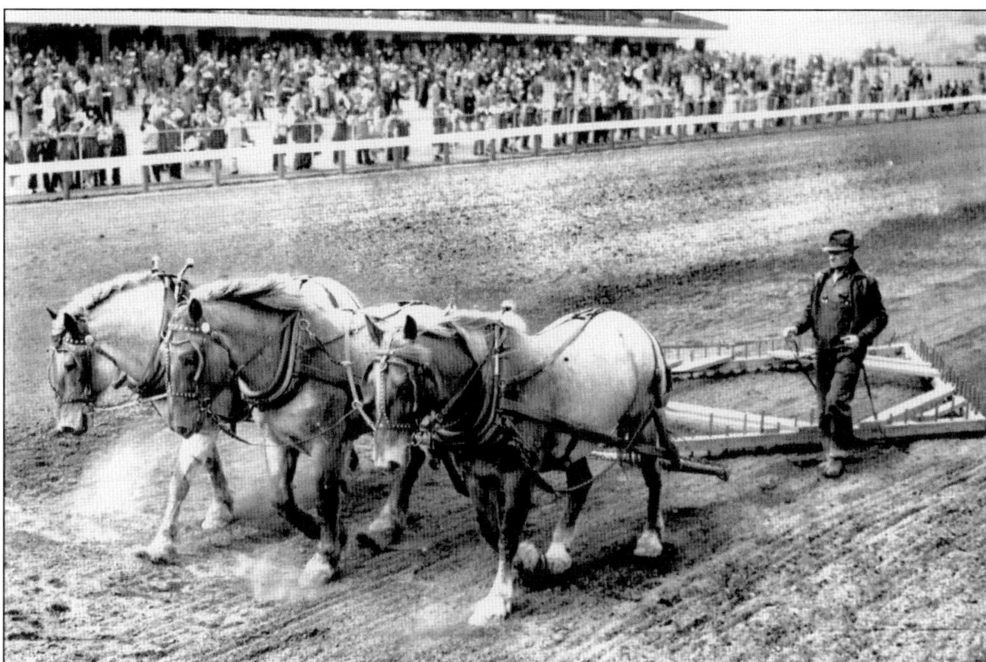

HORSEPOWER. Workhorses groomed the track surface when gas-rationing measures, made necessary due to World War II, put tractors out of commission in 1942. (*Boston Herald-Traveler* photograph, courtesy Boston Public Library Print Department.)

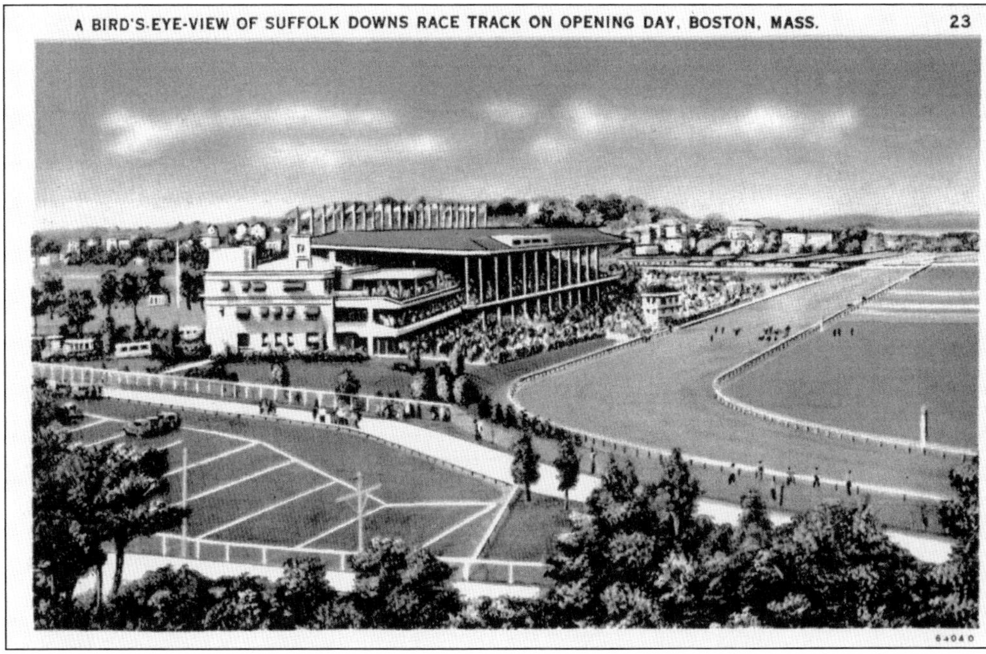

A TRACK POSTCARD. The track was included in a series of postcards created by the Tichnor Postcard Company in the 1940s featuring area landmarks. This one depicts the track's opening day. (Tichnor Postcard Company image, courtesy Boston Public Library Print Department.)

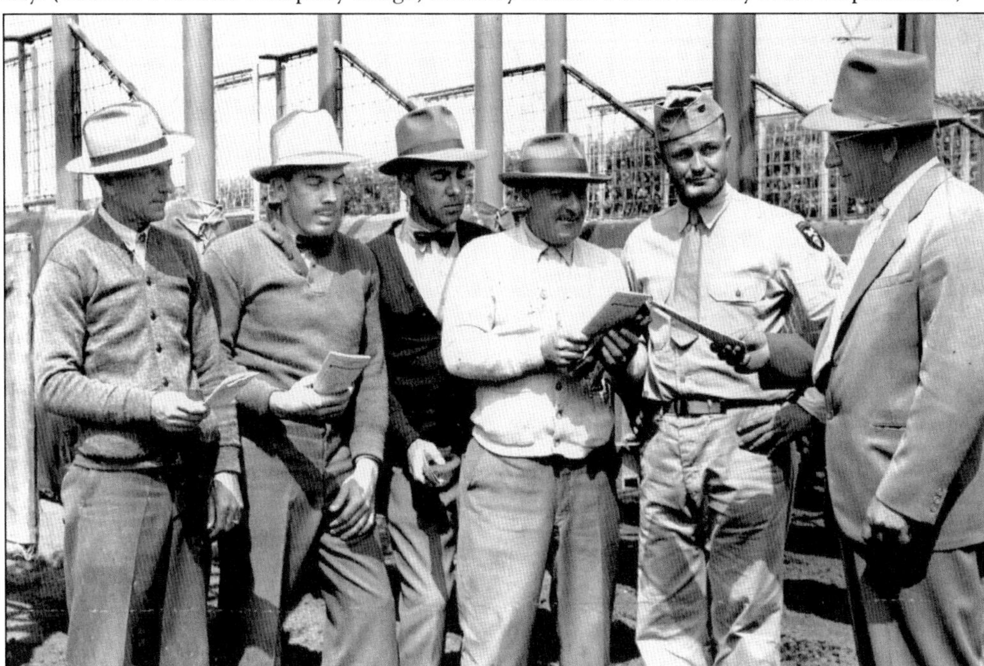

THE GATE CREW. Four unidentified members of the gate crew join Corp. Morris Kuykendall (in uniform, wearing a necktie) of the Airborne Command in receiving instructions from starter Bob Frend (far right) prior to a race in June 1943. (*Boston Herald-Traveler* photograph, courtesy Boston Public Library Print Department.)

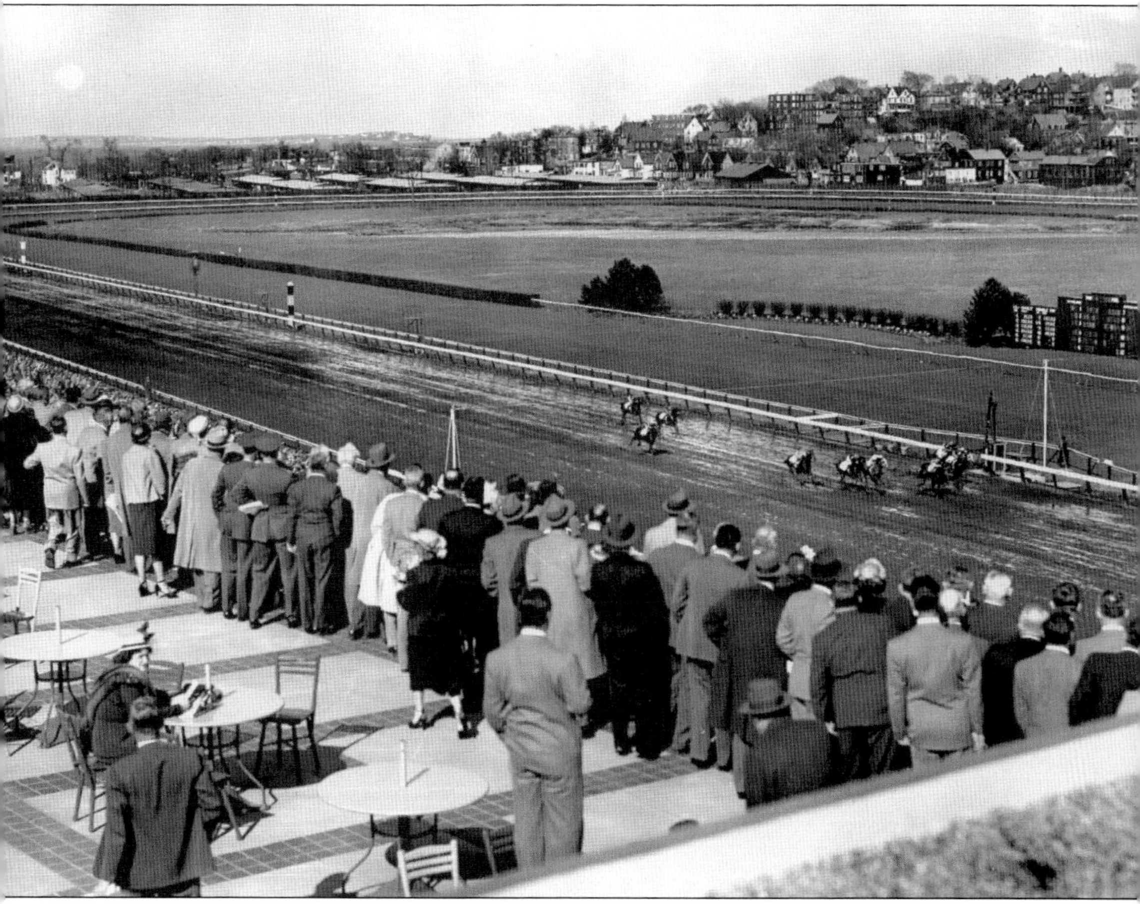

A Bird's-Eye View. The balcony atop the clubhouse provides an excellent vantage point for watching the races. (Leslie Jones photograph, courtesy Boston Public Library Print Department.)

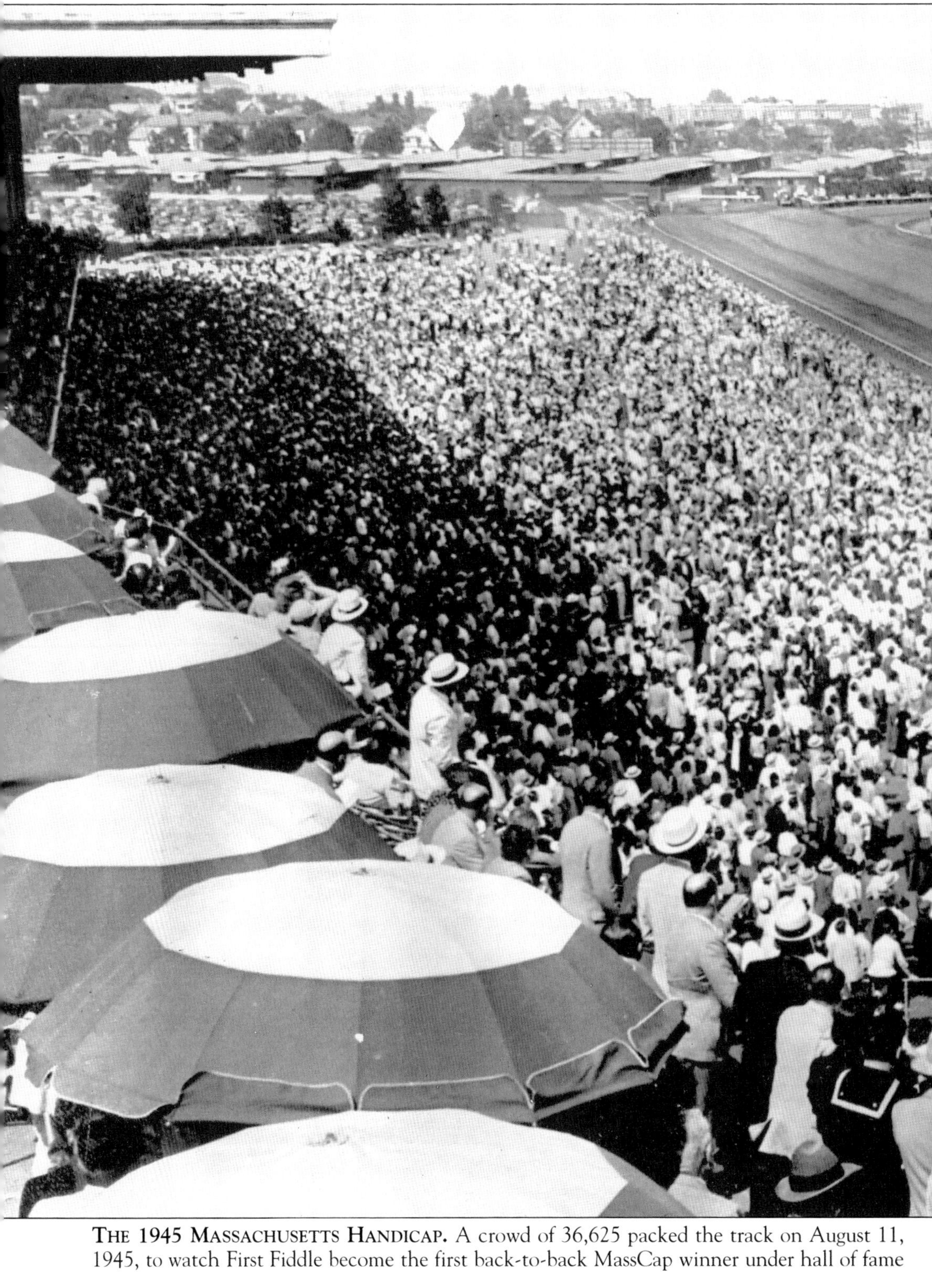

The 1945 Massachusetts Handicap. A crowd of 36,625 packed the track on August 11, 1945, to watch First Fiddle become the first back-to-back MassCap winner under hall of fame

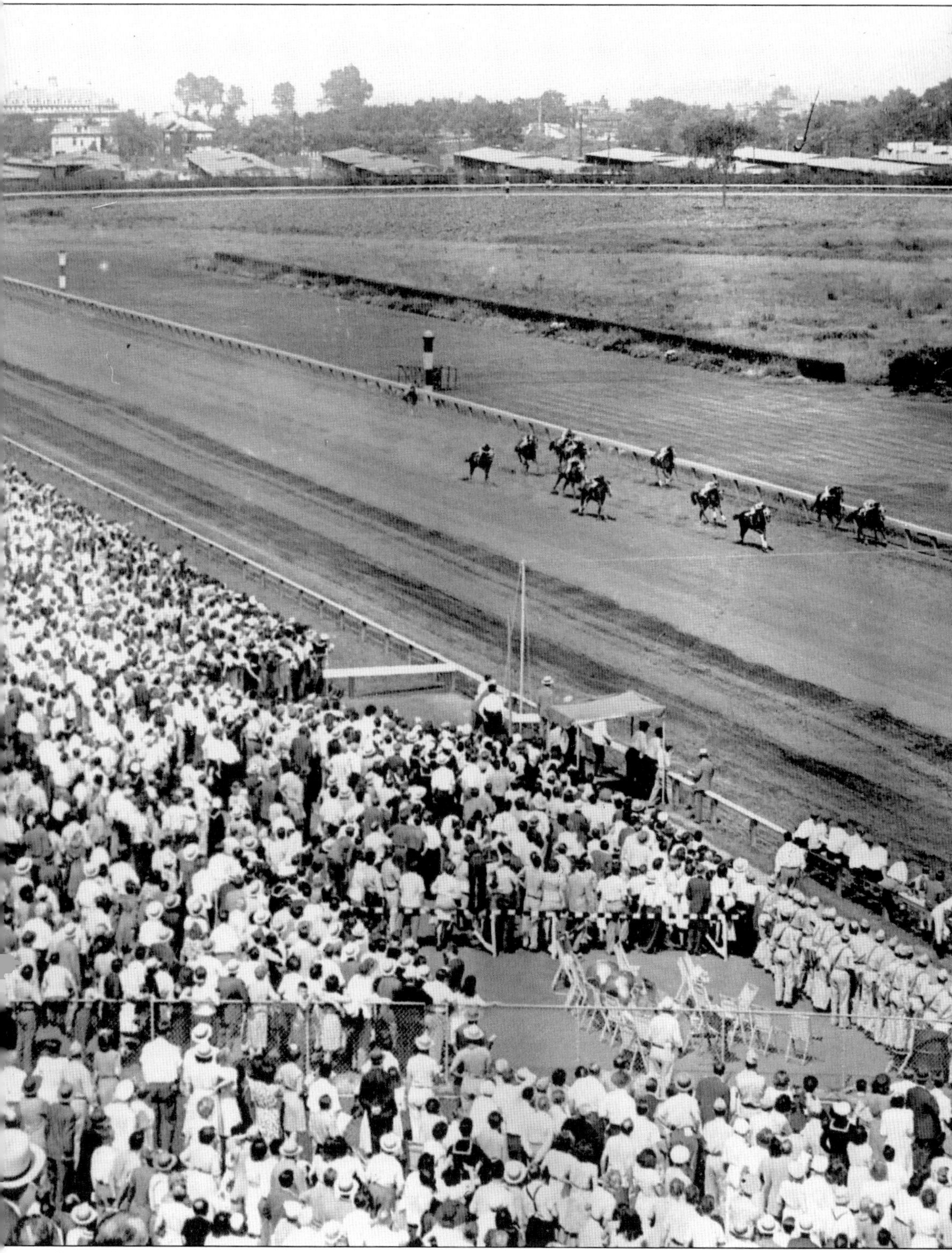

jockey Johnny Longden. (Courtesy Suffolk Downs.)

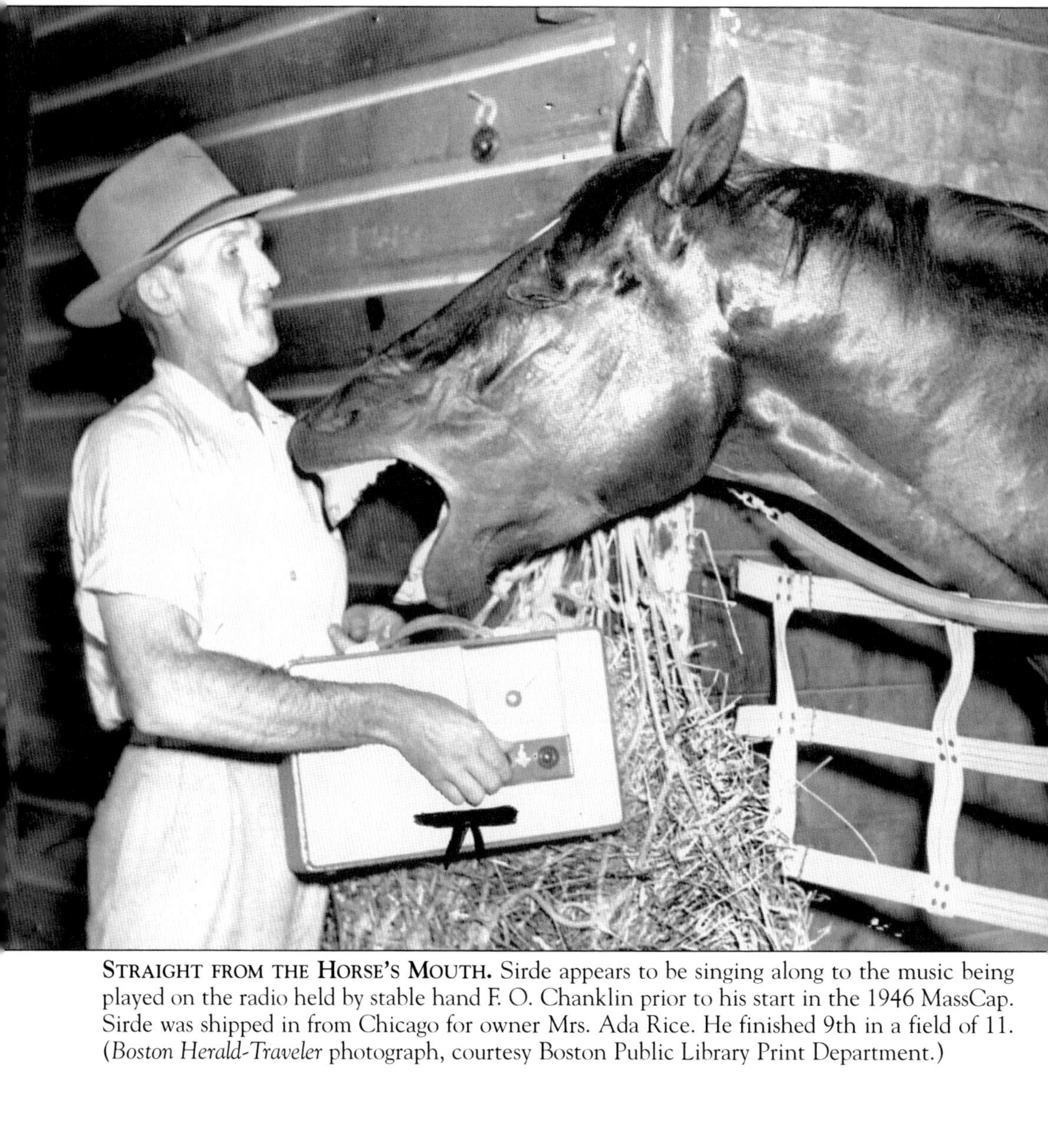

STRAIGHT FROM THE HORSE'S MOUTH. Sirde appears to be singing along to the music being played on the radio held by stable hand F. O. Chanklin prior to his start in the 1946 MassCap. Sirde was shipped in from Chicago for owner Mrs. Ada Rice. He finished 9th in a field of 11. (*Boston Herald-Traveler* photograph, courtesy Boston Public Library Print Department.)

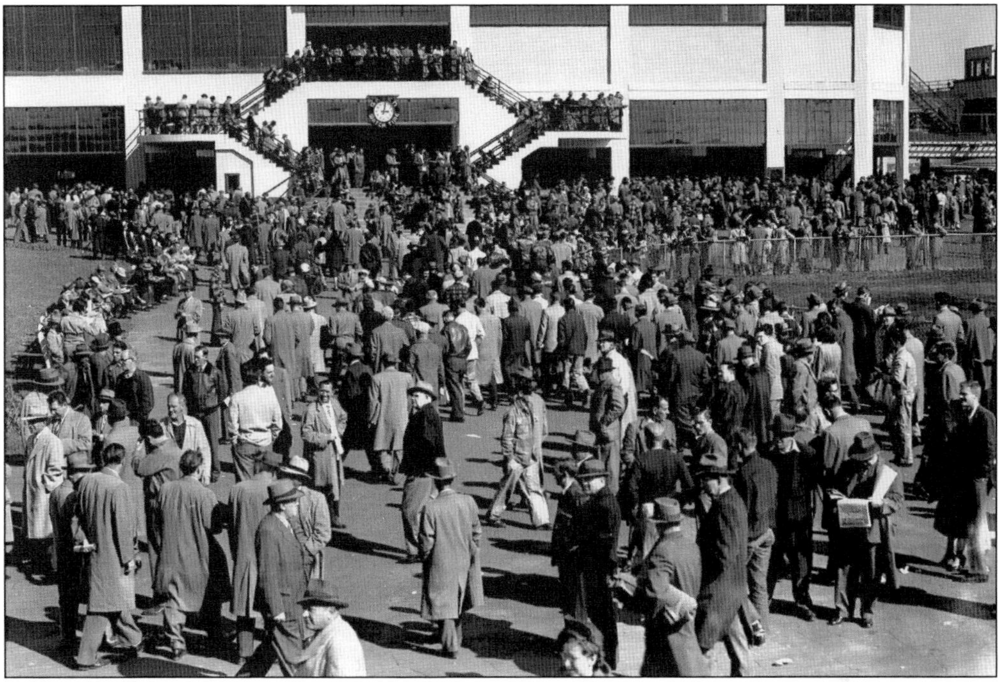

A BOOMING BUSINESS. Legions of fans make their way to the entrance of the grandstand. The track's three highest average attendance figures were posted from 1945 to 1947, including an all-time high of 18,388 in 1945. (Leslie Jones photograph, courtesy Boston Public Library Print Department.)

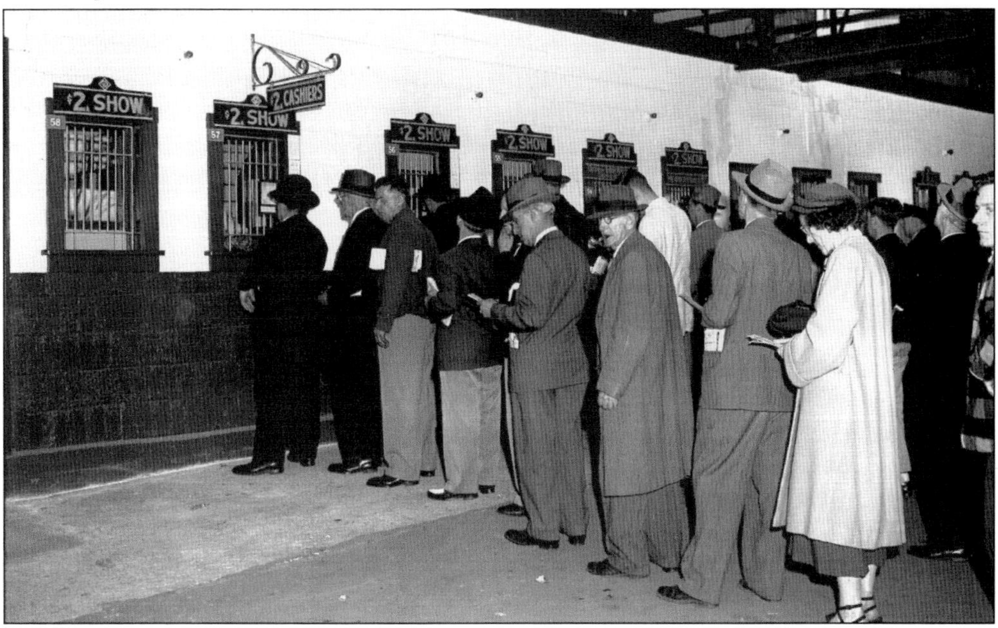

TWO DOLLARS TO SHOW. Horseplayers line up at a $2 show window. Windows were set up for each specific wager at the time. Patrons sent a daily average of $1,164,240 through the windows in 1946, a record that still stands. (Leslie Jones photograph, courtesy Boston Public Library Print Department.)

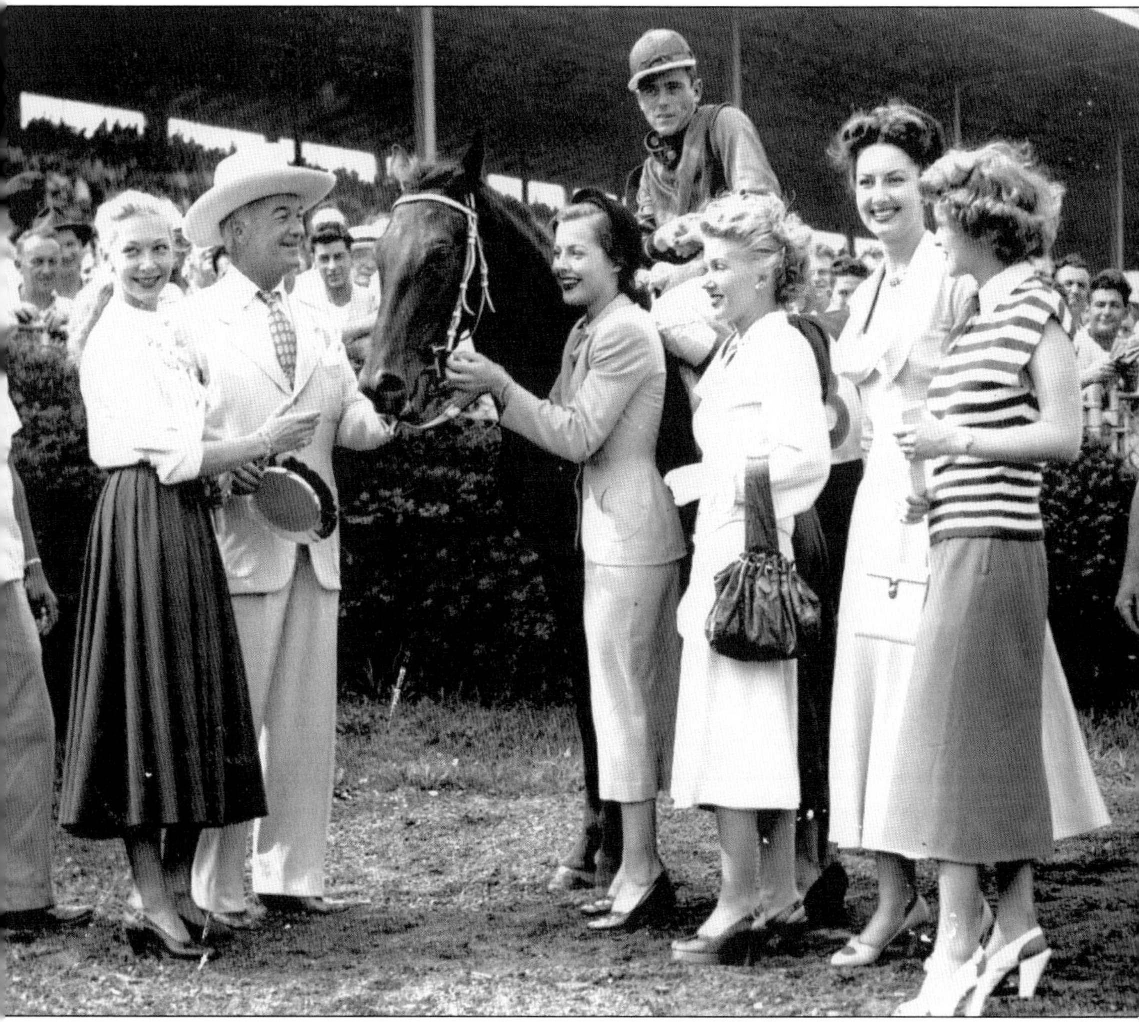

A Hollywood Ending. A group of movie stars joins Friendly Frank and jockey Jimmy Peres in the winner's circle after the feature race on July 18, 1949. Standing from left to right are Belita, Bill Boyd, Laura Elliot, Grace Bradley, Virginia O'Brien, and Lois James. The stars were in Boston for a charity softball game. (*Boston Herald-Traveler* photograph, courtesy Boston Public Library Print Department.)

Three

The 1950s

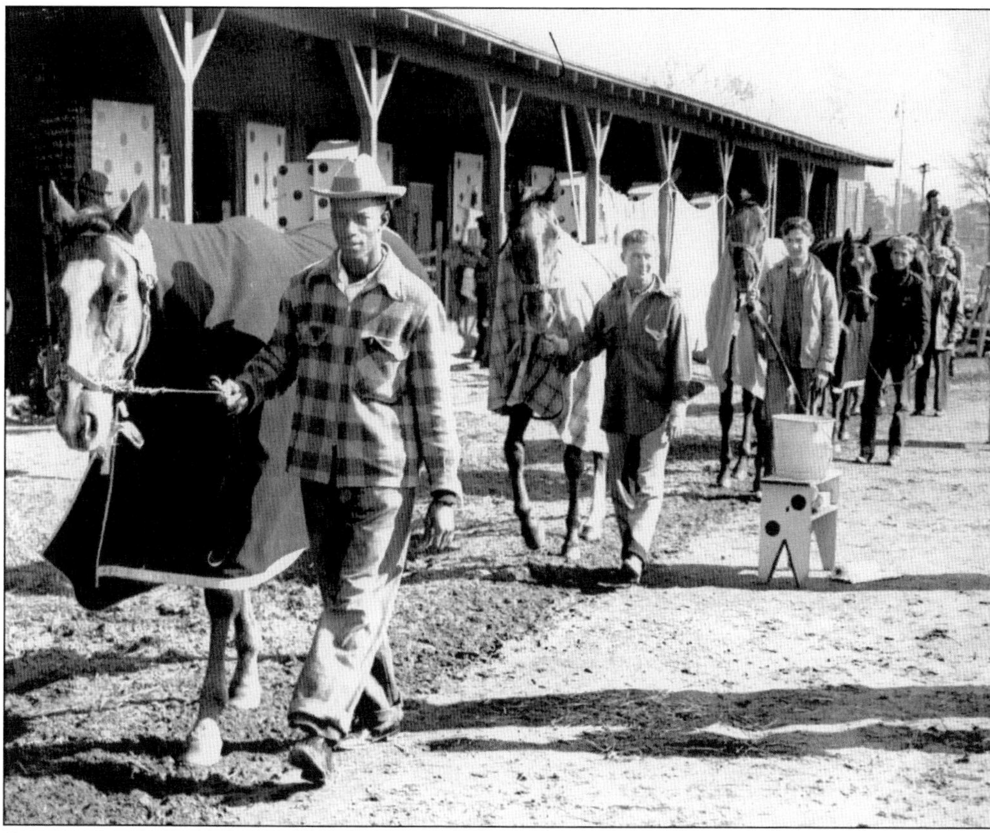

Chilling Out. Stable hands cool down the horses after their morning workouts in May 1950. Upon completion of a workout or a race, Thoroughbreds are walked to give them time to relax prior to returning to their stalls. (*Boston Herald-Traveler* photograph, courtesy Boston Public Library Print Department.)

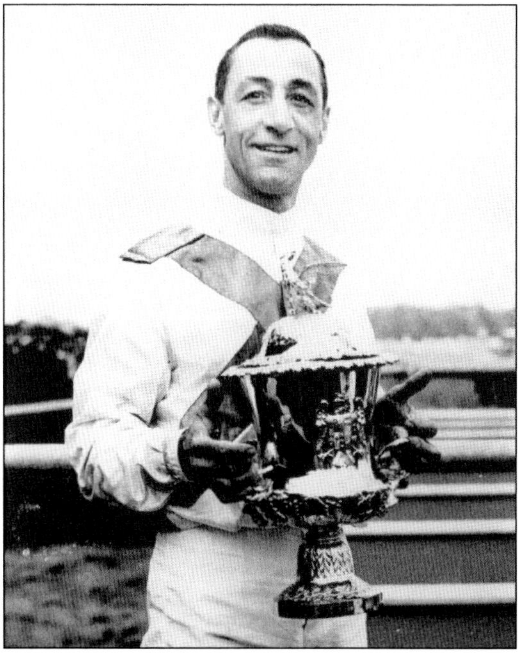

EDDIE ARCARO. Legendary jockey Eddie Arcaro holds the MassCap trophy after his winning ride aboard Cochise on June 7, 1950. It was the first of two MassCap wins for Arcaro, who won with Polylad in 1961. Arcaro is the only jockey to have won two Triple Crowns, doing so in 1941 with Whirlaway and in 1948 with Citation. (Courtesy Suffolk Downs.)

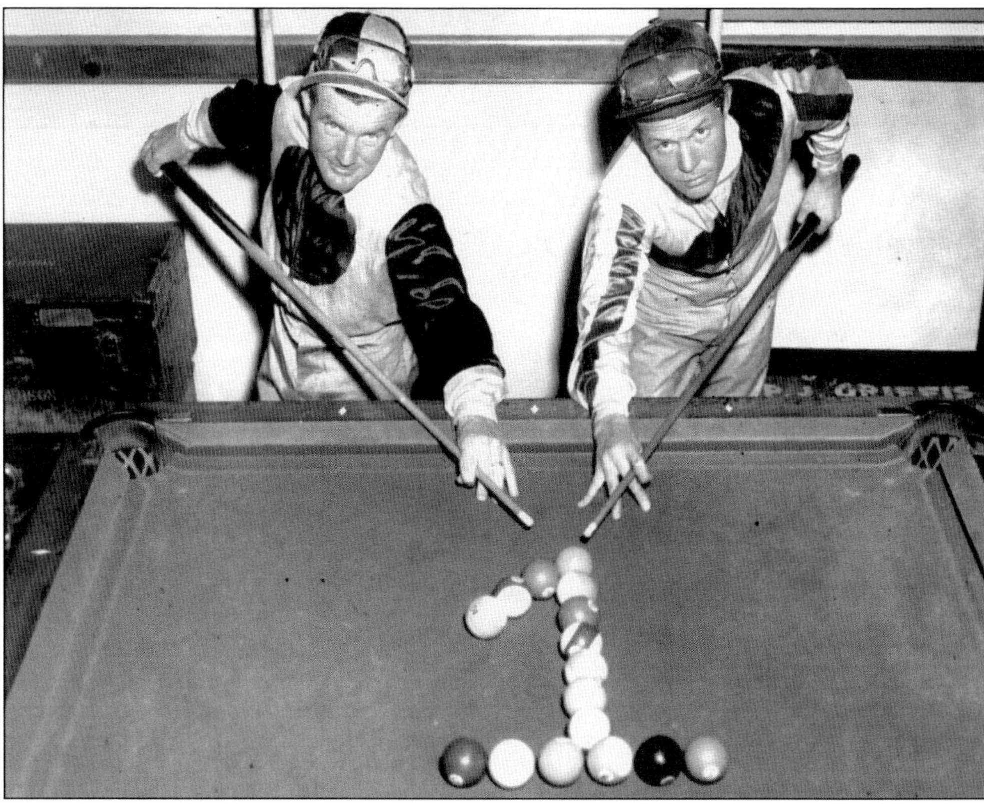

WHO'S NUMBER ONE? Jockeys Harold Keene (left) and Darrell Madden take their competition off the track and onto the pool table. Keene was the track's leading rider in 1950, while Madden shared that distinction with Henry Wajda in 1966. (Courtesy Suffolk Downs.)

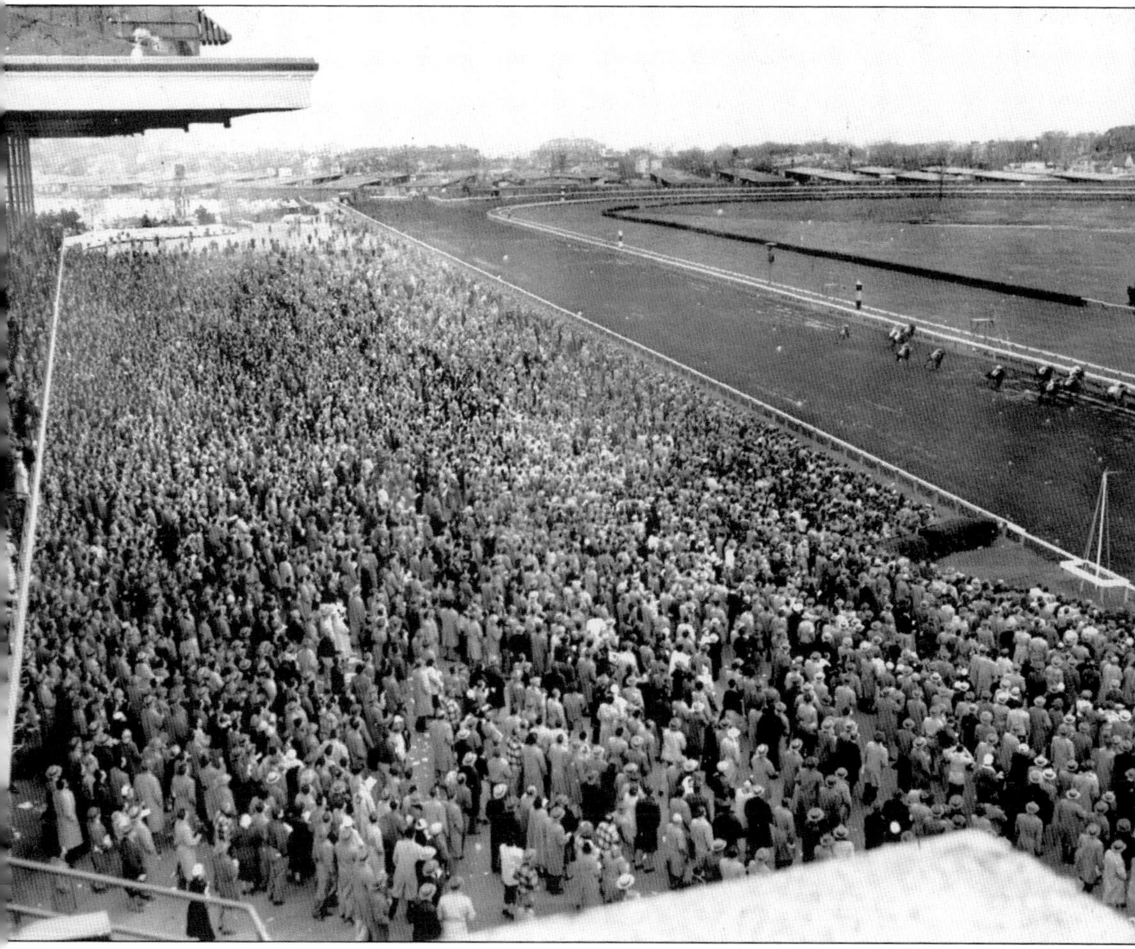

OPENING DAY, 1953. A crowd of 29,853 looks on as horses near the wire on April 20, 1953, the opening day of the racing season. Average attendance for the 60-day meet was 13,050. (Courtesy Suffolk Downs.)

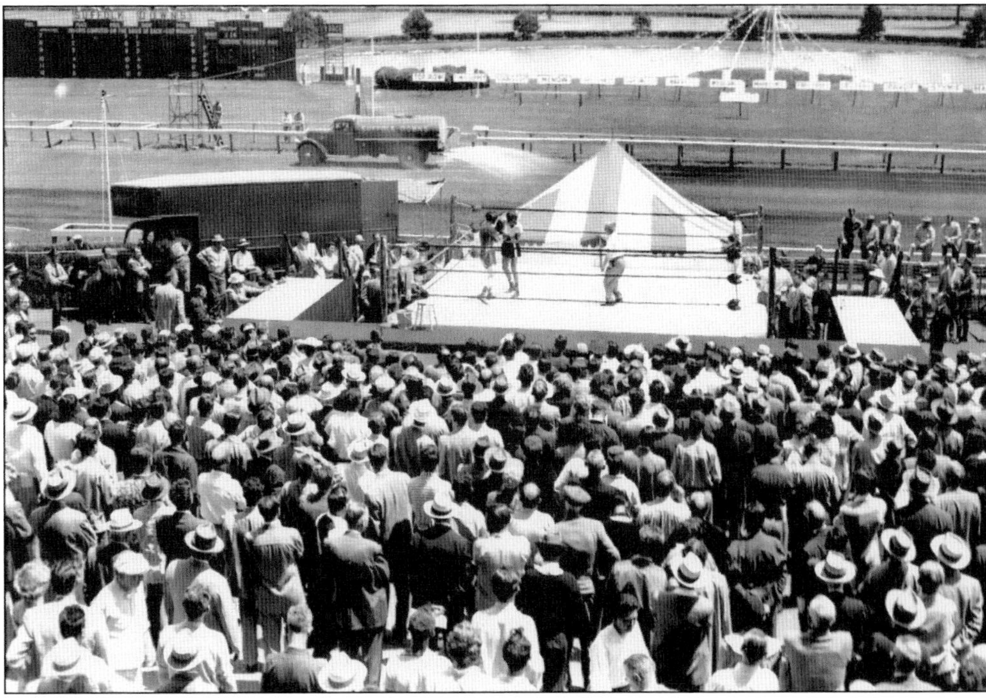

BOXING. The track has hosted numerous boxing matches over the years, including this one, which was part of the 1953 MassCap festivities. (Courtesy Suffolk Downs.)

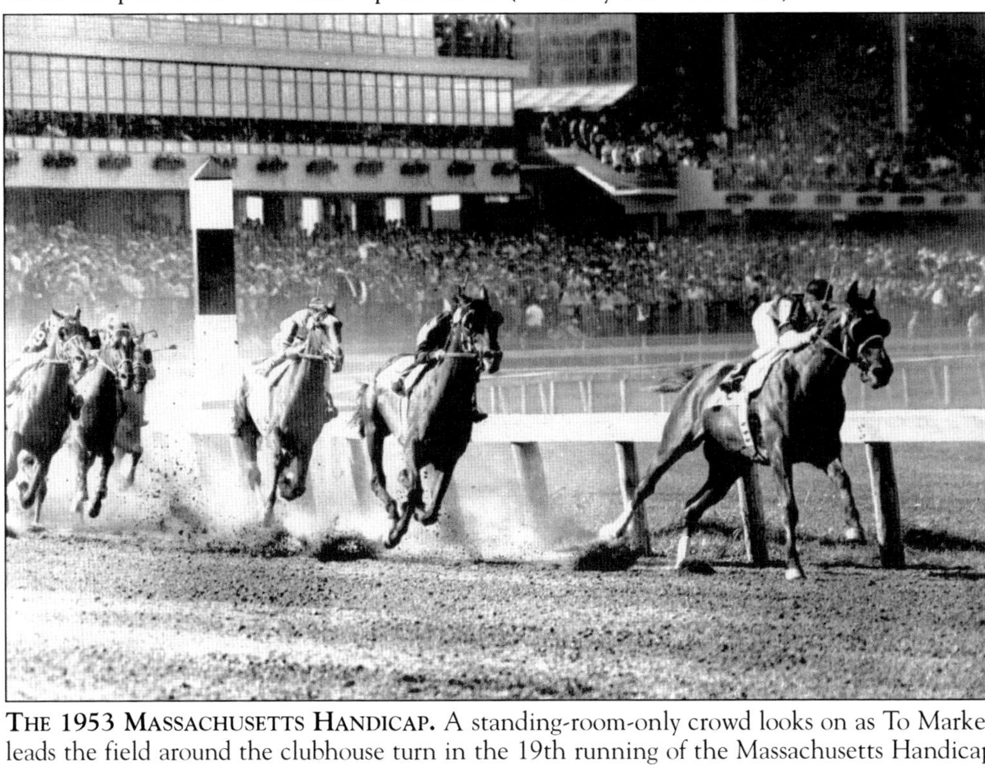

THE 1953 MASSACHUSETTS HANDICAP. A standing-room-only crowd looks on as To Market leads the field around the clubhouse turn in the 19th running of the Massachusetts Handicap on June 10, 1953. (Courtesy Suffolk Downs.)

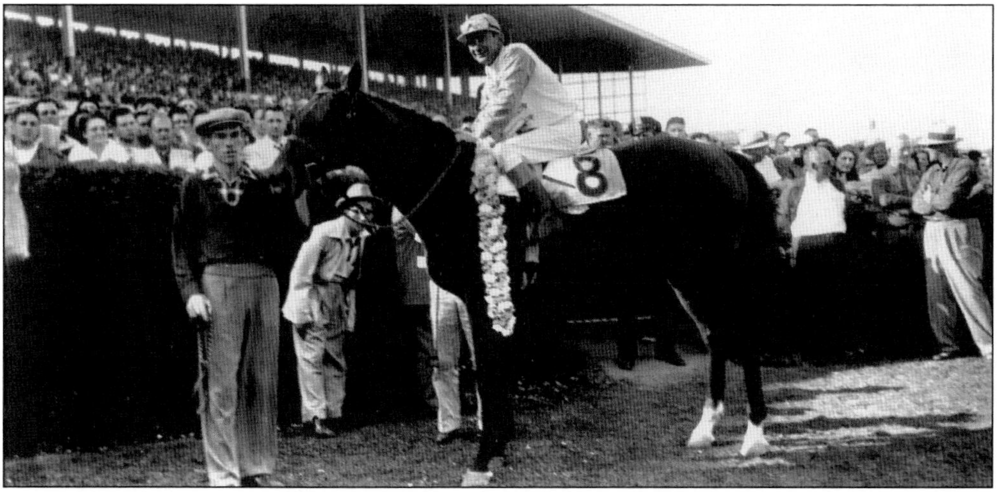

Royal Vale and Jack Westrope. Hall of fame jockey Jack Westrope sits atop Royal Vale in the winner's circle after their 1953 MassCap victory. Bred in England, Royal Vale joined 1948 MassCap champion Beauchef, from Chile, as the only foreign-bred winners of the race at the time. (Courtesy Suffolk Downs.)

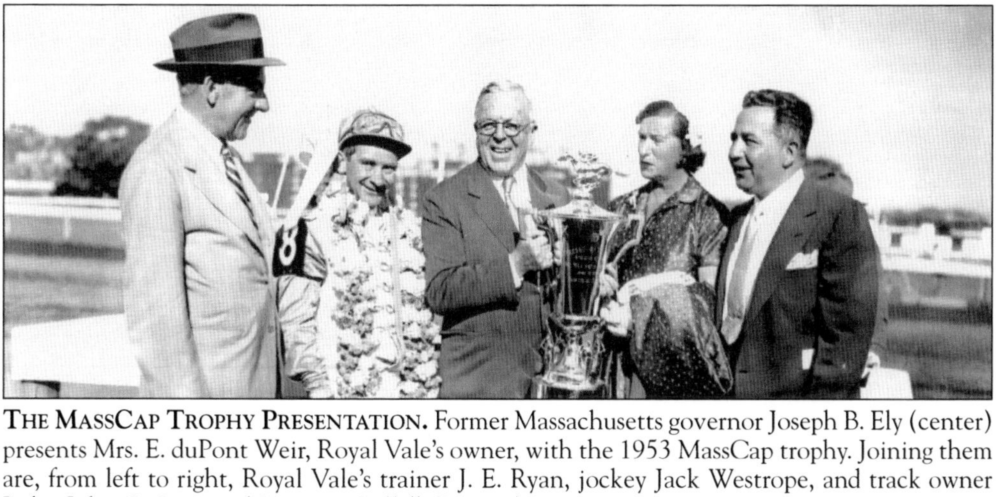

The MassCap Trophy Presentation. Former Massachusetts governor Joseph B. Ely (center) presents Mrs. E. duPont Weir, Royal Vale's owner, with the 1953 MassCap trophy. Joining them are, from left to right, Royal Vale's trainer J. E. Ryan, jockey Jack Westrope, and track owner Judge John C. Pappas. (Courtesy Suffolk Downs.)

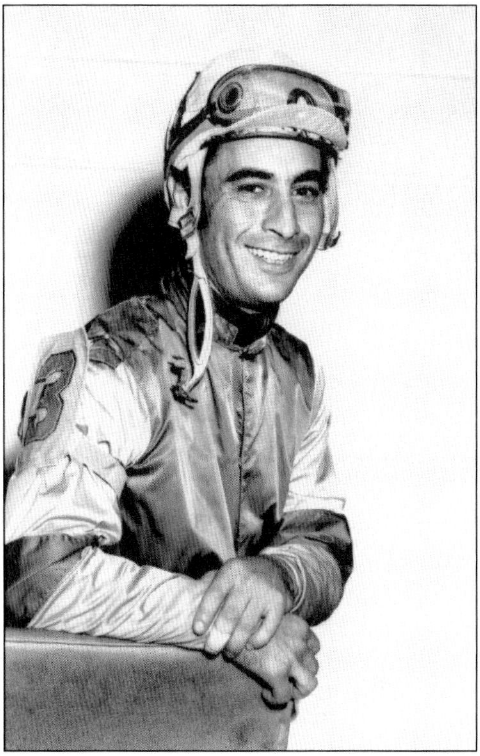

TONY DESPIRITO. A native of Lawrence, jockey Tony DeSpirito captured his lone Suffolk Downs riding title in 1954, two years after winning a record 390 races as a 16-year-old apprentice. (Courtesy Suffolk Downs.)

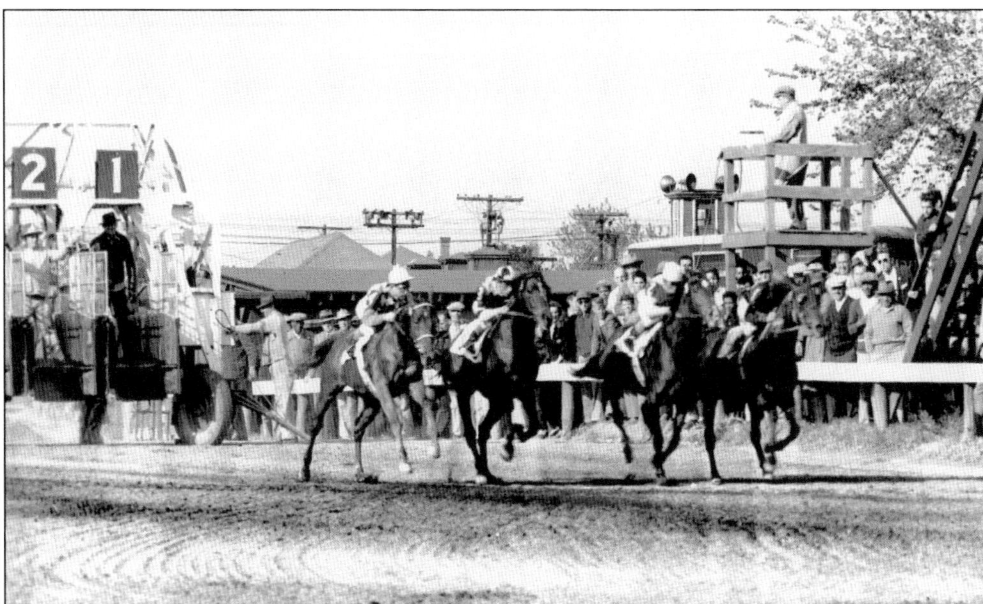

THE 1955 MASSACHUSETTS HANDICAP. Seen here from left to right, Social Outcast, Wise Margin, Helioscope, and Bassanio compete for the early lead in the 21st running of the MassCap on May 19, 1955. Helioscope, with jockey Sammy Boulmetis, stopped the clock at 2:01, setting a track record for 1¼ miles that still stands. The four-horse field remains the smallest in MassCap history. (Courtesy Suffolk Downs.)

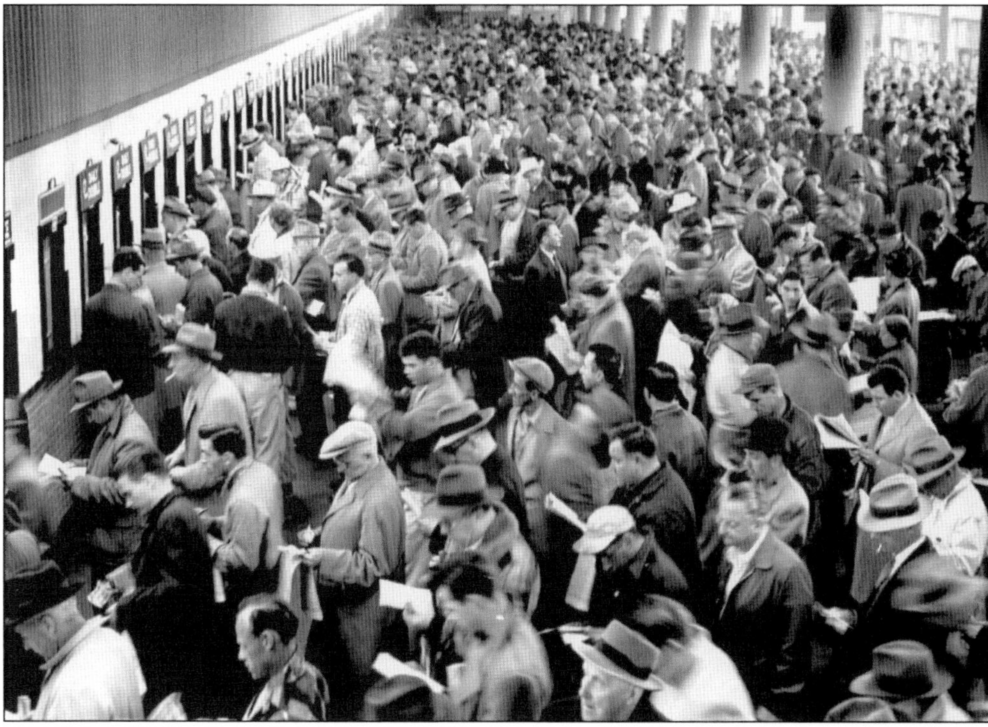

THE DAILY DOUBLE WINDOW. Bettors flock to the Daily Double window on opening day of the 1956 racing season. The first double of the meet paid $381.80 on 144 winning tickets when Pyongyang and Clay's Choice won races one and two, respectively. (*Boston Herald-Traveler* photograph, courtesy Boston Public Library Print Department.)

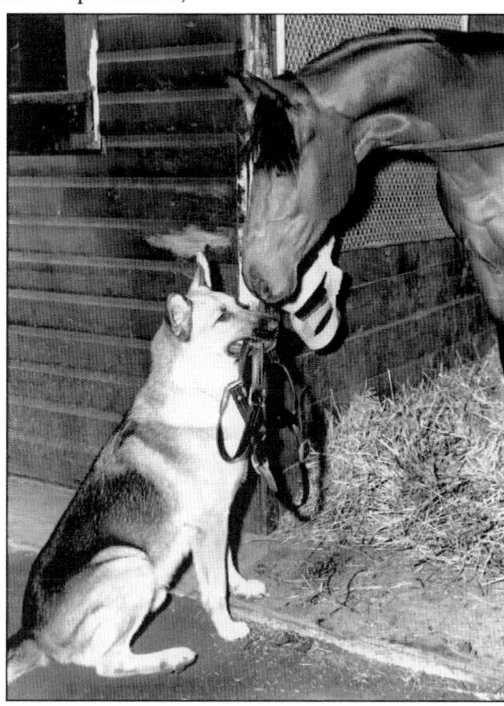

RIN TIN TIN. The canine star of the hit television series *Adventures of Rin Tin Tin* visits the stall of Brandywine Stable's Bora in October 1956. Rin Tin Tin was in town for an appearance in the rodeo at the Boston Garden. (*Boston Herald-Traveler* photograph, courtesy Boston Public Library Print Department.)

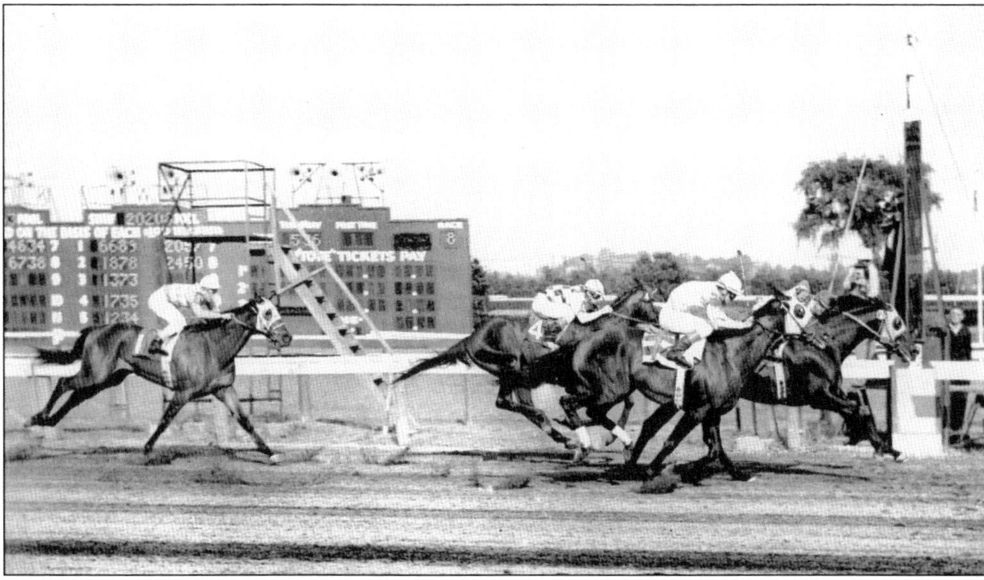

THE 1959 MASSACHUSETTS HANDICAP. Day Court crossed the wire first, but it was Air Pilot (No. 7) who came away the winner of the 25th MassCap when Day Court was disqualified. The stewards ruled that Day Court's jockey, Henry Moreno, grabbed Jack Leonard, the rider of Air Pilot, several times in the stretch, resulting in Day Court being placed second and Air Pilot winning the first of his two MassCaps. His second win came in 1962. (Courtesy Suffolk Downs.)

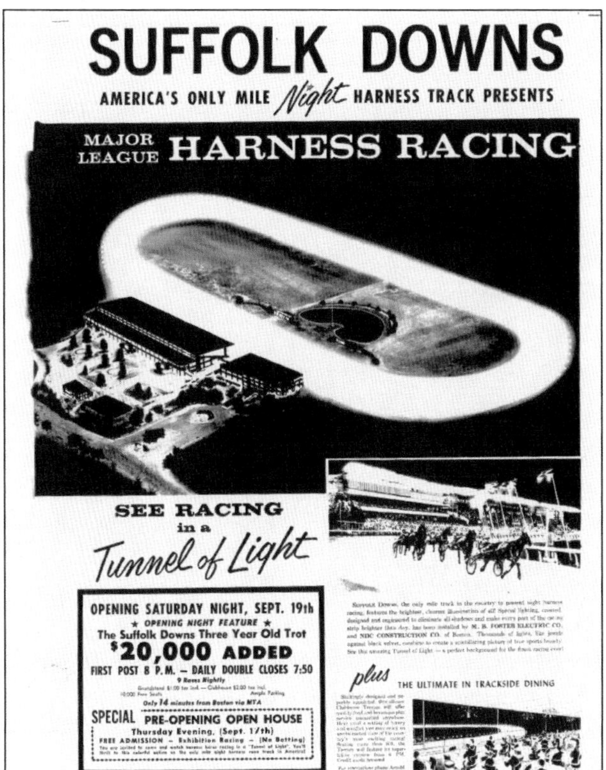

A TUNNEL OF LIGHT. The track boasts its status as the nation's only one-mile night harness track in a print advertisement in September 1959. (Courtesy *Boston Herald*.)

Four

THE 1960S

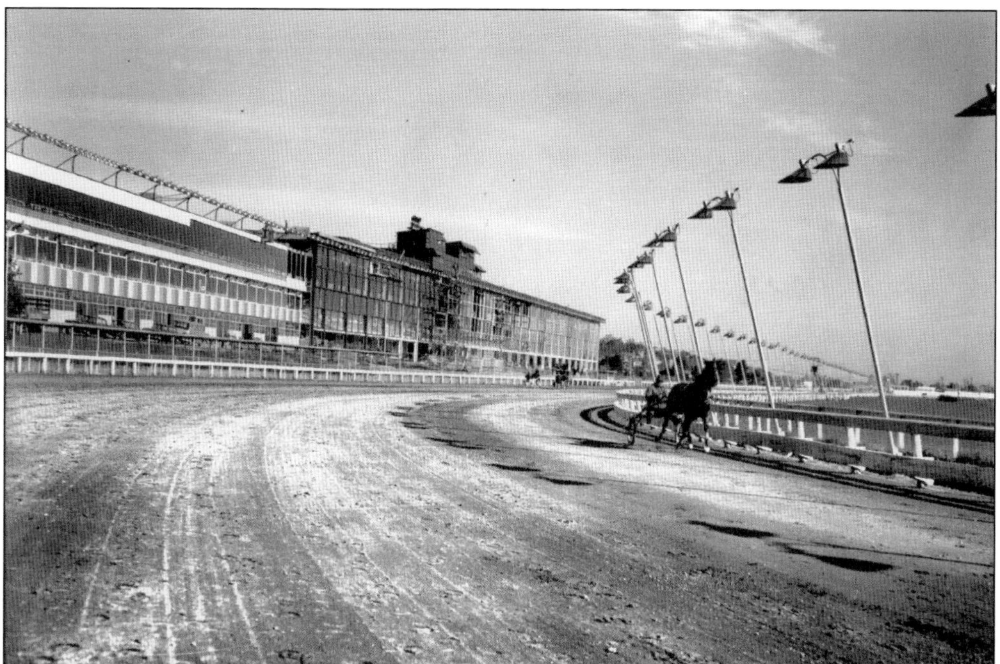

HARNESS RACING. Trotters get in some exercise prior to the day's races in October 1962. Harness racing was conducted under the lights on a regular basis from 1959 to 1970. (*Boston Herald-Traveler* photograph, courtesy Boston Public Library Print Department.)

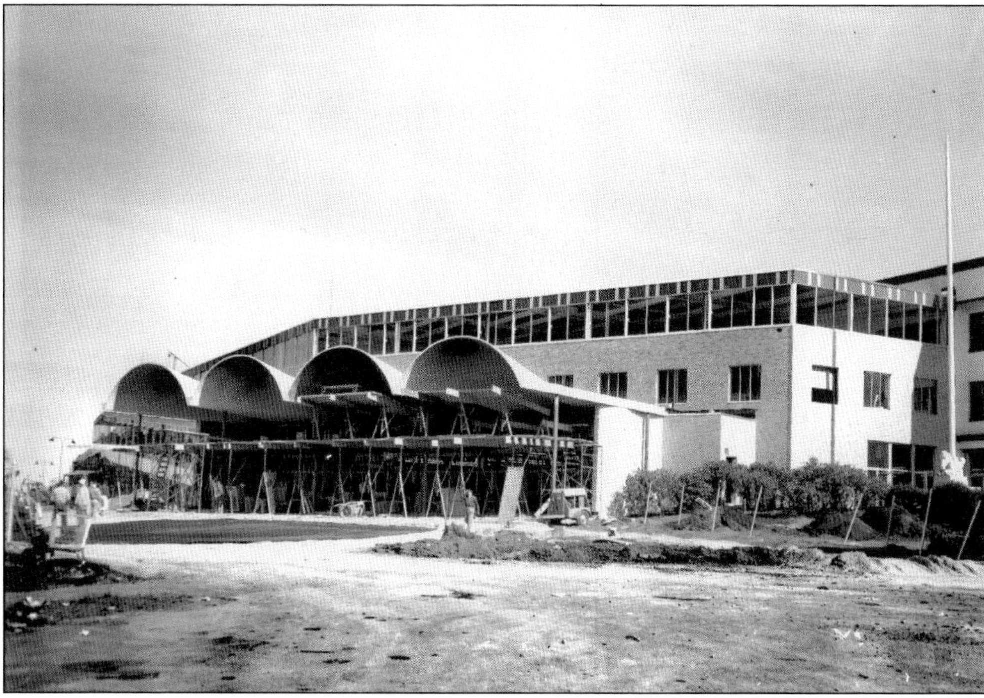

UNDER CONSTRUCTION. The facility underwent a major renovation after the conclusion of the 1962 Thoroughbred meet. The project drastically changed the look of the main entrance, which had remained the same since it was built in 1935. (Above, *Boston Herald-Traveler* photograph, courtesy Boston Public Library Print Department; below, courtesy Suffolk Downs.)

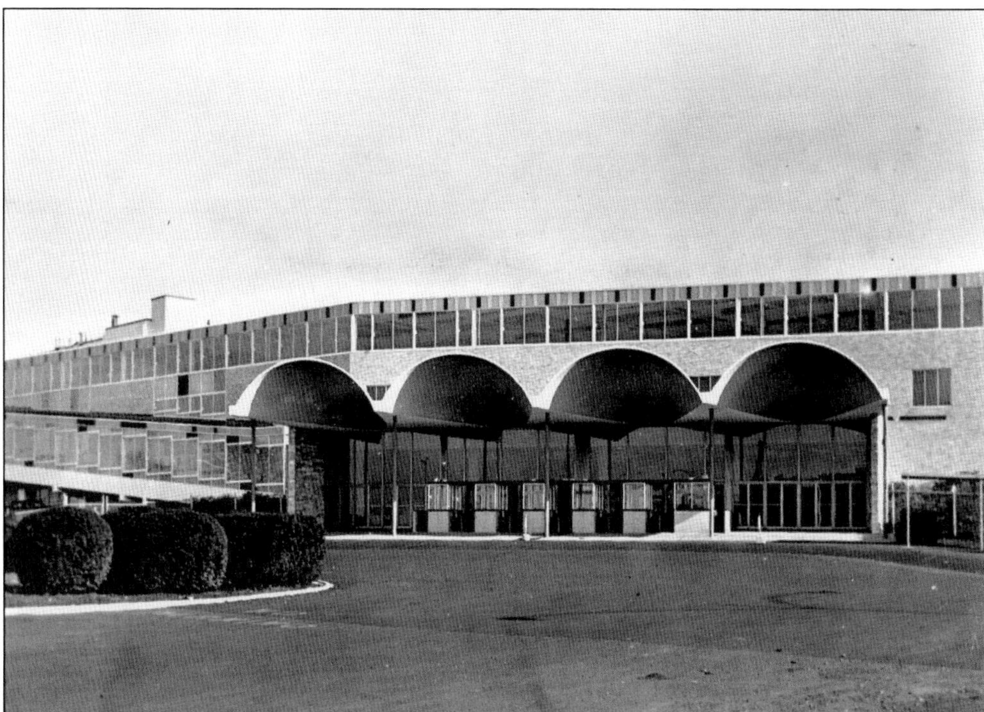

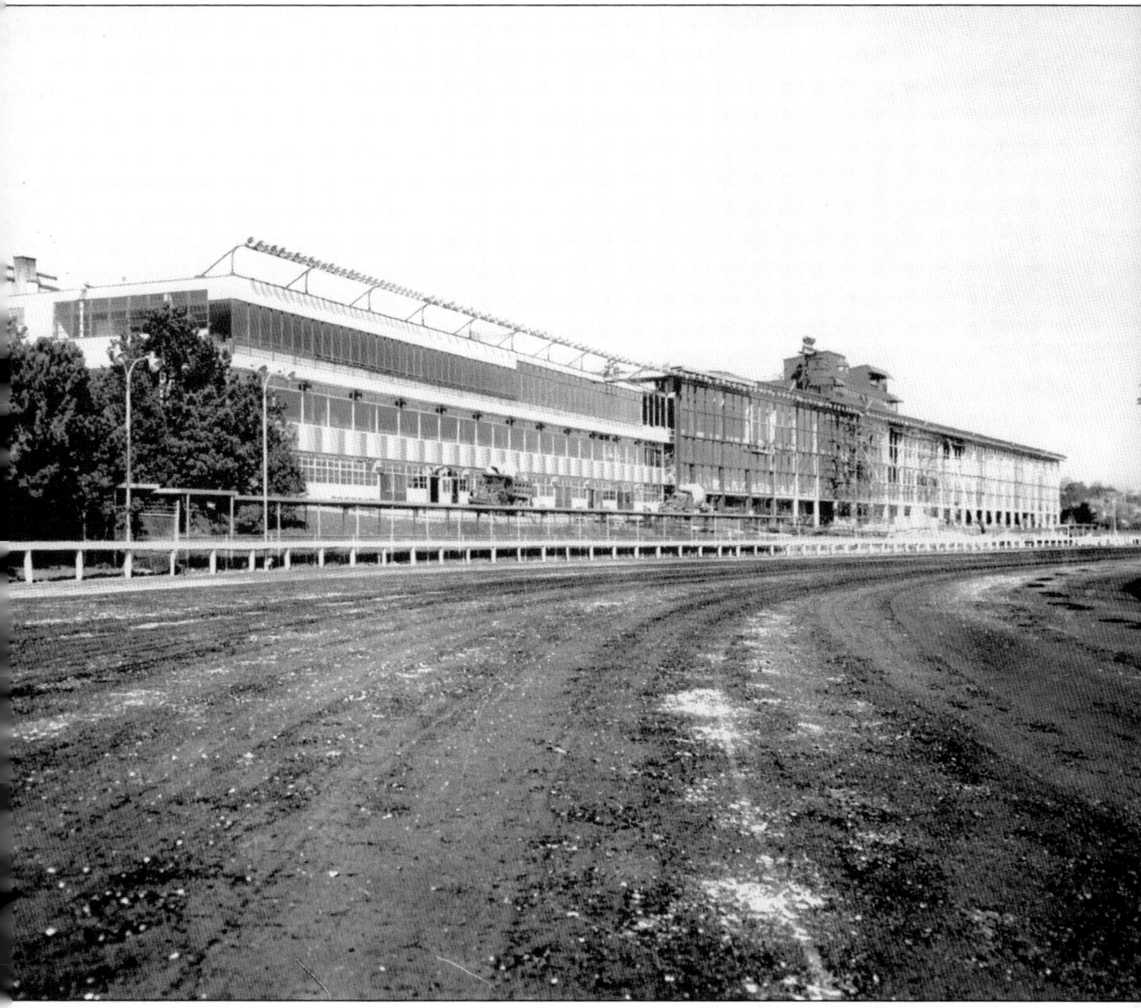

The Clubhouse and the Grandstand. As part of the renovation project, the clubhouse and grandstand were joined together and completely enclosed. (*Boston Herald-Traveler* photograph, courtesy Boston Public Library Print Department.)

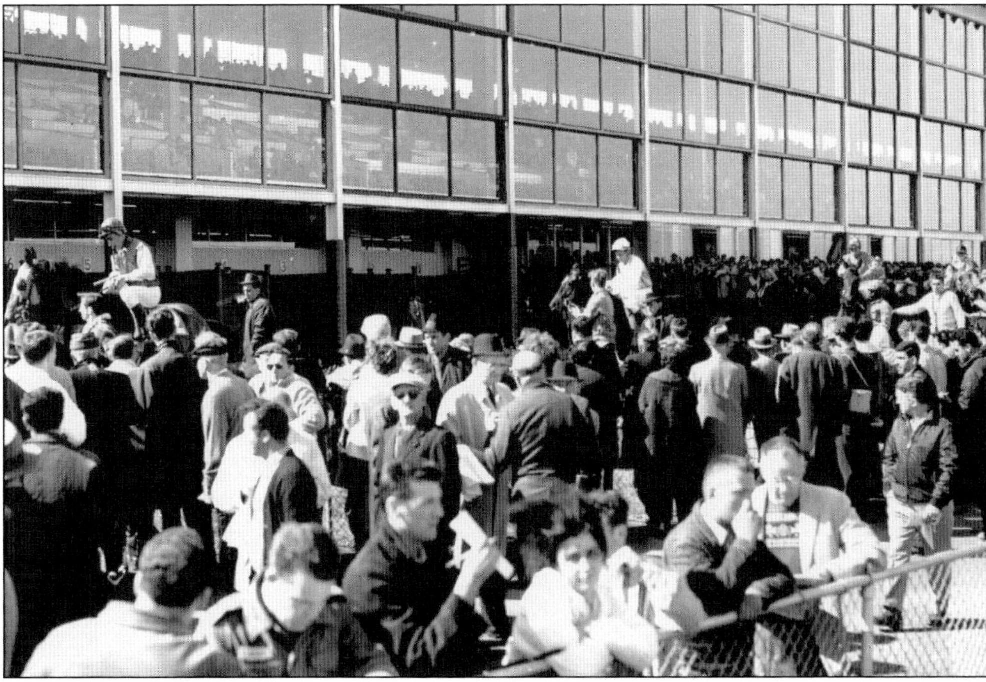

THE WALKING RING. Fans get a closer look at the horses in the new walking ring, located on the track side of the grandstand, on opening day of the 1963 racing season. Before the new walking ring was constructed, the horses were saddled on the opposite side of the grandstand and paraded directly onto the track. Below is a closeup view of the new walking ring and paddock area. (Above, *Boston Herald-Traveler* photograph, courtesy Boston Public Library Print Department; below, *Boston Herald* photograph.)

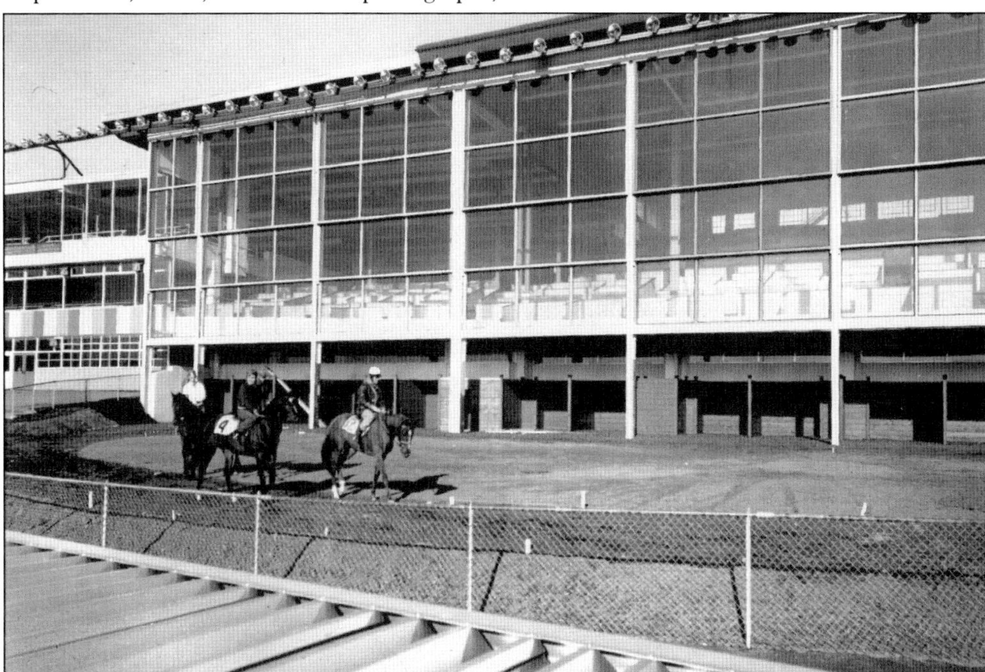

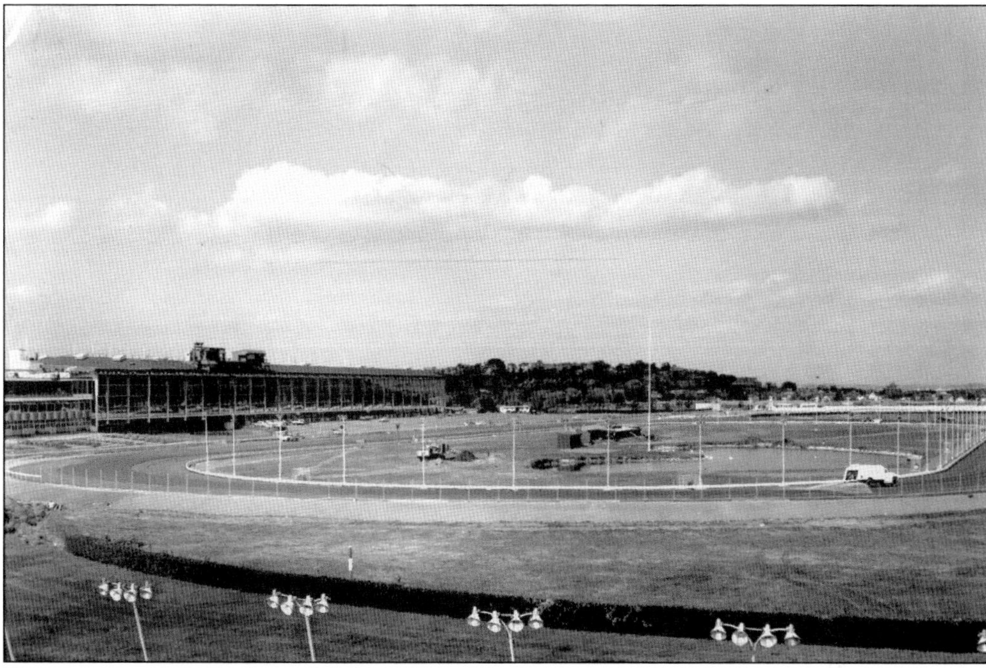

THE INNER OVAL. A lighted half-mile harness oval was constructed inside of the one-mile main track prior to the start of the 1964 meet. (*Boston Herald-Traveler* photograph, courtesy Boston Public Library Print Department.)

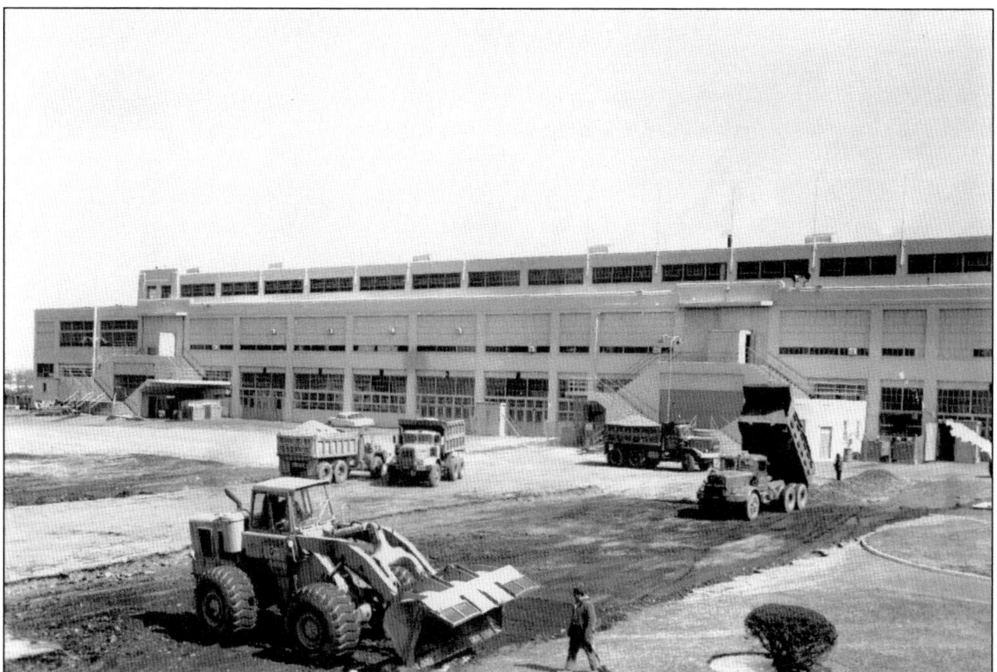

MORE PARKING. The grassy area behind the grandstand was converted to a parking lot prior to opening day of the 1965 meet. The lot accommodated 500 cars. (*Boston Herald-Traveler* photograph, courtesy Boston Public Library Print Department.)

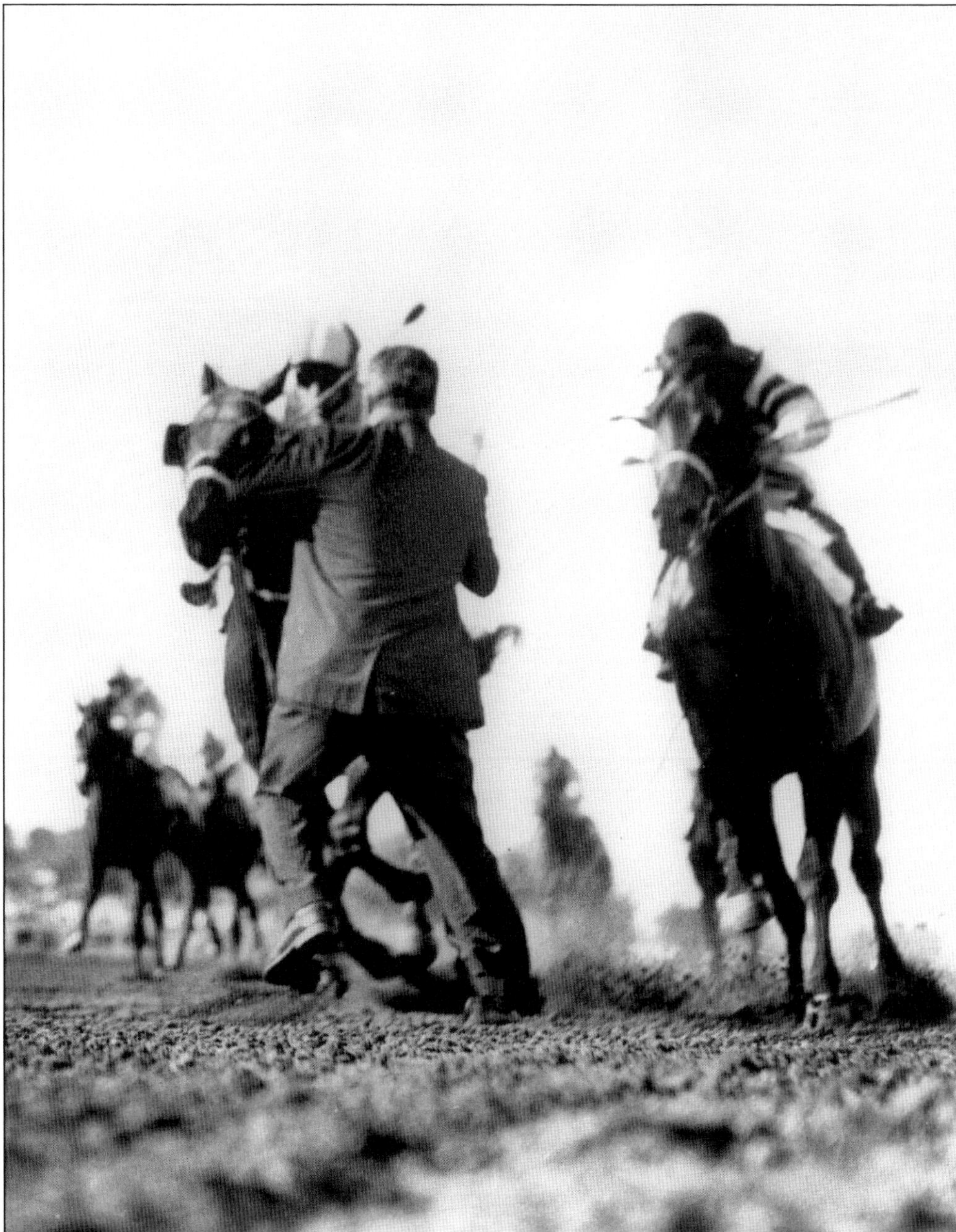

THE 1966 MAYFLOWER STAKES. A disoriented fan made his way onto the racetrack during the 32nd running of the Mayflower Stakes on July 4, 1966. The fan, Theodore Luppino, made contact with three horses and was hospitalized for observation. Miraculously, he was not injured. The outcome of the race, won by Happy Voter, was not affected. (Henry Carfagna photograph, courtesy Suffolk Downs.)

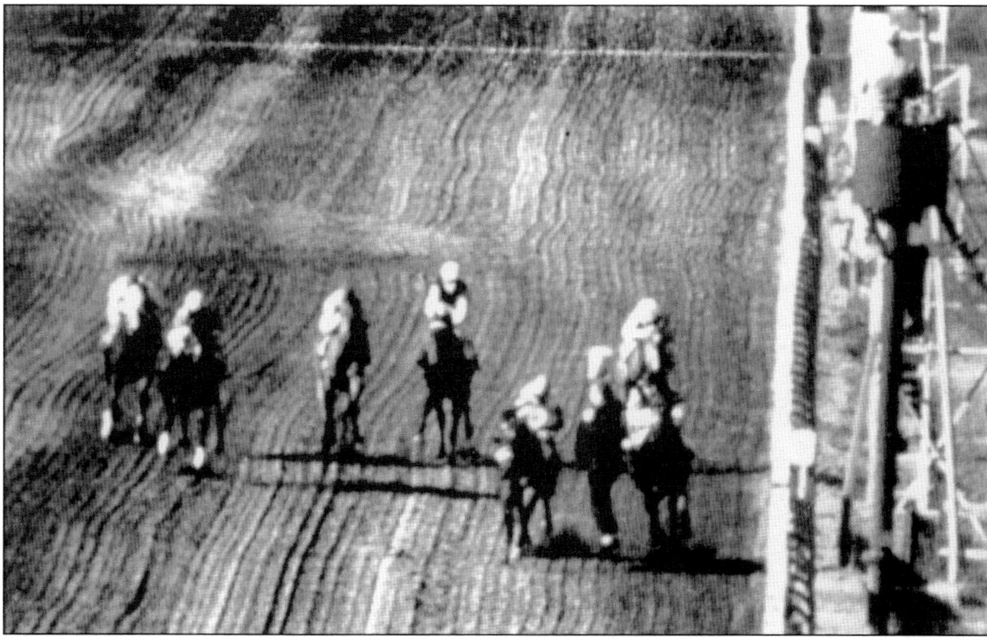

A Head-On View. These photographs of the 1966 Mayflower Stakes show the fan between horses (above) and standing with his arms out once the horses passed him (below). (Courtesy Boston Public Library Print Department.)

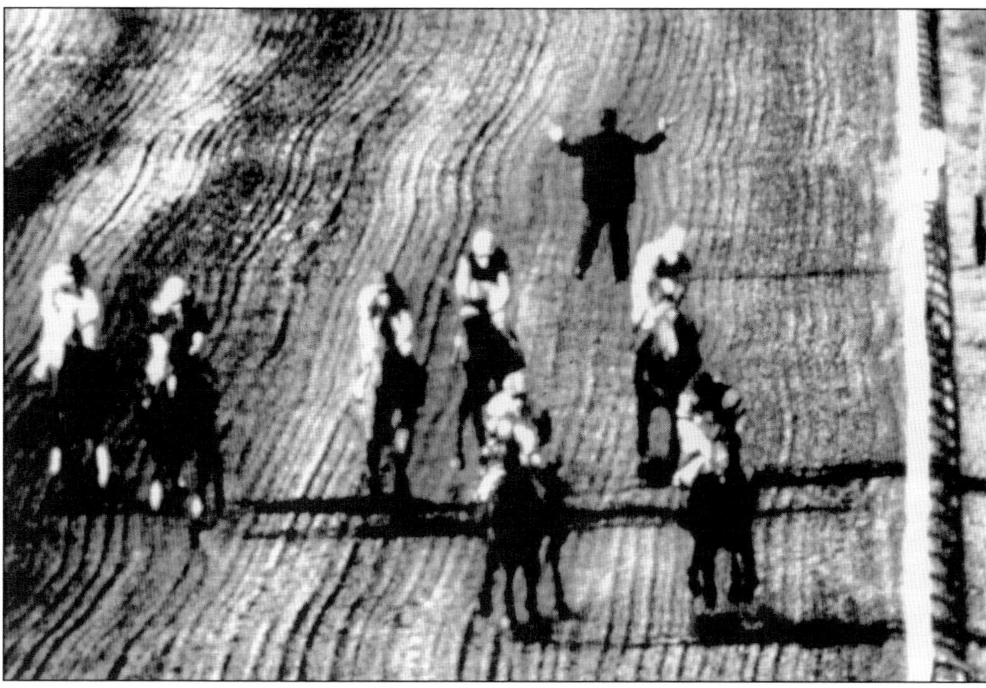

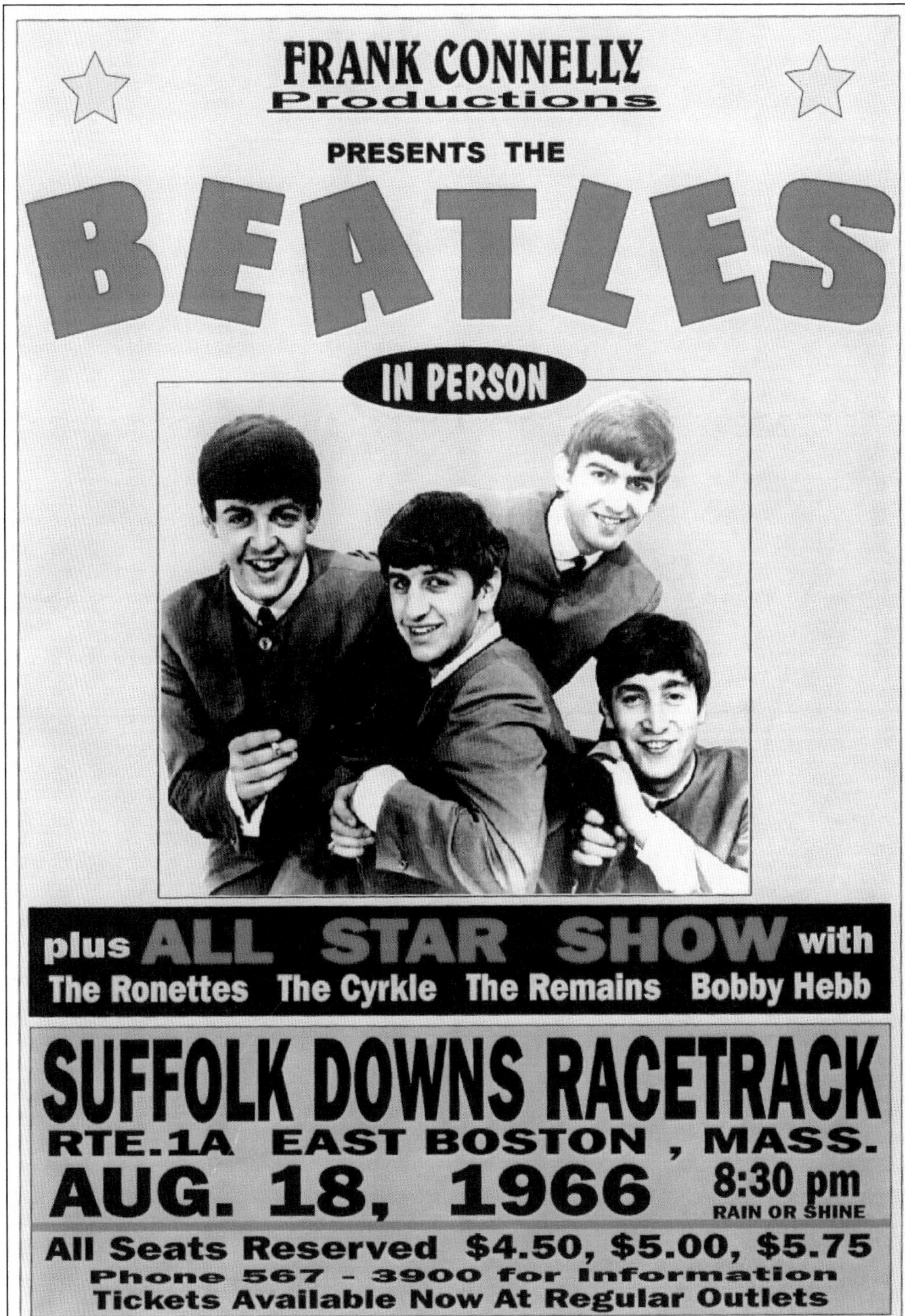

THE BEATLES. A promotional poster advertises the Beatles' 1966 concert at the track. (Courtesy Suffolk Downs.)

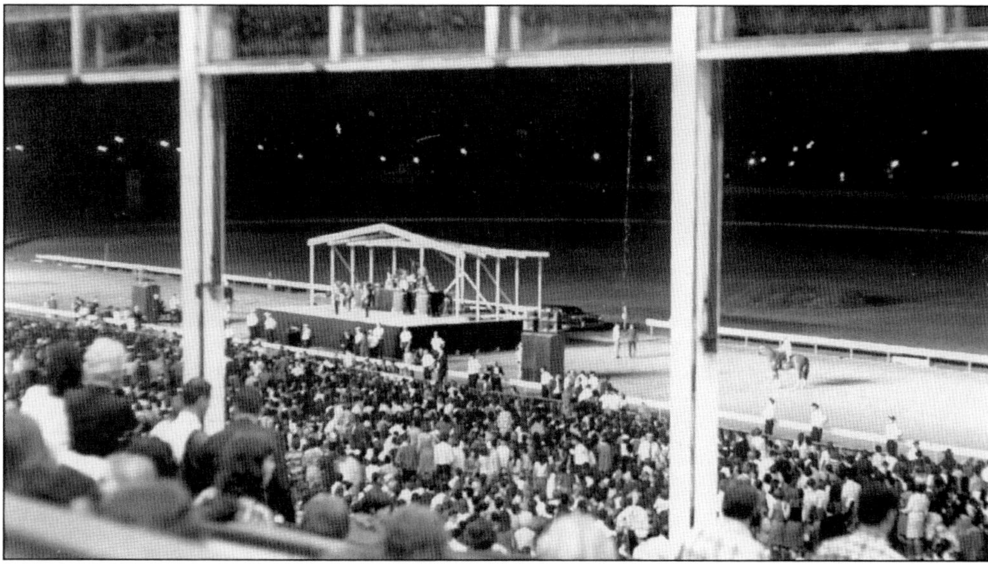

The Fab Four in Concert. The Beatles made their final Boston appearance on August 18, 1966, before a packed crowd of over 25,000. (*Boston Herald-Traveler* photograph, courtesy Boston Public Library Print Department.)

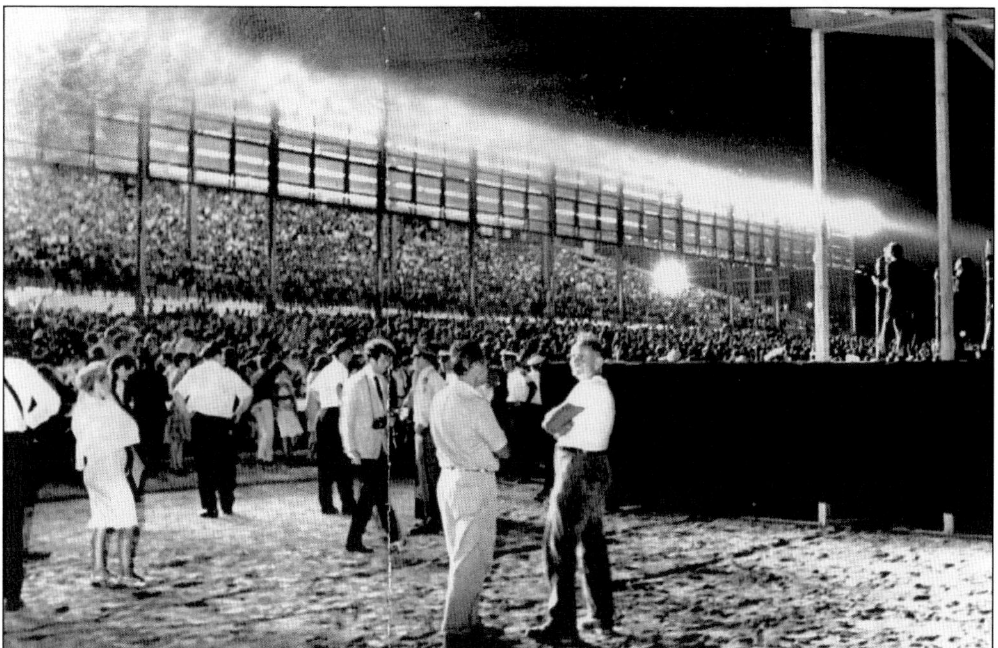

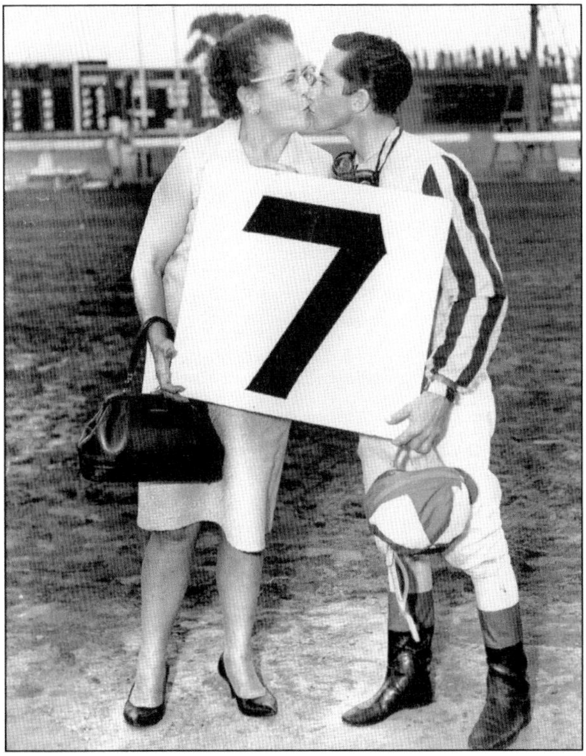

LUCKY SEVEN. Jockey Leroy Moyers gets a kiss from his mother after tallying a track-record seven wins in one day on July 4, 1967. His feat has yet to be equaled. (Courtesy Suffolk Downs.)

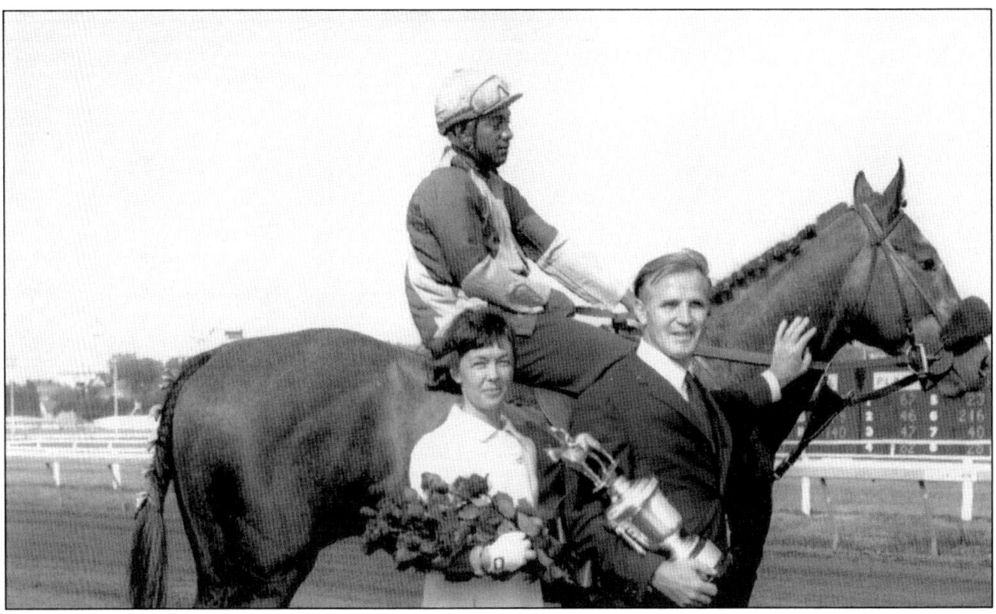

DANCER'S IMAGE. Dancer's Image, the only Kentucky Derby winner ever to be disqualified, makes his final public appearance on June 19, 1968. Earlier that year, Dancer's Image crossed the wire first in the Kentucky Derby, but he was stripped of his title when a post-race drug test allegedly revealed traces of a banned painkiller. Joining him are owner Peter Fuller (holding the trophy), his wife, Joan, and exercise rider Richard Mitchell. Fuller was a prominent Boston businessman. (United Press International photograph, courtesy the Sports Museum.)

WILLIAM ALMY JR. William "Bunny" Almy Jr. was one of first officials hired by the track, serving as its superintendent during the construction of the facility in 1935. The following year, he became a steward at the track, a position he held until 1974. A consummate horseman, Almy was also a breeder, owner, trainer, and jockey, riding primarily in steeplechase races. Additionally, Almy served for 10 years as president of the Masters of Foxhounds Association of America. (Courtesy Suffolk Downs.)

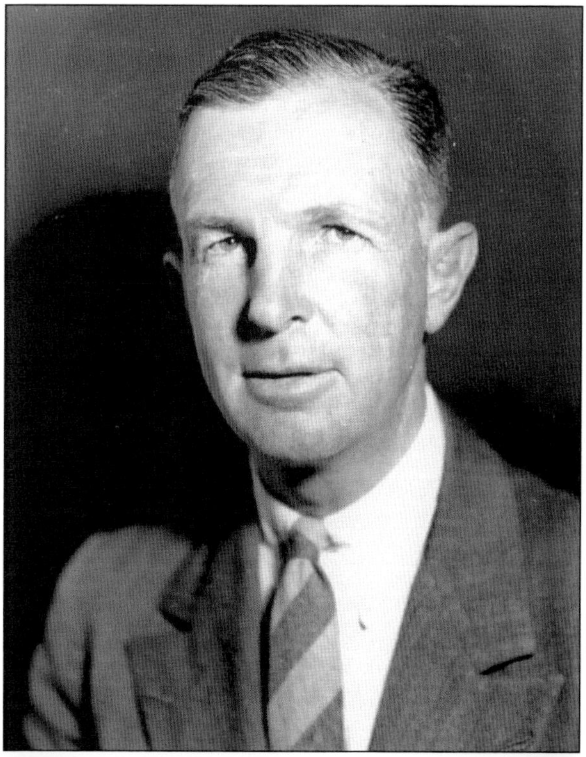

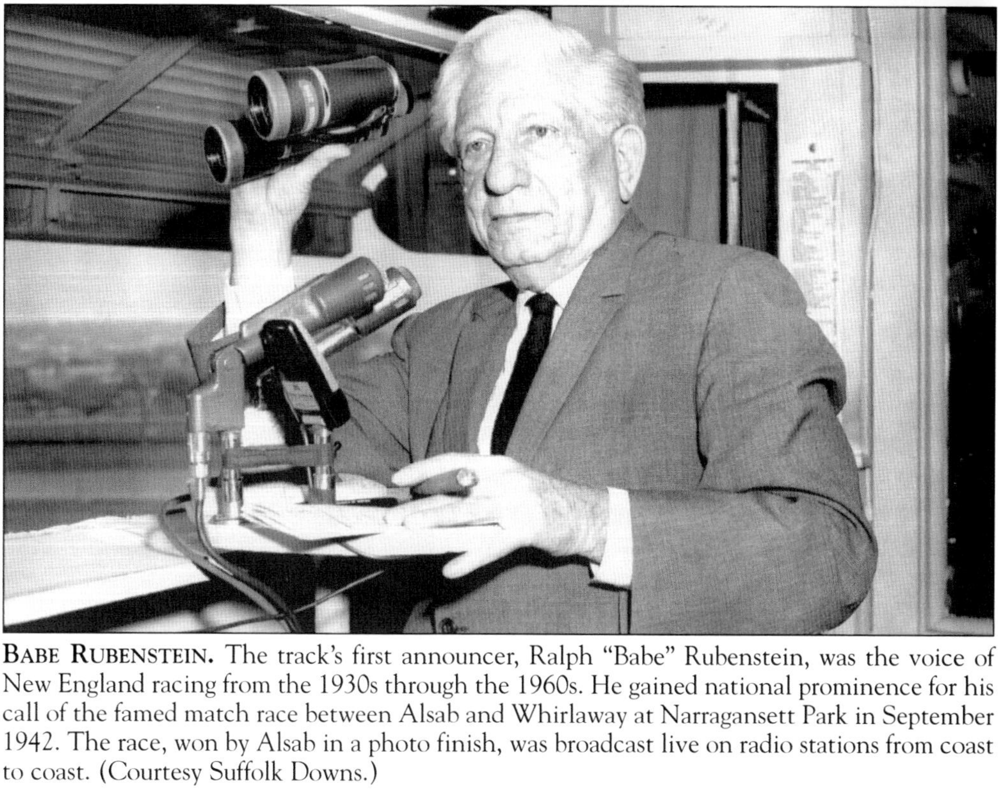

BABE RUBENSTEIN. The track's first announcer, Ralph "Babe" Rubenstein, was the voice of New England racing from the 1930s through the 1960s. He gained national prominence for his call of the famed match race between Alsab and Whirlaway at Narragansett Park in September 1942. The race, won by Alsab in a photo finish, was broadcast live on radio stations from coast to coast. (Courtesy Suffolk Downs.)

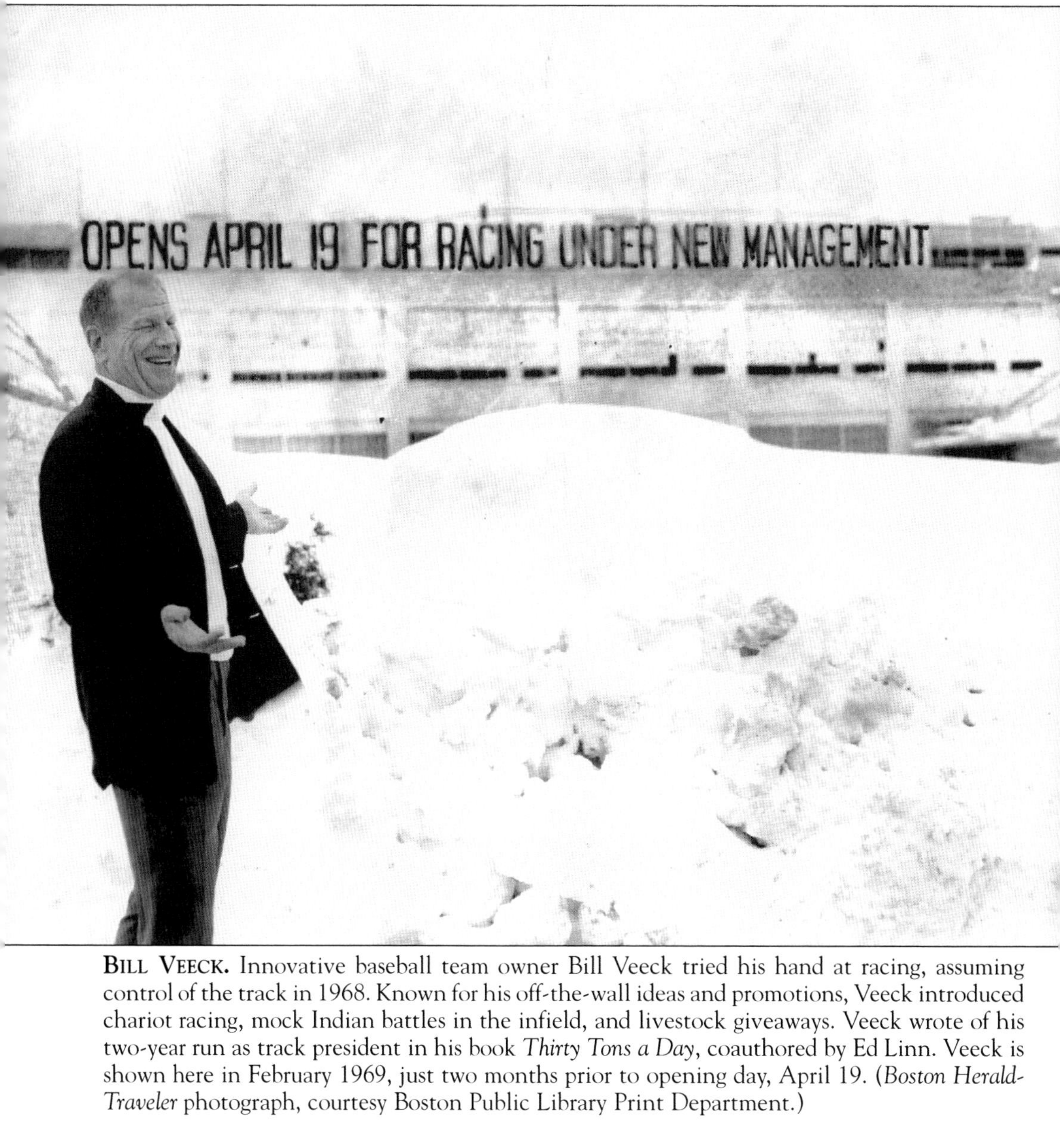

BILL VEECK. Innovative baseball team owner Bill Veeck tried his hand at racing, assuming control of the track in 1968. Known for his off-the-wall ideas and promotions, Veeck introduced chariot racing, mock Indian battles in the infield, and livestock giveaways. Veeck wrote of his two-year run as track president in his book *Thirty Tons a Day*, coauthored by Ed Linn. Veeck is shown here in February 1969, just two months prior to opening day, April 19. (*Boston Herald-Traveler* photograph, courtesy Boston Public Library Print Department.)

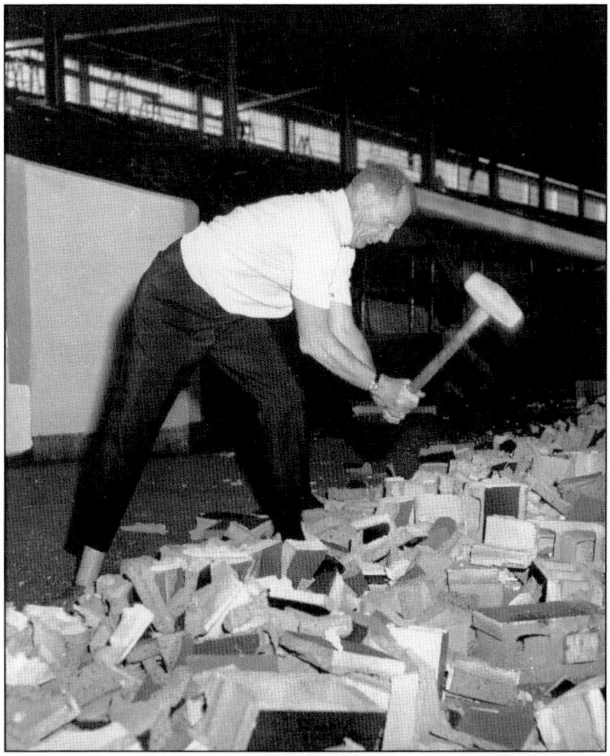

SLEDGEHAMMER. No job was too small for Veeck. Seen here in March 1969, he contributes to the demolition of the existing box seat area to make way for a more open seating arrangement. (Right, *Boston Herald-Traveler* photograph, courtesy Boston Public Library Print Department; below, courtesy Suffolk Downs.)

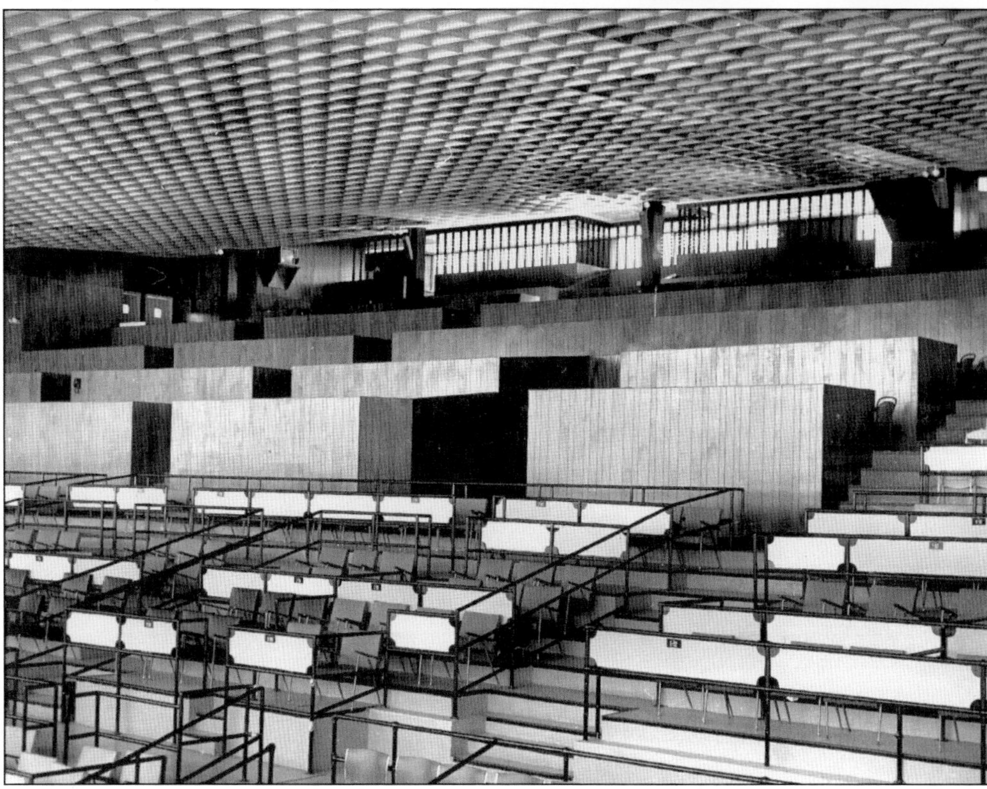

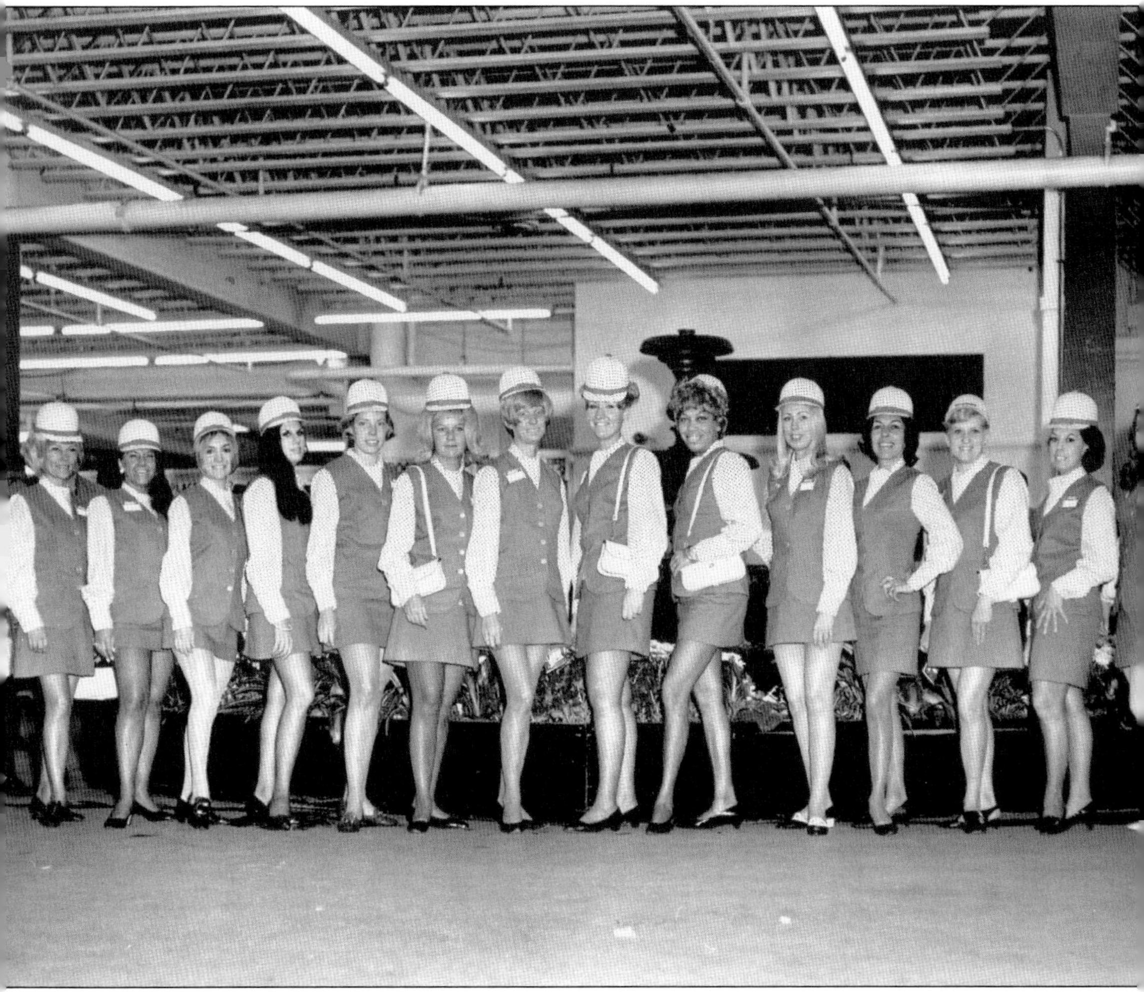

Mutuel Messengers. Veeck assembled a group of mini-skirted mutuel messengers to make wagering easier, and more attractive, to certain patrons. (*Boston Herald-Traveler* photograph, courtesy Boston Public Library Print Department.)

Five

THE 1970S

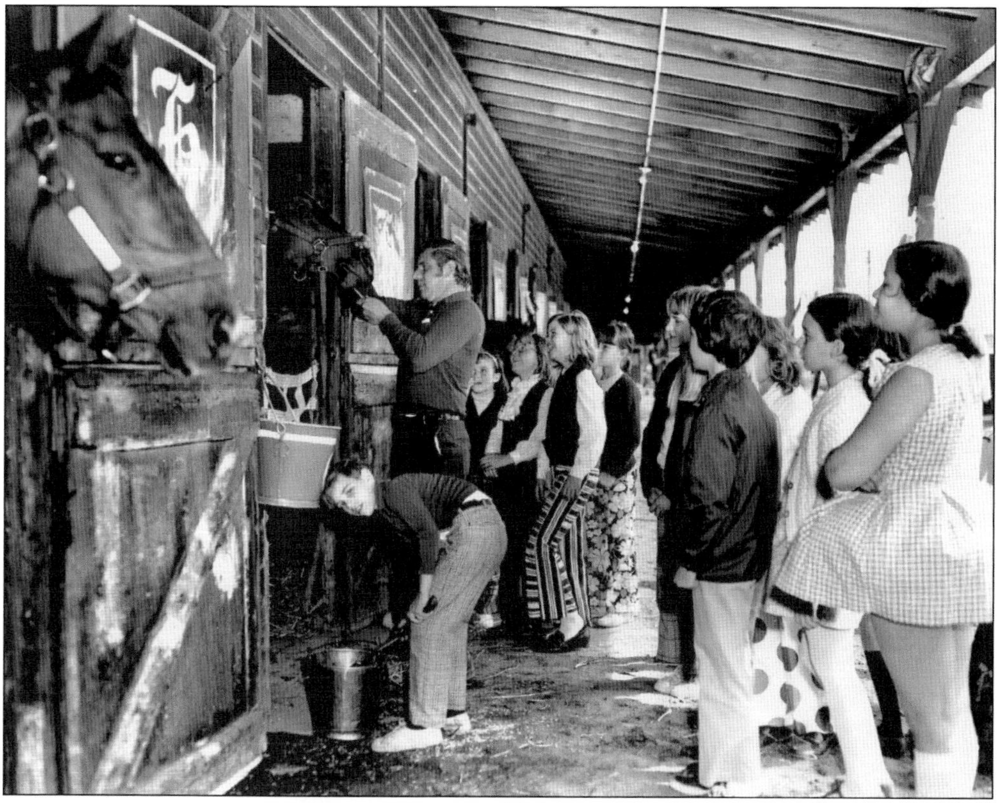

SCHOOLING. Fifth-grade students from the Bell School in Marblehead visit a barn as part of their tour of the stable area in May 1970. (Courtesy Suffolk Downs.)

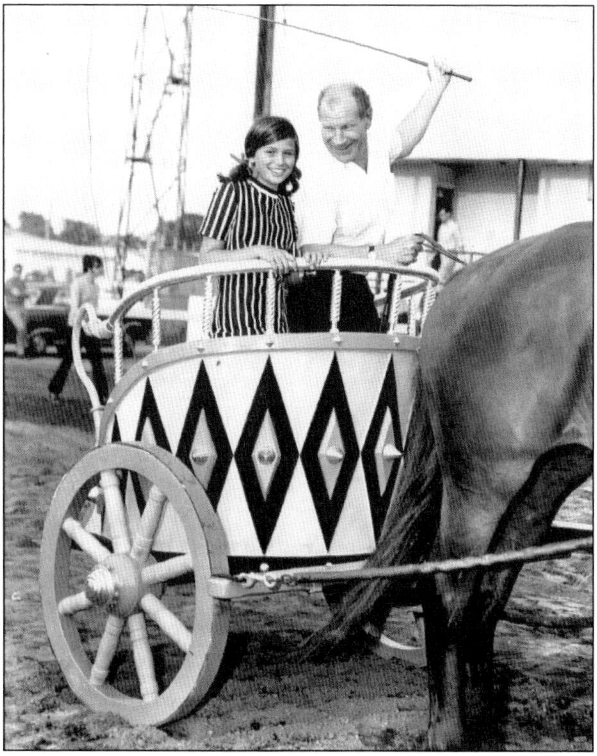

CHARIOT RACING. Bill Veeck and his daughter Lisa take a test ride prior to a chariot race for media celebrities in July 1970. During his brief reign, Veeck successfully challenged a Massachusetts law that did not allow children to attend the track, making the sport family friendly. (*Boston Herald* photograph.)

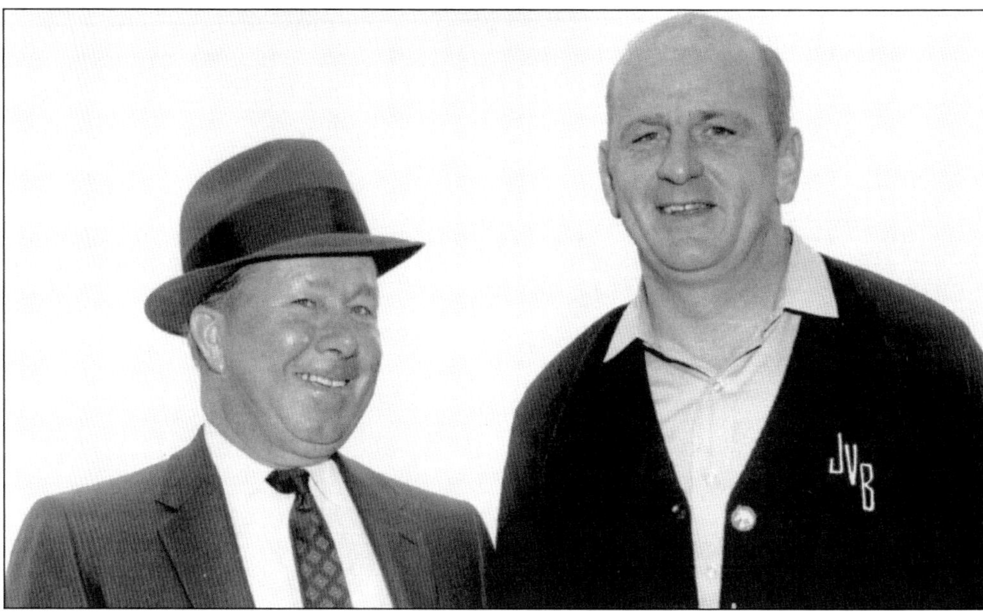

LEADING TRAINERS. Eddie Anspach (left) and Jack Van Berg (right) had reason to smile, as both trainers enjoyed great success at the track in the early part of the decade. Anspach captured five meet titles from 1966 to 1972. Van Berg saddled 78 winners at the track in 1970, amassing 282 victories nationwide on his way to leading the country for the third straight year. Van Berg was inducted into racing's hall of fame in 1985. He is the second-winningest trainer of all time, with over 6,300 victories. (Courtesy Suffolk Downs.)

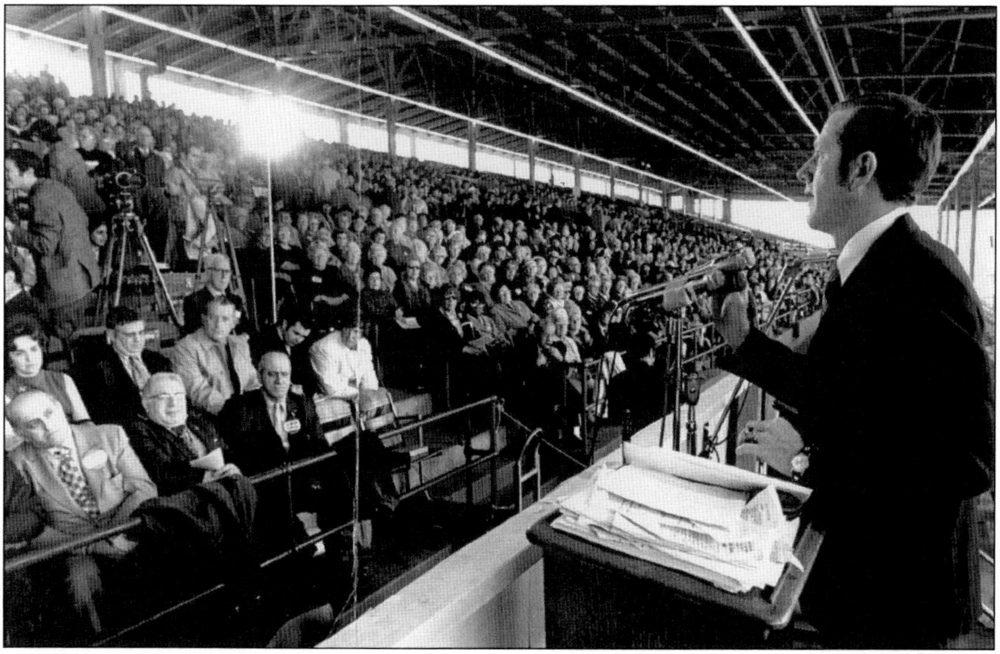

THE HOUSE SPEAKER. David M. Bartley, Speaker of the Massachusetts House of Representatives, addresses a group of senior citizens assembled in the grandstand in April 1971. (*Boston Herald-Traveler* photograph, courtesy Boston Public Library Print Department.)

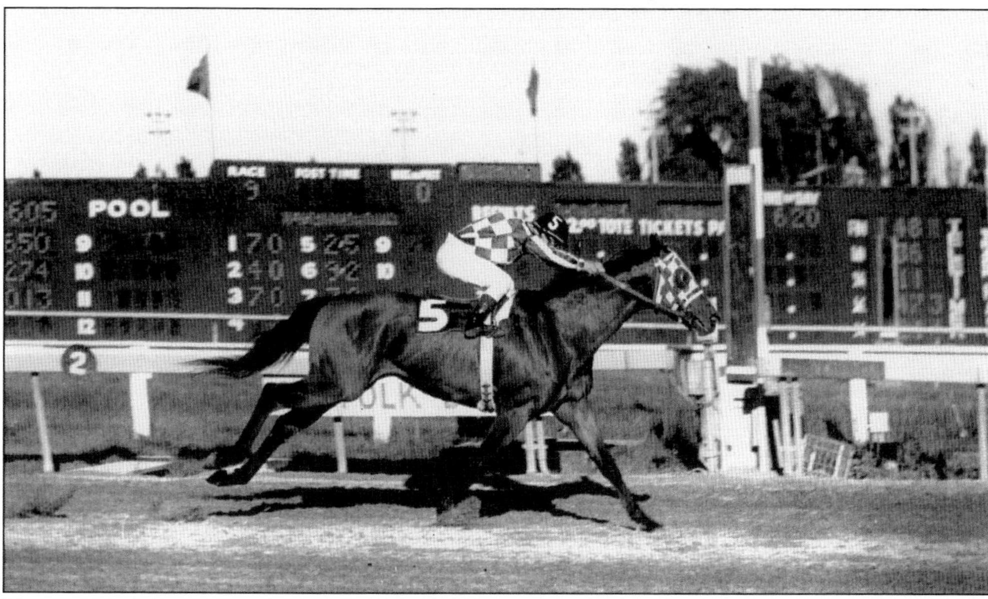

THE 1973 MASSACHUSETTS HANDICAP. Riva Ridge powers home under Ron Turcotte to win the 1973 MassCap. Having captured the Kentucky Derby and the Belmont Stakes in 1972, he became just the second Derby winner to win the MassCap. The win was yet another success for Riva Ridge's owner Meadow Stable, trainer Lucien Laurin, and Turcotte—the same connections as Secretariat. Just eight days earlier, Secretariat had made history with his epic performance in the Belmont Stakes, becoming the first Triple Crown winner since Citation in 1948. (Courtesy Suffolk Downs.)

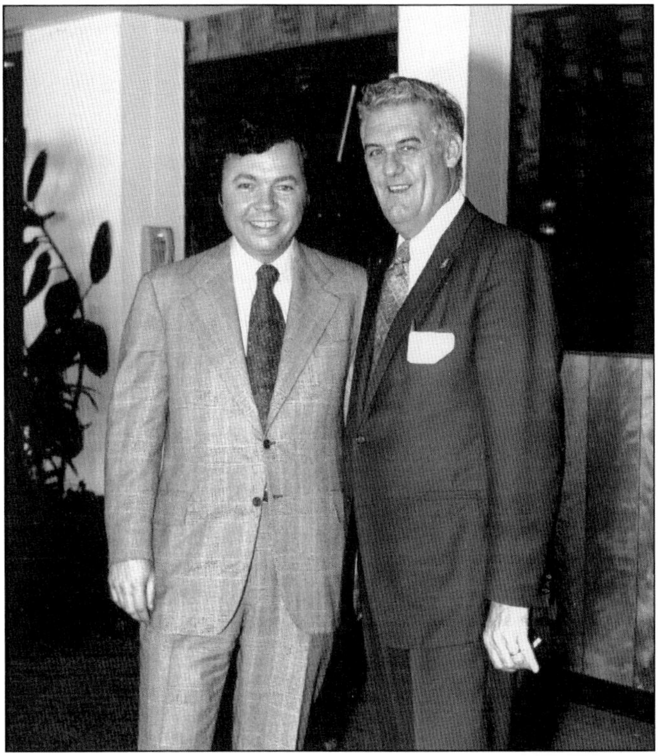

WILLIAM F. CONNELL AND BOB VAREY. William F. Connell (left) of Lynn became the track's youngest president in 1972 at the age of 33. Connell later became track chairman during Ogden Corporation's ownership run, which concluded in 1986. He is joined here by longtime publicity director Bob Varey. (Courtesy Suffolk Downs.)

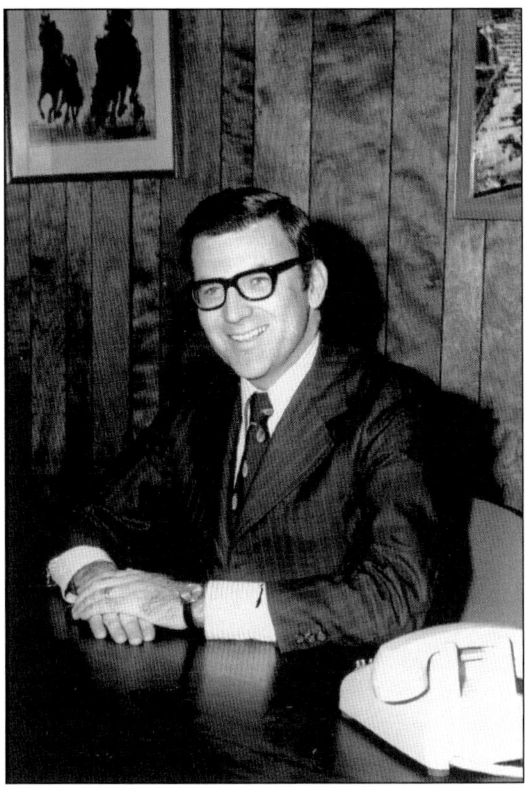

JOHN MACANIFF. John MacAniff served as track president for the Ogden Corporation ownership group from 1975 to 1985. (Courtesy Suffolk Downs.)

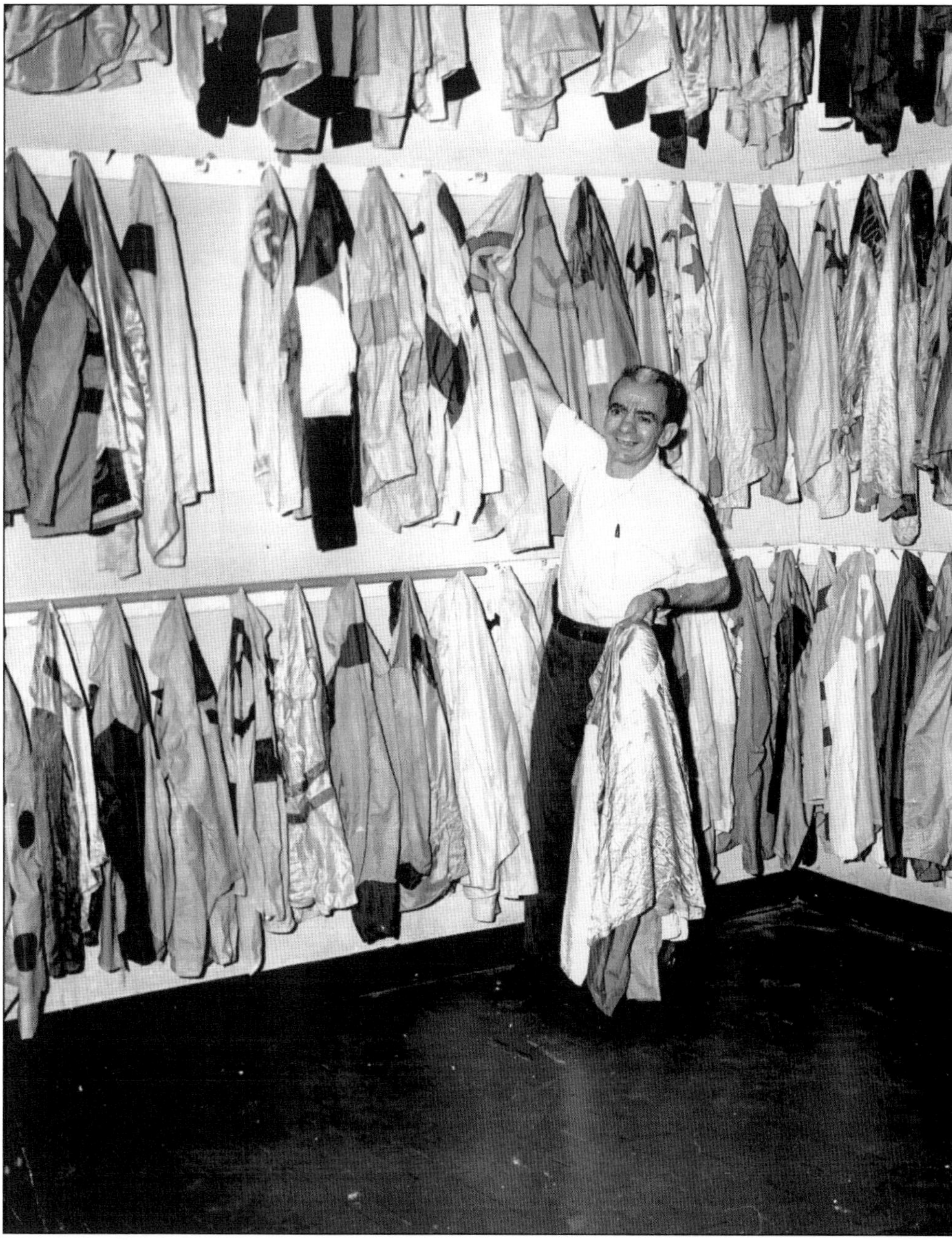

The Silks Room. Former jockey Joey DeLucia gathers the silks for the day's races. All horse owners have their own silks, which feature the colors and patterns of their choice. The silks' descriptions are included in the racing program. It is the responsibility of the silks room attendant to review the program each day and bring the appropriate silks into the jockeys' room. (Courtesy Suffolk Downs.)

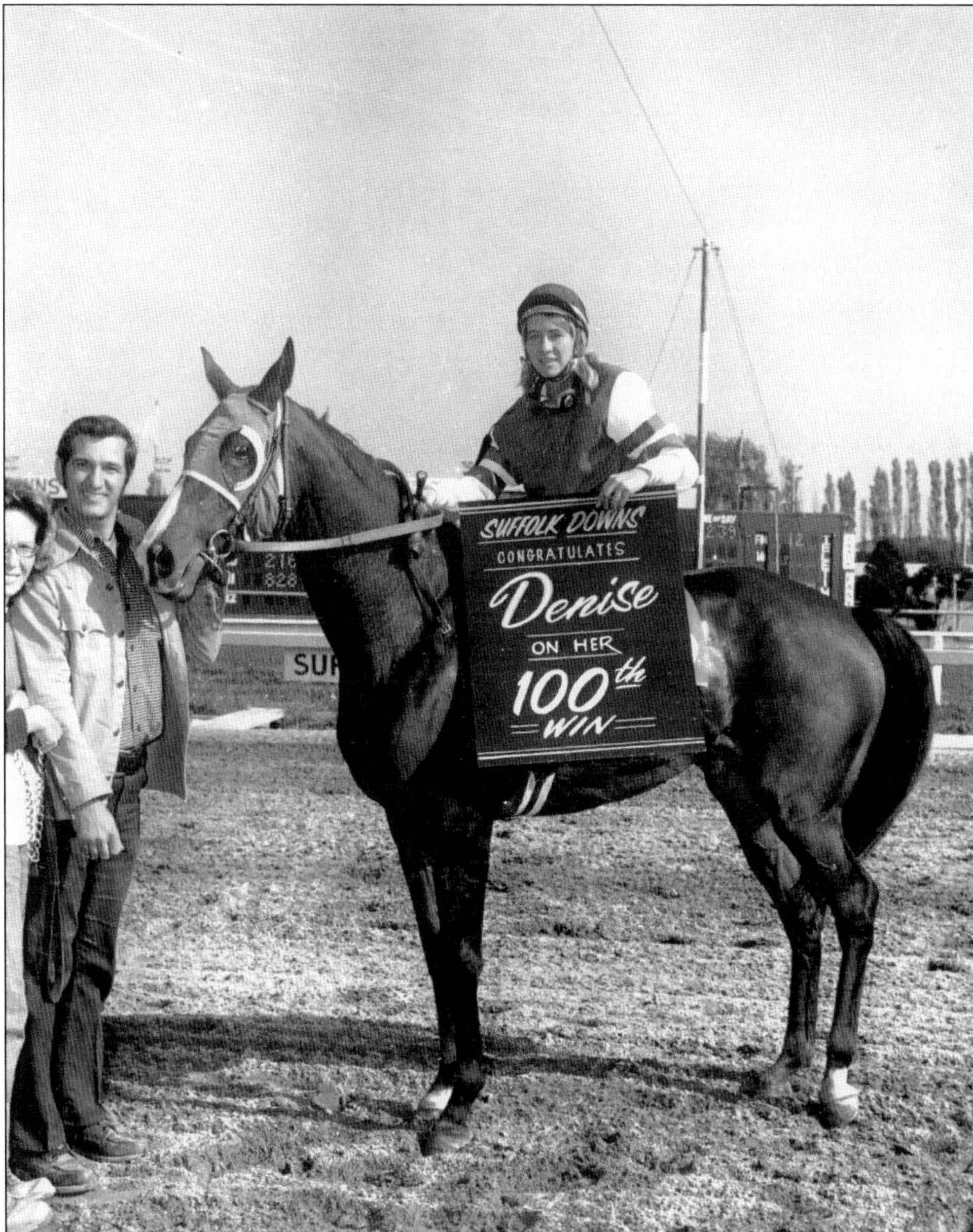

DENISE BOUDROT. In the fall of 1974, 22-year-old Denise Boudrot became the first woman to win a riding title at a major Thoroughbred racetrack, recording 94 wins in 92 racing days while still an apprentice. She began her riding career in 1972 and retired in 1985. (Courtesy Suffolk Downs.)

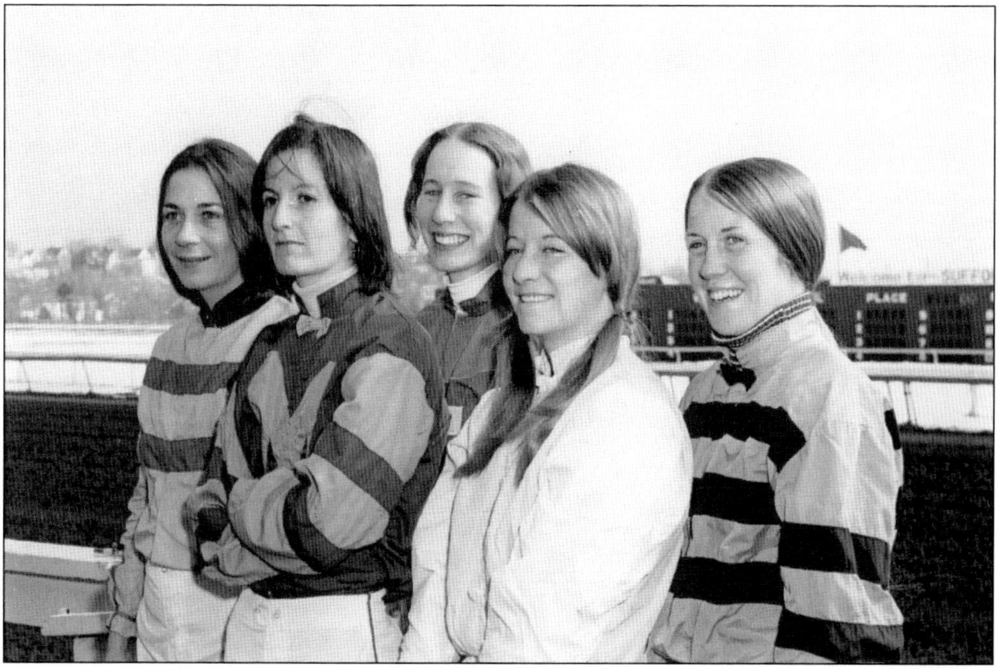

"JOCKETTES." The track was one of the first to welcome female riders, or "Jockettes," as they were popularly referred to at the time. From left to right are Susanna Pye, Barbara Smith, Nancy Beilan, Denise Boudrot, and Christine Derby. (Courtesy Suffolk Downs.)

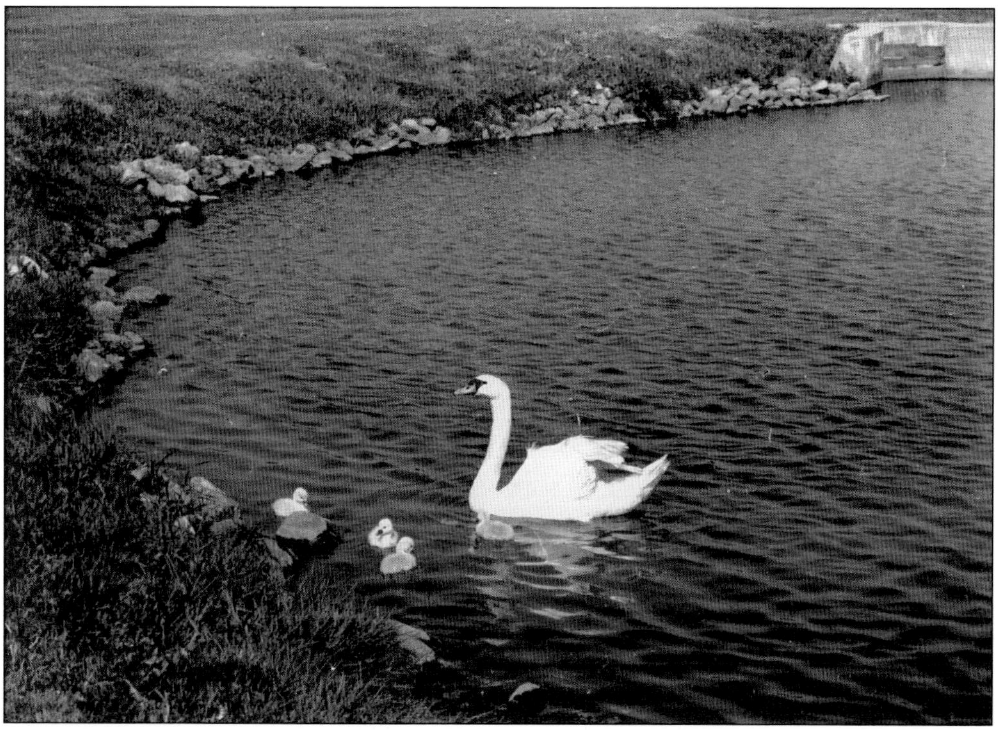

SWAN LAKE. A mother swan watches over her babies in the infield pond in 1976. (Courtesy Suffolk Downs.)

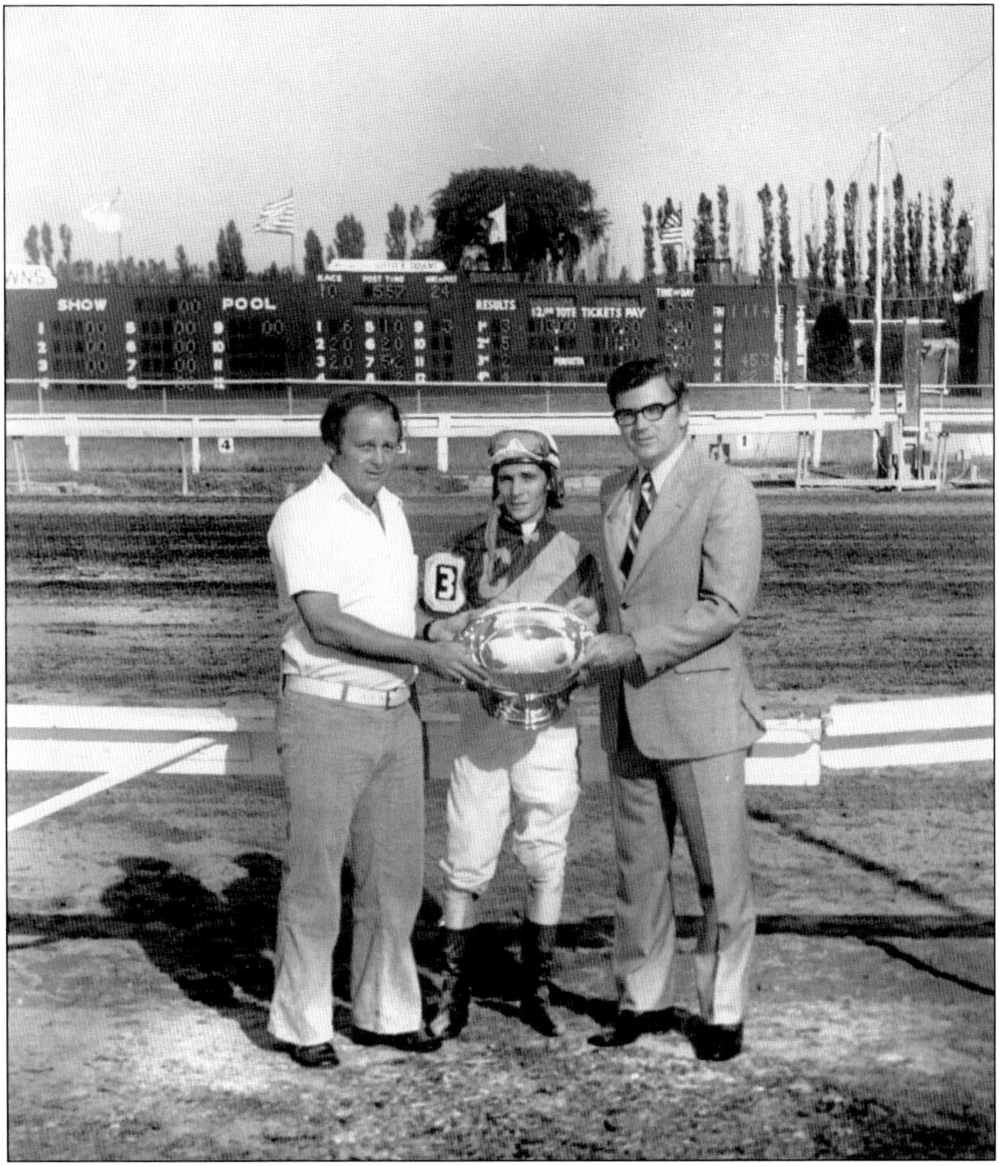

GERRY CHEEVERS. Boston Bruin great and hockey hall of famer Gerry Cheevers (left) poses in the winner's circle with jockey Don Meade Jr. and track president John MacAniff after Cheevers's two-year-old colt Royal Ski won the 1976 Mayflower Stakes. (Courtesy Suffolk Downs.)

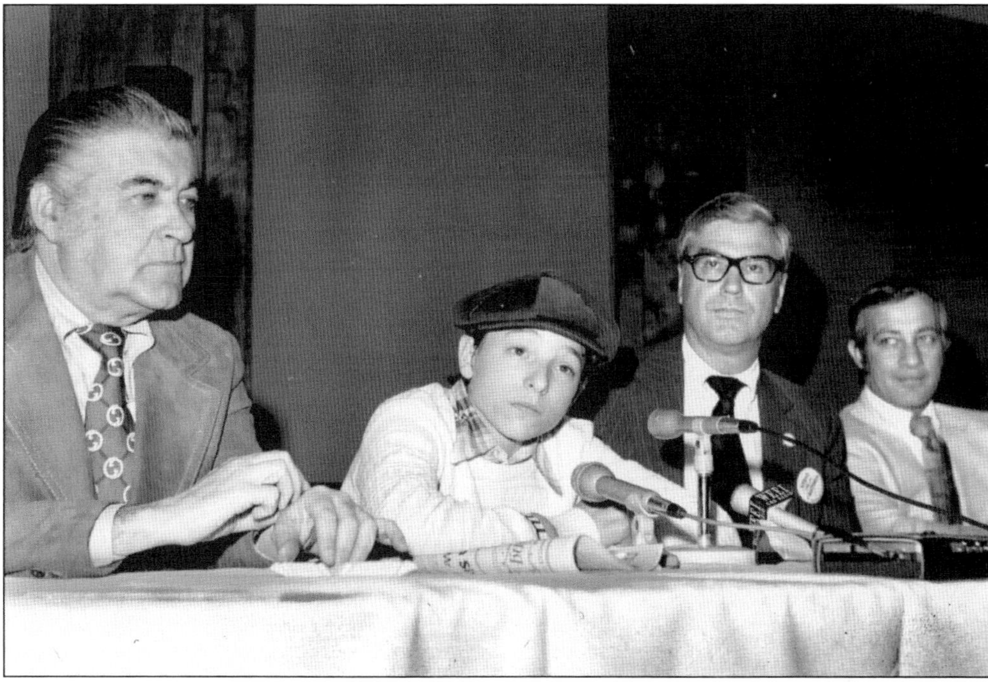

"THE KID." Steve Cauthen (wearing the hat) addresses the media on April 3, 1977. Cauthen, age 16, was the leading jockey in North America at the time, riding primarily at Aqueduct Race Track in New York. He rode Affirmed to the Triple Crown the following year. Steve Cauthen Day attracted a crowd of 15,797. The betting public made five of his six mounts favorites, but he failed to win a race. Joining Cauthen at the press conference are, from left to right, his agent Lennie Goodman, track vice president Richard Donovan, and racing secretary Robert DeStasio. (Courtesy Suffolk Downs.)

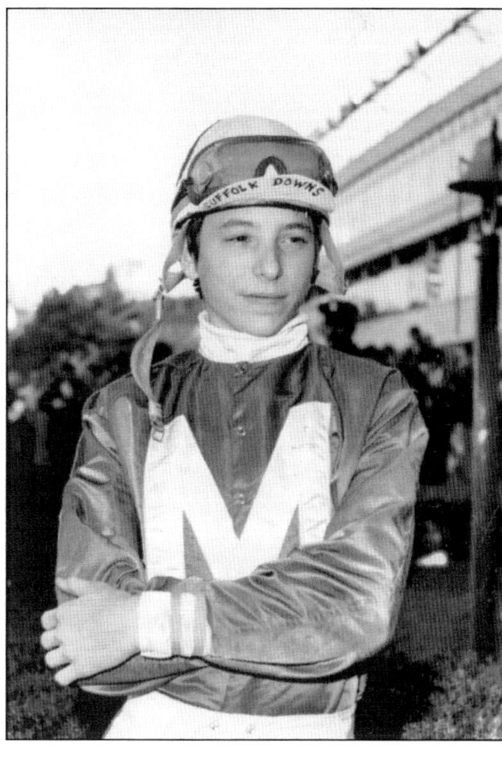

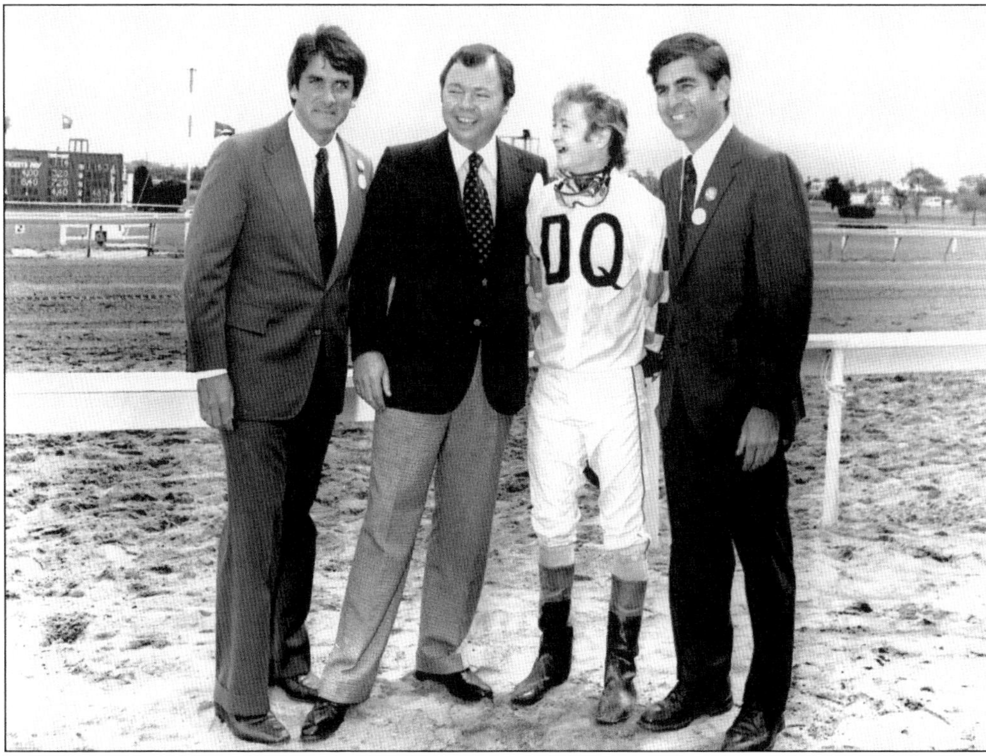

MICHAEL DUKAKIS. Posing in the winner's circle in 1978 are, from left to right, Massachusetts lieutenant governor Tommy O'Neill, track chairman William Connell, jockey Rick Luhr, and Massachusetts governor Michael Dukakis. (Courtesy Suffolk Downs.)

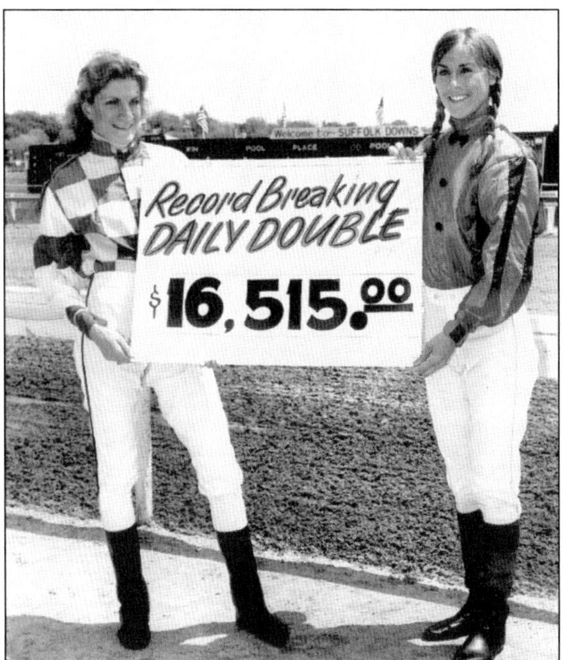

A RECORD DAILY DOUBLE. Jockeys Suzanne Kelly (left) and Linda Salinas (right) display the record-breaking daily double payoff that they produced on May 25, 1979. Salinas rode Green Gina (136-1) to victory in race one, and Kelly piloted Duc de Idiot (38-1) in race two, resulting in a return of $16,515 for the exotic wager, a record that still stands. (Courtesy Suffolk Downs.)

Six

The 1980s

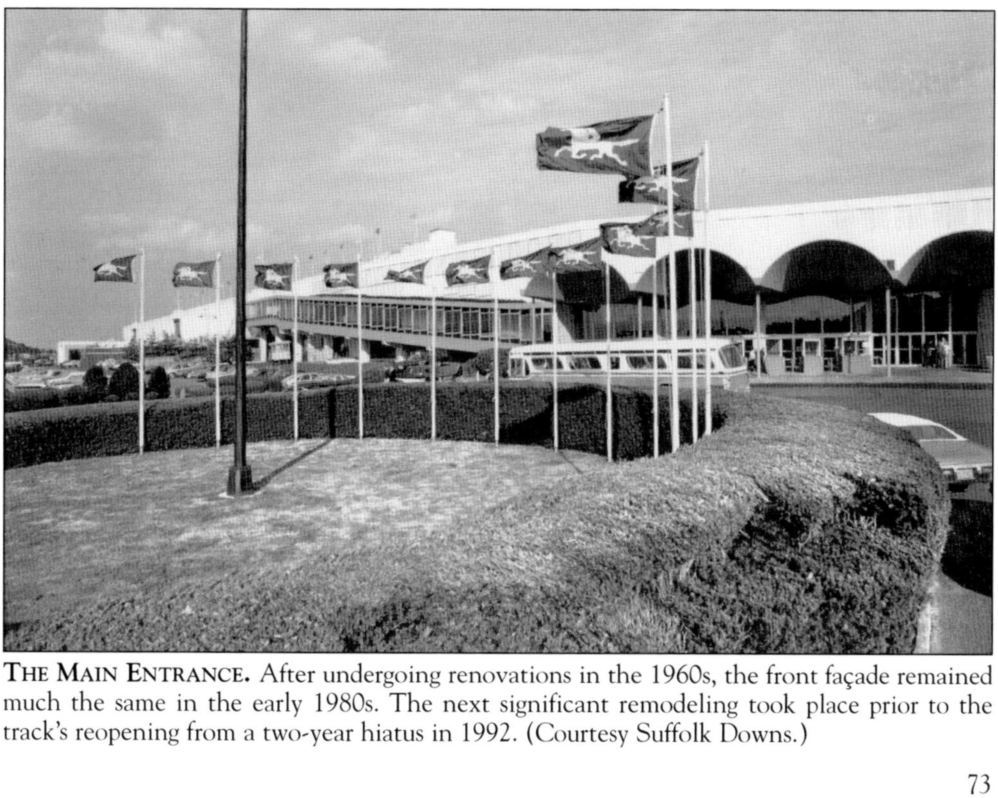

The Main Entrance. After undergoing renovations in the 1960s, the front façade remained much the same in the early 1980s. The next significant remodeling took place prior to the track's reopening from a two-year hiatus in 1992. (Courtesy Suffolk Downs.)

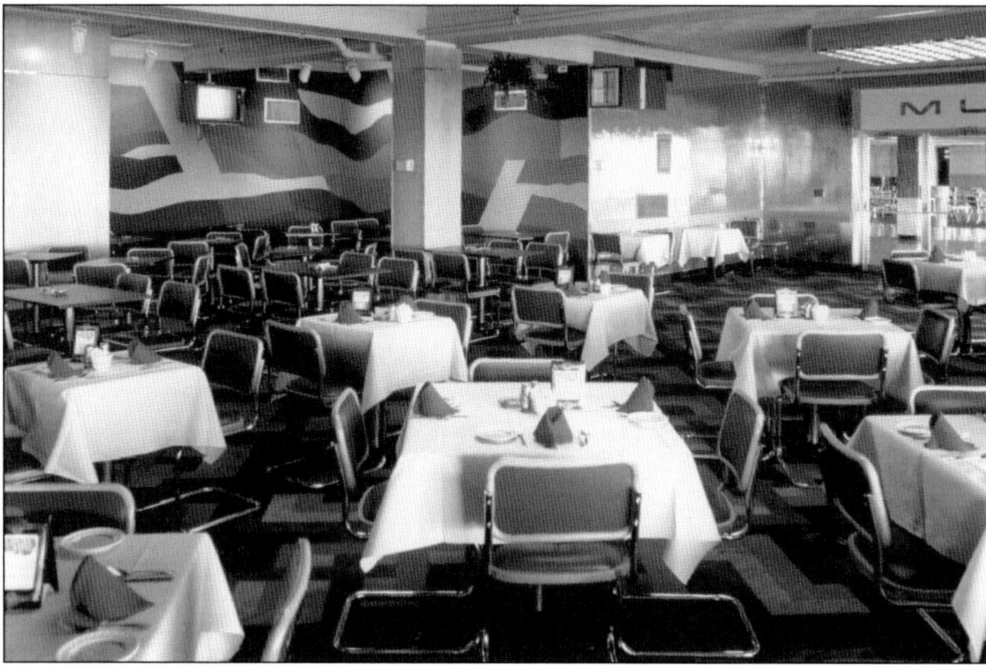

The Futurity Dining Room. The Futurity Dining Room, on the second floor of the clubhouse, allows race fans to enjoy a nice meal as well as a great view of the racetrack. The room is now home to Legends Bar & Grill. (Courtesy Suffolk Downs.)

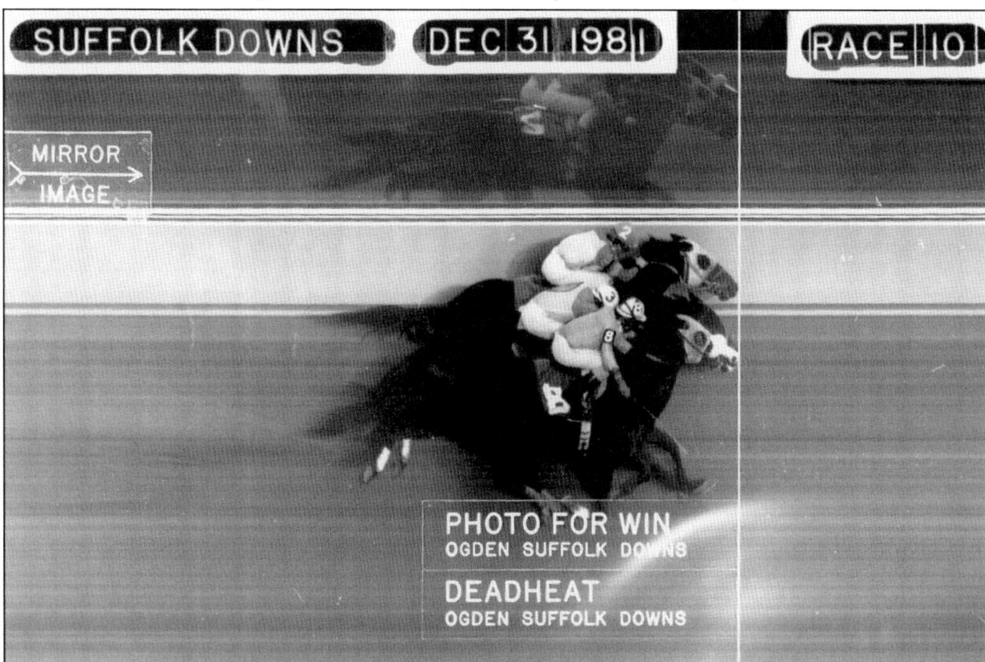

A Triple Dead Heat. In the ultimate photo finish, Great Combination (No. 2), Dawn's Count (No. 3), and Needachant (No. 8) cross the wire as one, creating a triple dead heat for the win in the final race of the year on December 31, 1981. (Courtesy Suffolk Downs.)

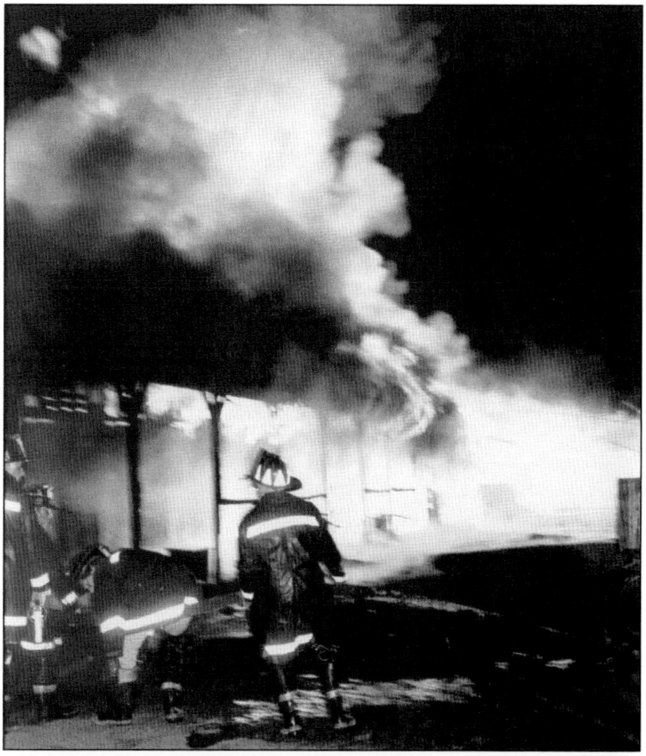

A Barn Fire. A fire engulfs a barn in the stable area on July 24, 1982. Eleven horses were killed, and several people were treated for injuries. (*Boston Herald* photograph.)

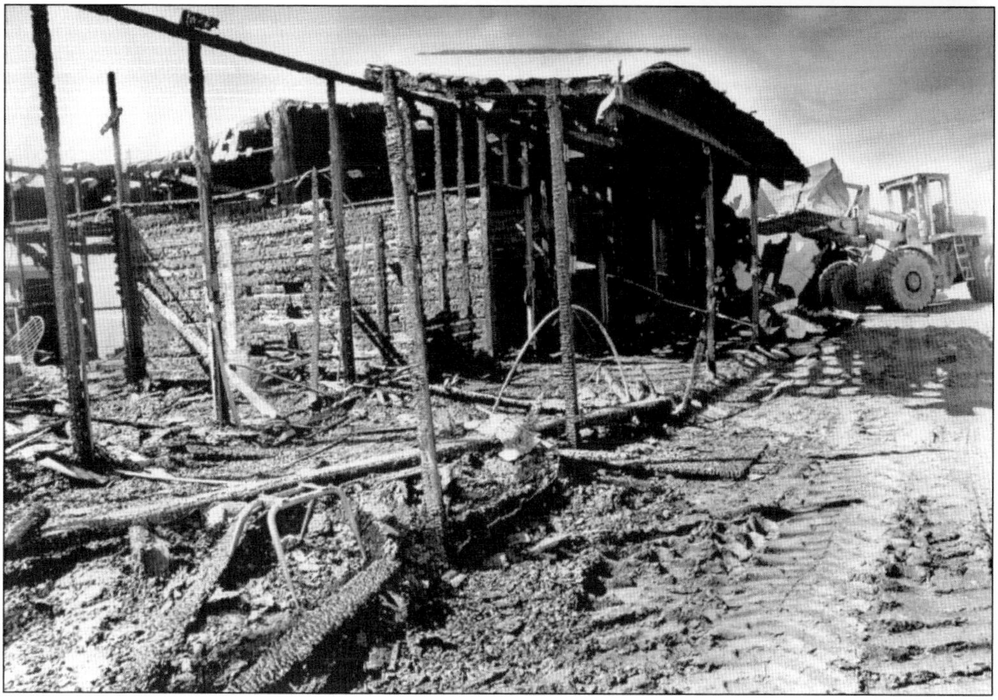

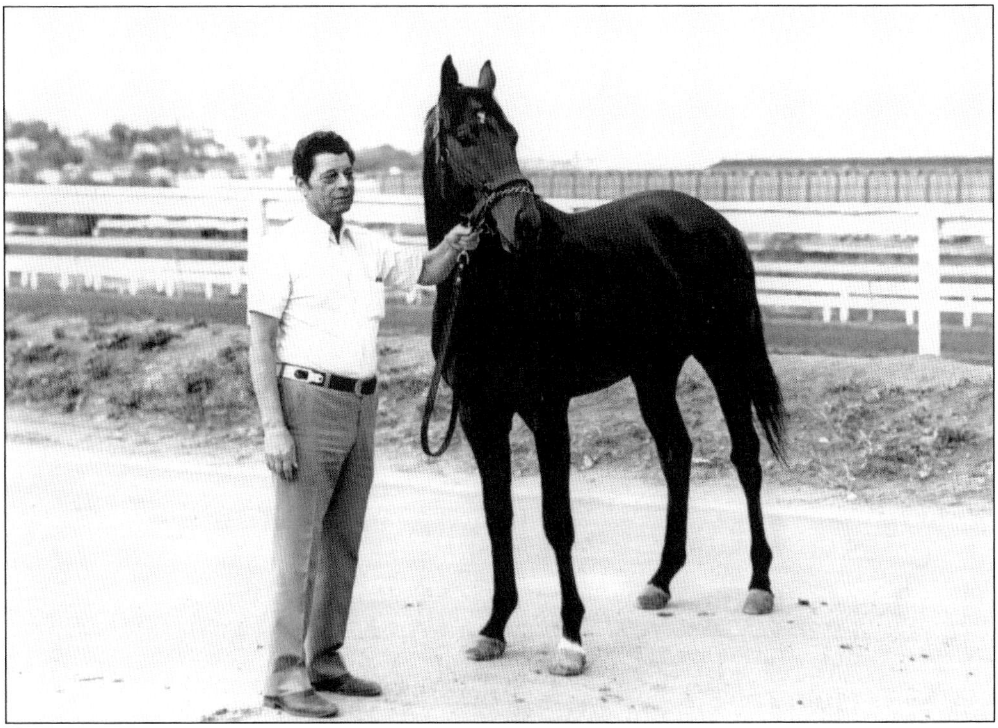

TIMELY WRITER. Trainer Dominic Imprescia stands with Timely Writer, who was voted a New England champion at age two and three. In 1982, Timely Writer won the Florida Derby and was a leading contender for the Kentucky Derby before an illness prevented him from competing in the race. He returned to Boston later that year to win the Yankee Handicap (below) before suffering a catastrophic injury in the Jockey Club Gold Cup at Belmont Park. The colt was owned by Francis and Peter Martin. (Courtesy Suffolk Downs.)

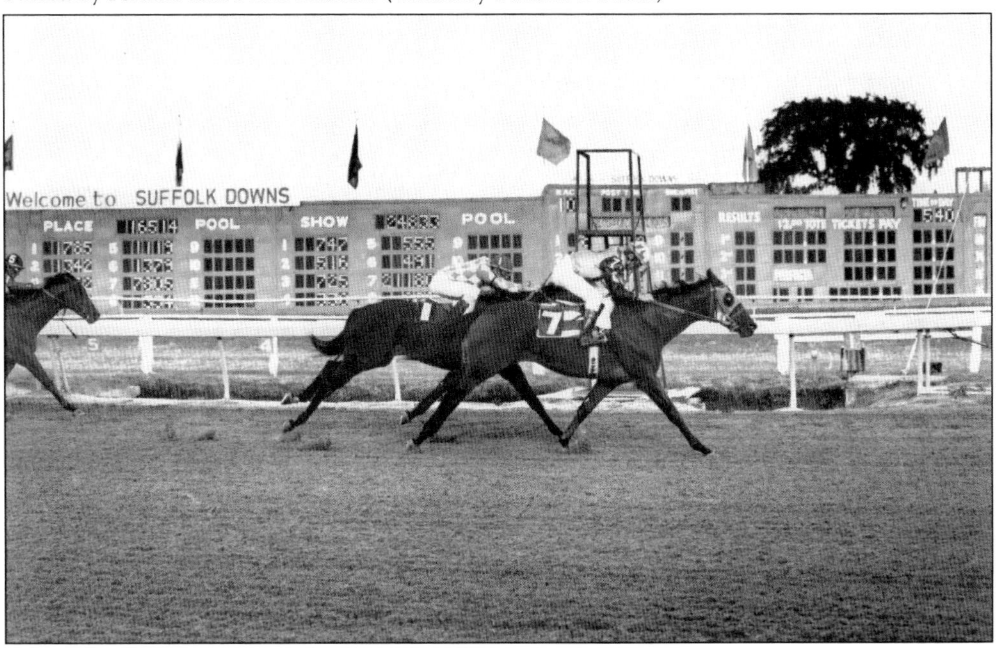

MICKEY ROONEY. Turf Club captain Joseph Gullifa (left) greets actor and horse owner Mickey Rooney. (Courtesy Suffolk Downs.)

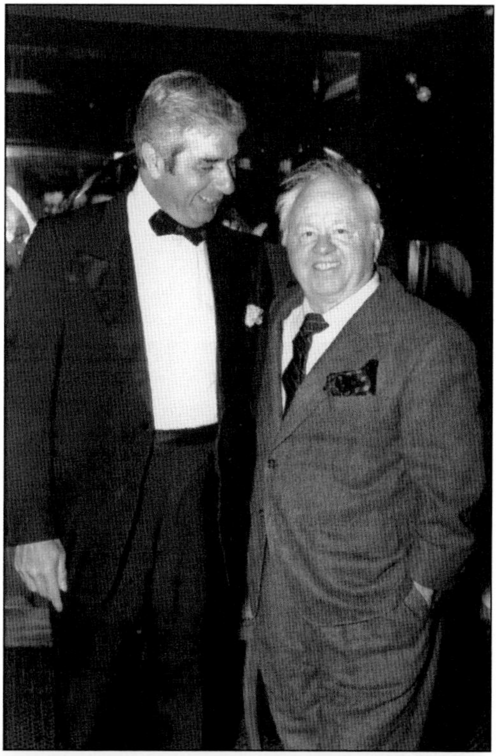

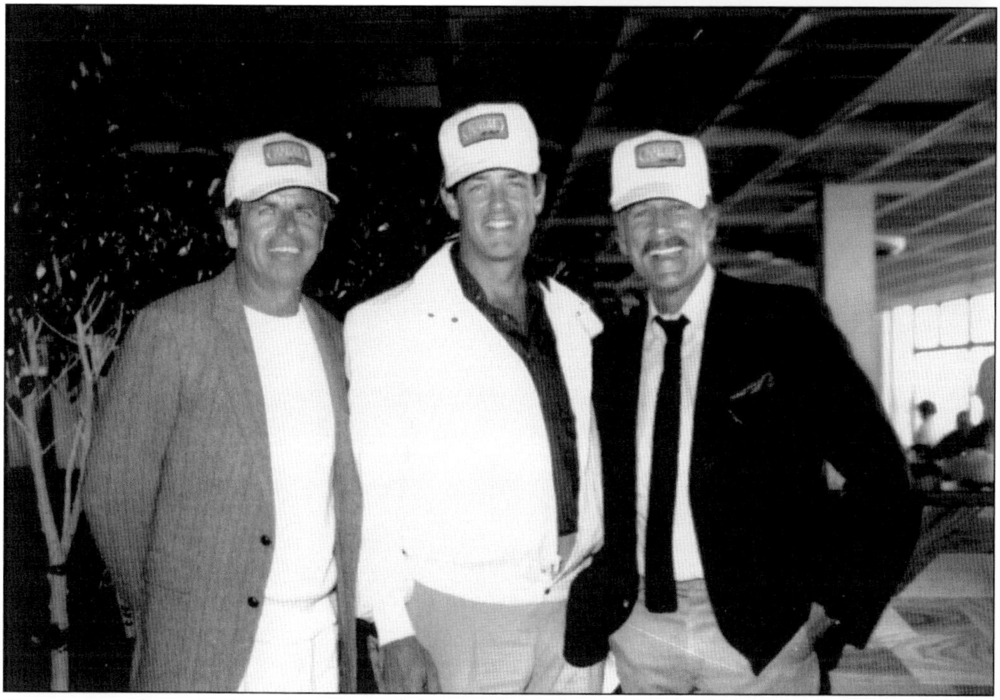

TELEVISION STARS. Seen here from left to right, television stars William Devane and Doug Sheehan of *Knots Landing* and Alex Cord of *Airwolf* sport Suffolk Downs hats during their visit to the Turf Club. (Courtesy Suffolk Downs.)

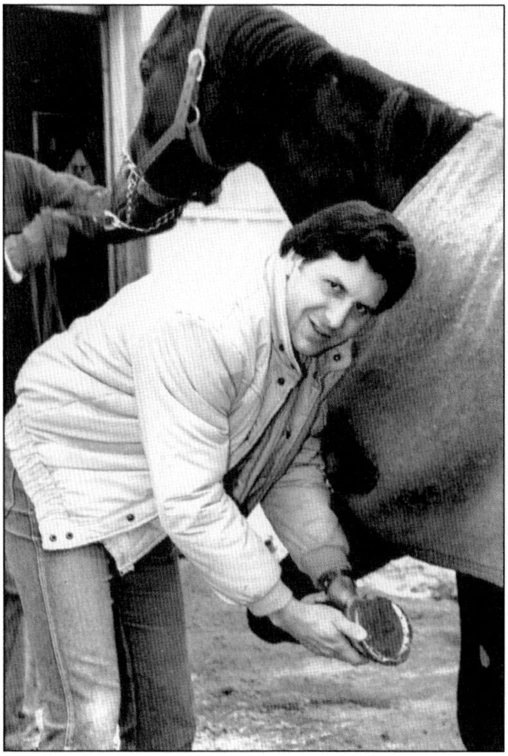

Bob Klesaris. Medford native Bob Klesaris became the first trainer to claim four straight meet titles at the track, accomplishing the feat from 1982 to 1983. He sent out 142 winners in 1983, establishing a track record at the time. Klesaris saddled what was believed to be a track record of five winners in one day on April 10, 1986. (Courtesy Suffolk Downs.)

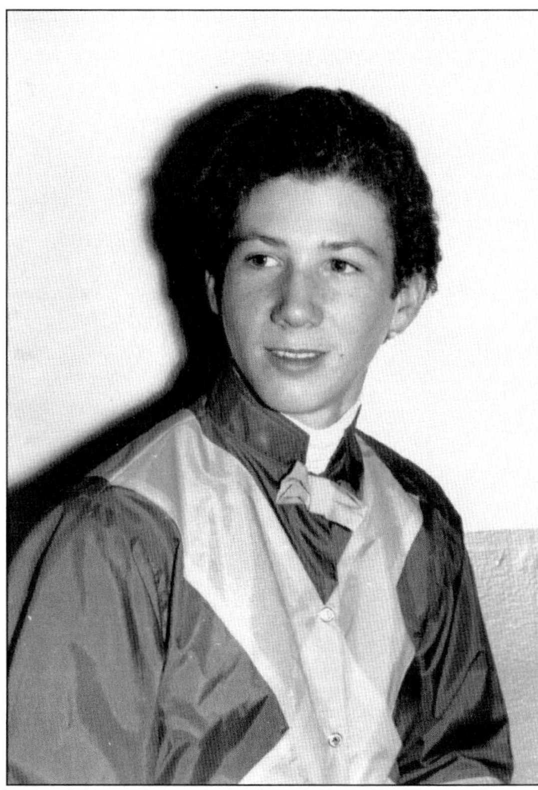

Stewart Elliott. Jockey Stewart Elliott became a regular rider at the track as a teenager in the early 1980s. He captured meet titles in 1984, 1985, and 1989. Elliott gained national attention in 2004, when he rode Smarty Jones to victories in the Kentucky Derby and the Preakness Stakes before narrowly missing out on the Triple Crown in the Belmont Stakes. (Courtesy Suffolk Downs.)

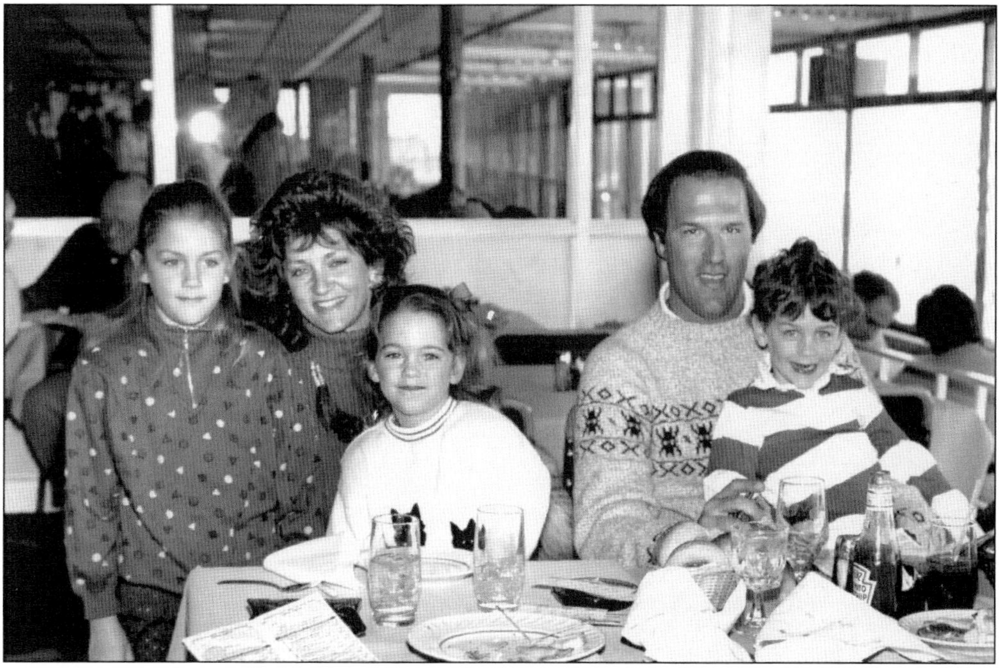

Bob Stanley. Boston Red Sox pitcher Bob Stanley (seated at right) and his family spend an afternoon in the Turf Club. From left to right are Stanley's daughter Kristin, wife Joan, daughter Kerri Ann, and son Kyle. (Courtesy Suffolk Downs.)

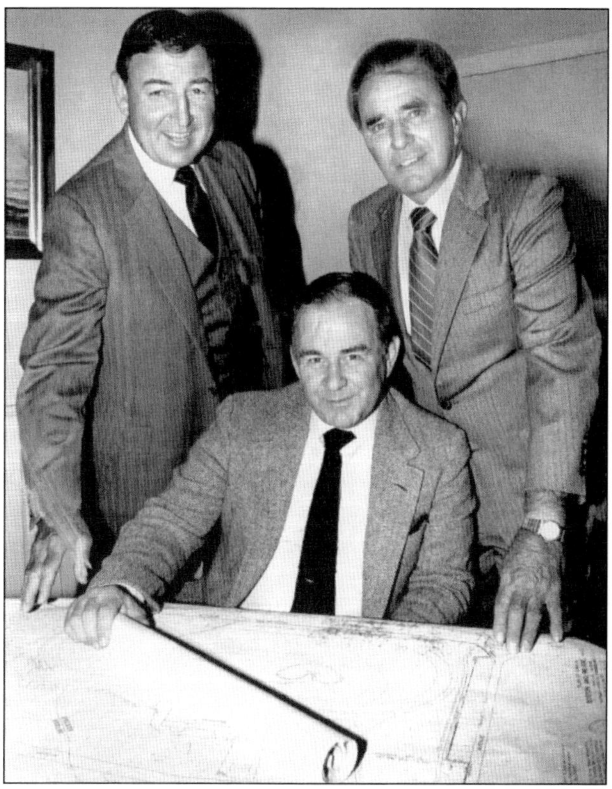

Belle Isle Limited. Edward "Buddy" LeRoux (seated), managing general partner of Belle Isle Limited, is joined by general partners Al Curran (left) and George Page (right) as they examine plans of the track property prior to finalizing their purchase of the track from Ogden Corporation in 1986. At the time, LeRoux was in the midst of a dispute concerning his share of ownership of the Boston Red Sox. (*Boston Herald* photograph.)

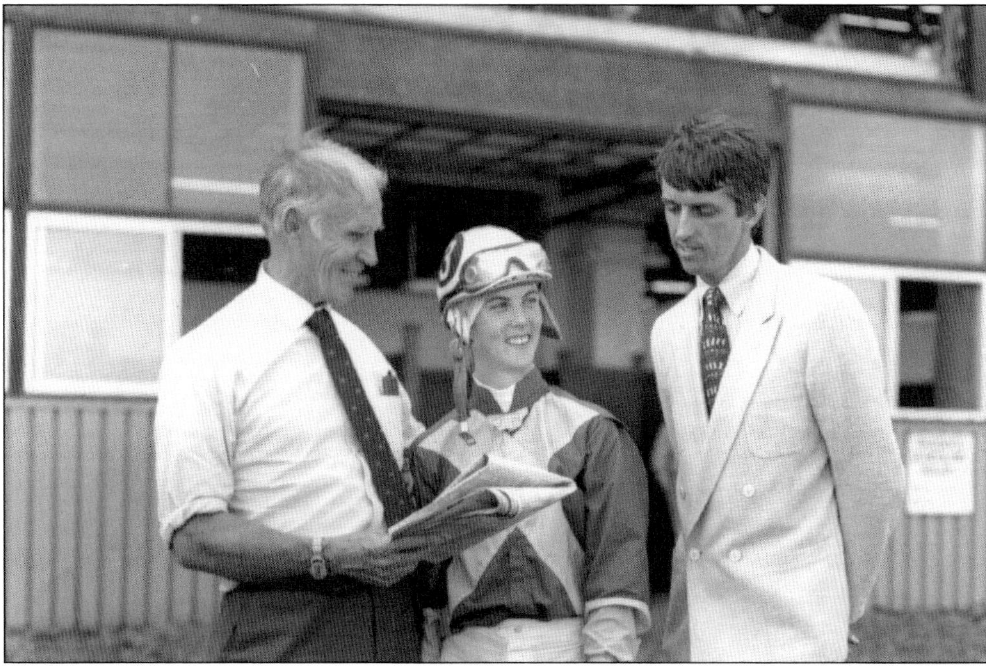

MOM'S COMMAND. Prominent local businessman and horse owner Peter Fuller (left), daughter and jockey Abby (center), and trainer Ned Allard (right) are in the paddock on Mom's Command Day, July 20, 1985. Mom's Command had just swept New York's prestigious Filly Triple Crown on her way to receiving the Eclipse Award for champion three-year-old filly. Abby rode Mom's Command in all nine of her starts that year, recording seven wins and two second-place finishes. Mom's Command was victorious in her lone local start, the 1984 Priscilla Stakes for two-year-old fillies, also with Abby aboard (below). (Courtesy Suffolk Downs.)

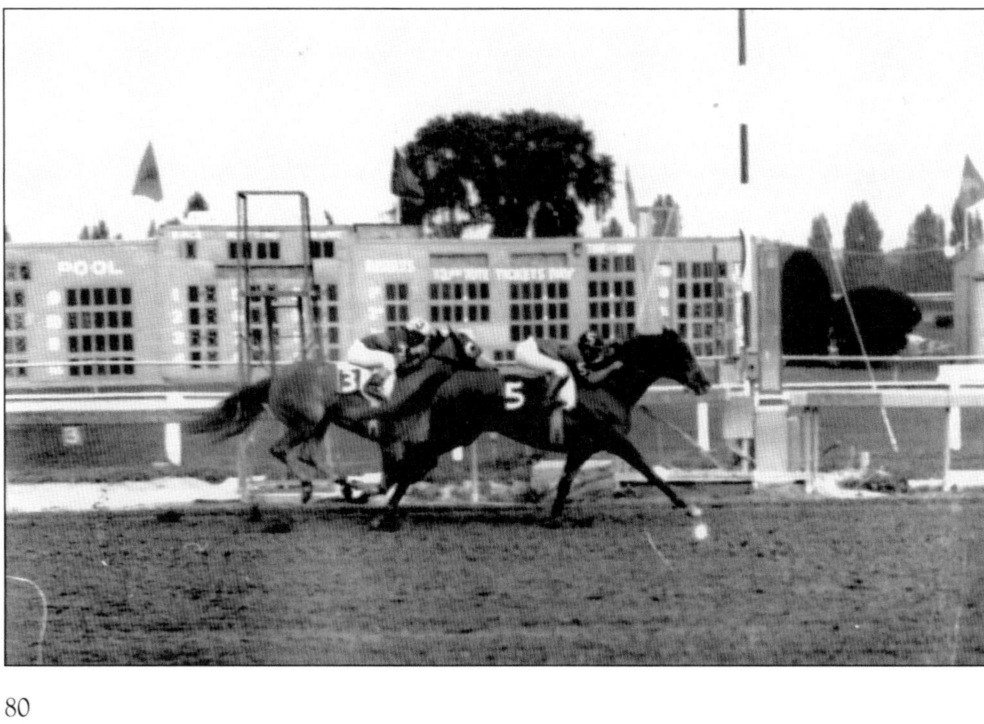

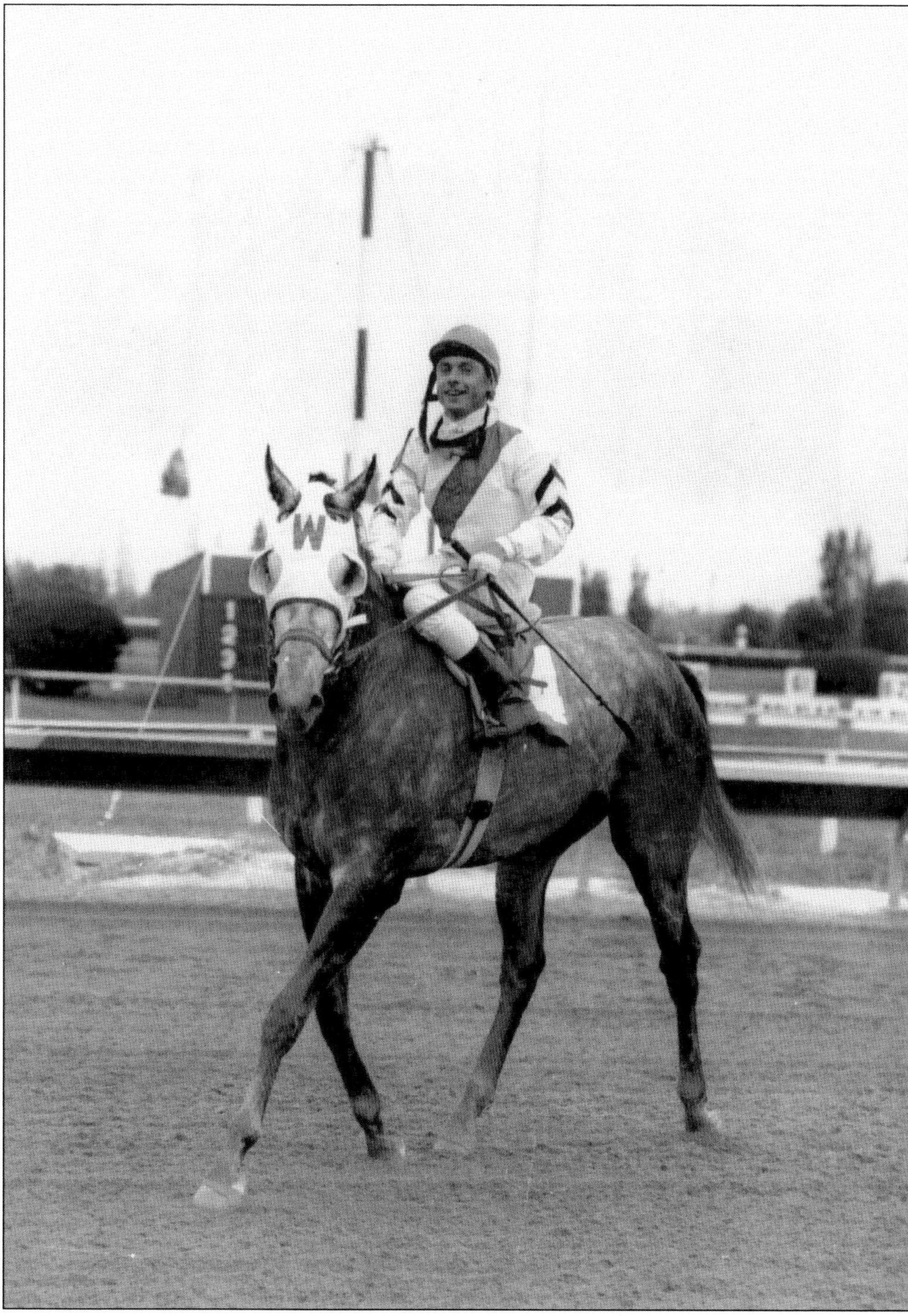

WAQUOIT. The Boston-based winner of the 1987 MassCap won 19 of 30 career starts for over $2.2 million in purse money. Waquoit was trained by Guido Federico for his cousin Joe Federico and was ridden in the MassCap by Dorchester native Chris McCarron. Guido Federico was born in Italy but was a longtime resident of Dorchester. (Courtesy Suffolk Downs.)

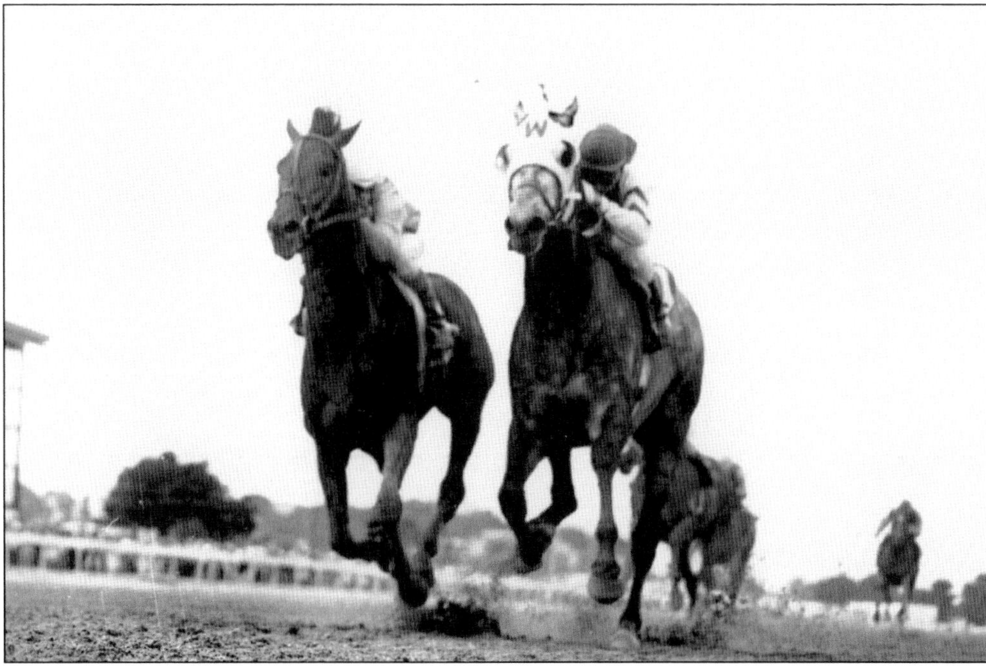

The 1987 Massachusetts Handicap. In arguably the greatest finish in MassCap history, hometown heroes Waquoit (right, with the *W*) and jockey Chris McCarron outdueled Broad Brush and Angel Cordero to win by a nose. The excitement level was perhaps best conveyed by track announcer Jim Hannon when his voice cracked at the conclusion of his call. (Courtesy Suffolk Downs.)

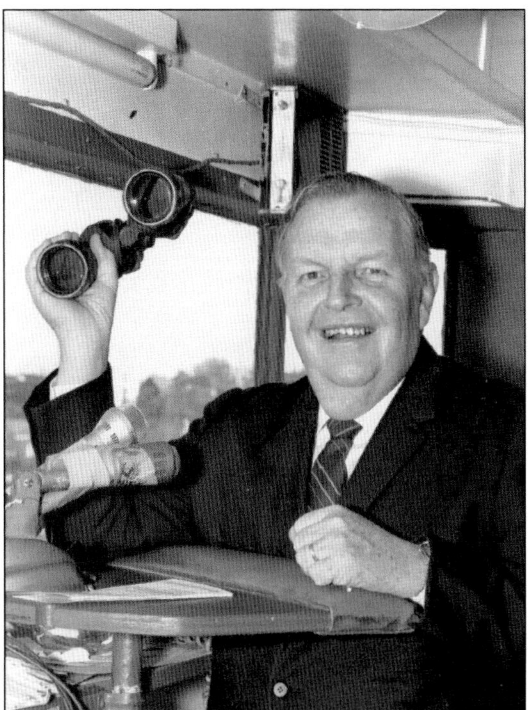

Jim Hannon. Jim Hannon manned the announcer's booth from 1969 to 1989, succeeding his mentor Babe Rubenstein upon his retirement. Hannon was hired by Bill Veeck to become just the second race caller in track history. Known for his booming voice, Hannon made his most famous call in the 1987 MassCap, when he exclaimed, "Ding-dong battle to the wire, Waquoit and Broad Brush!" (Courtesy Suffolk Downs.)

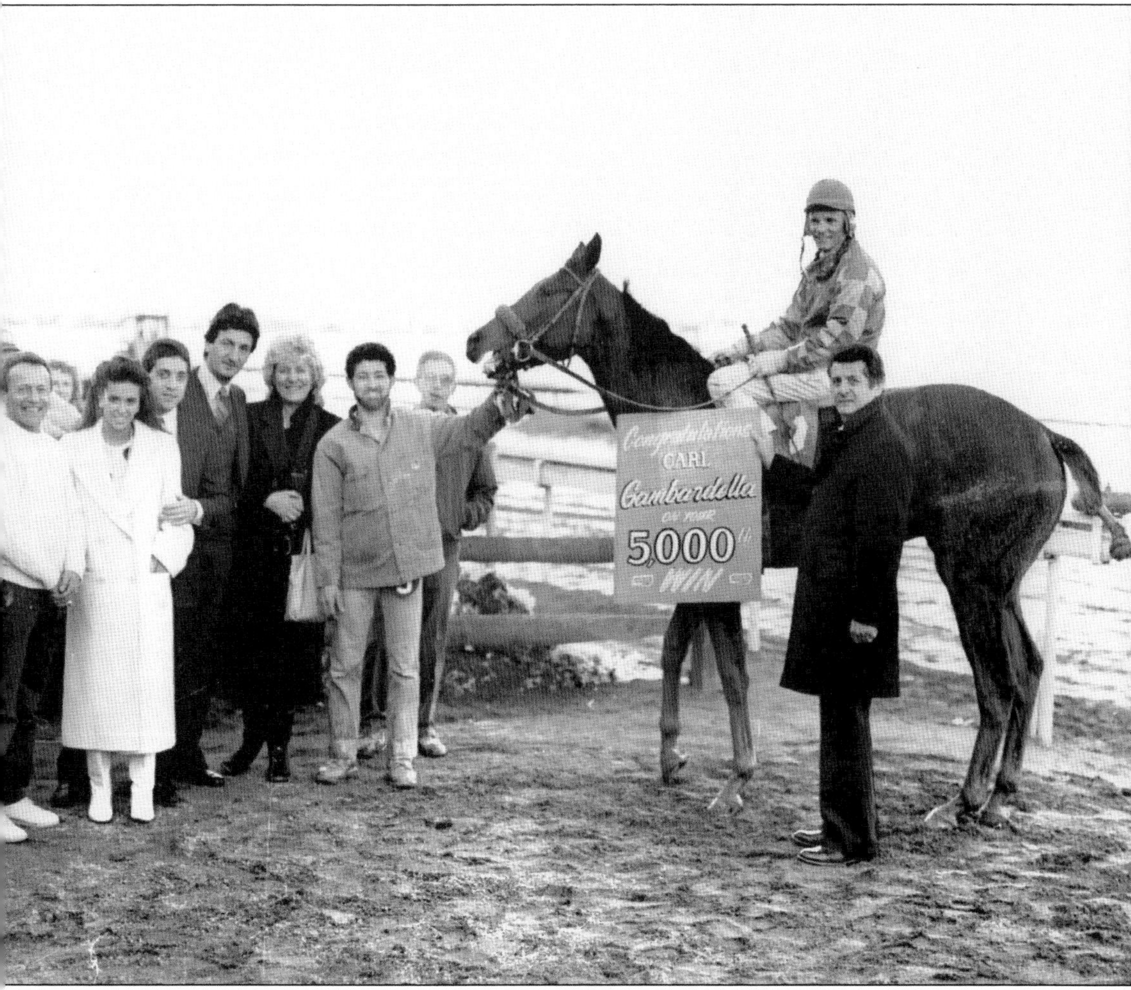

CARL GAMBARDELLA. Jockey Carl Gambardella celebrates career win number 5,000 on March 5, 1988. Gambardella is aboard John's Goldenapple, trained by Charlie Assimakopoulos (holding the sign). "Gamby," who recorded his first win in 1956, became just the ninth rider in history to reach that mark at the time. He would retire in 1994 with 6,349 victories and 12 meet riding titles at the track. (Courtesy Suffolk Downs.)

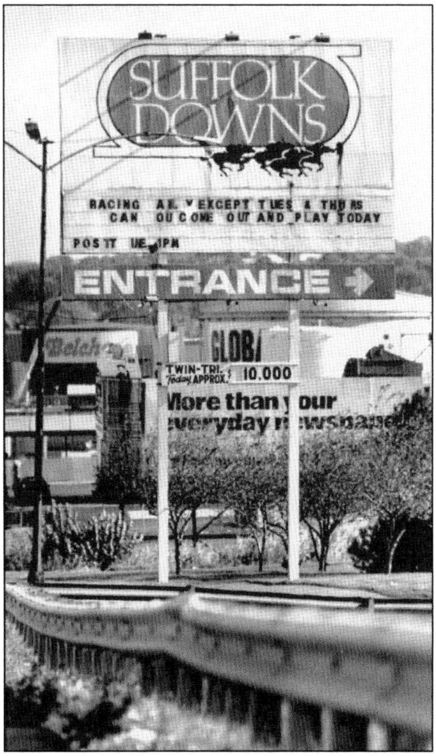

THE ROUTE 1A ENTRANCE. Travelers on Route 1A are notified of an approximate carryover of $10,000 in the Twin Trifecta pool on September 29, 1989. A Twin Trifecta produced the highest payout in track history on May 22, 1988, when one winning ticket returned $374,876.10. (*Boston Herald* photograph.)

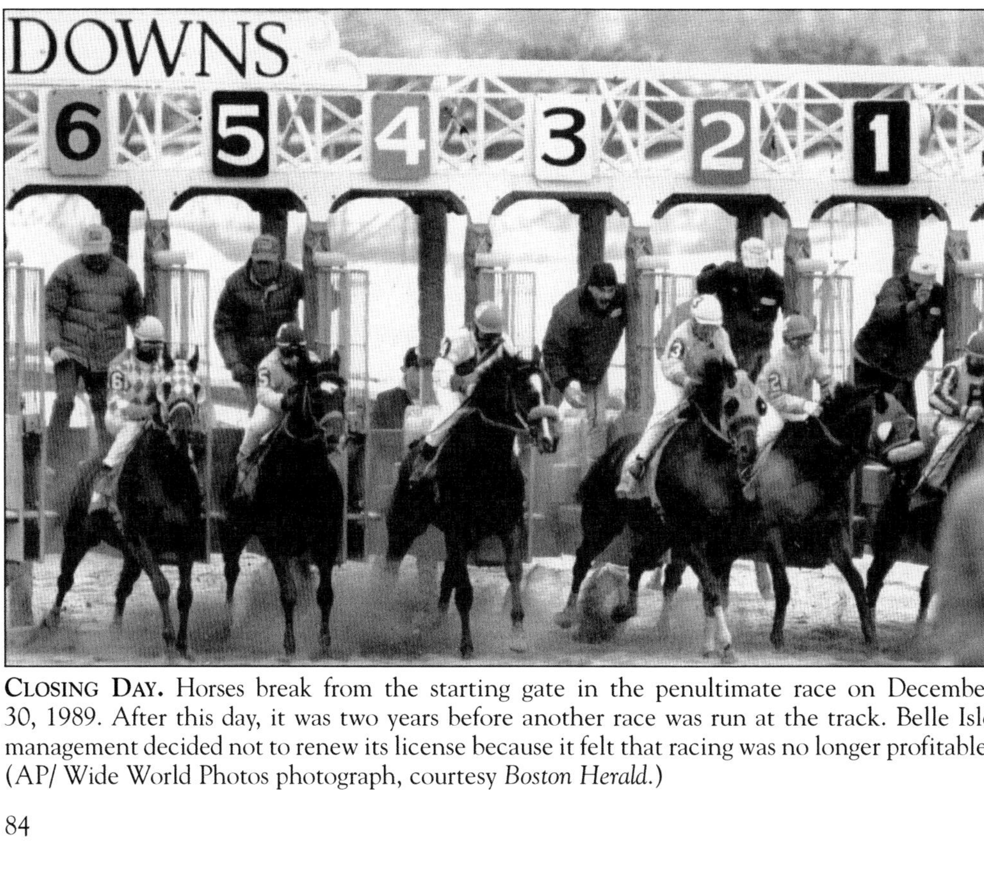

CLOSING DAY. Horses break from the starting gate in the penultimate race on December 30, 1989. After this day, it was two years before another race was run at the track. Belle Isle management decided not to renew its license because it felt that racing was no longer profitable. (AP/ Wide World Photos photograph, courtesy *Boston Herald*.)

Seven

THE 1990S

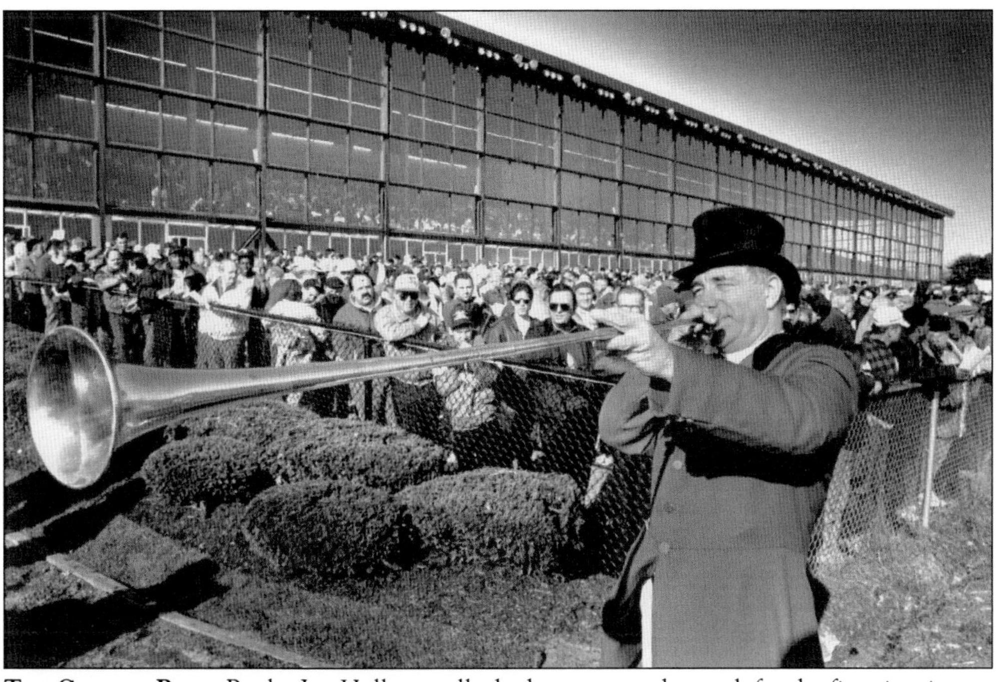

THE CALL TO POST. Bugler Joe Hollerer calls the horses onto the track for the first time in two years as the track reopens on January 1, 1992, in front of 15,212 fans. The first race was won by Larry of Florida with Rudy Baez in the saddle. (*Boston Herald* photograph.)

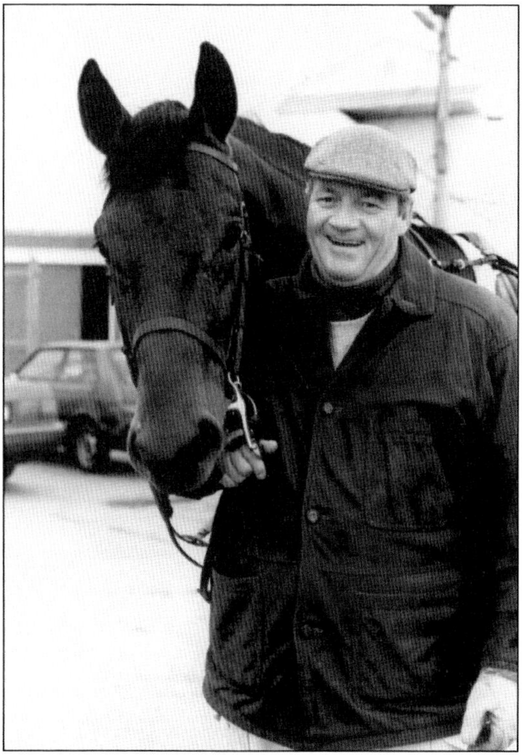

James B. Moseley. James B. Moseley played a leading role in the reopening of the track in 1992, after it had been closed for two years. With Moseley as chairman, Sterling Suffolk Racecourse assumed control of the track in May 1991 and obtained racing dates from the state legislature for 1992. Moseley directed an enormous reconstruction project prior to the track's reopening on January 1, 1992, and he was instrumental in the revival of the MassCap in 1995. (Bill Denver/Equi-Photo photograph.)

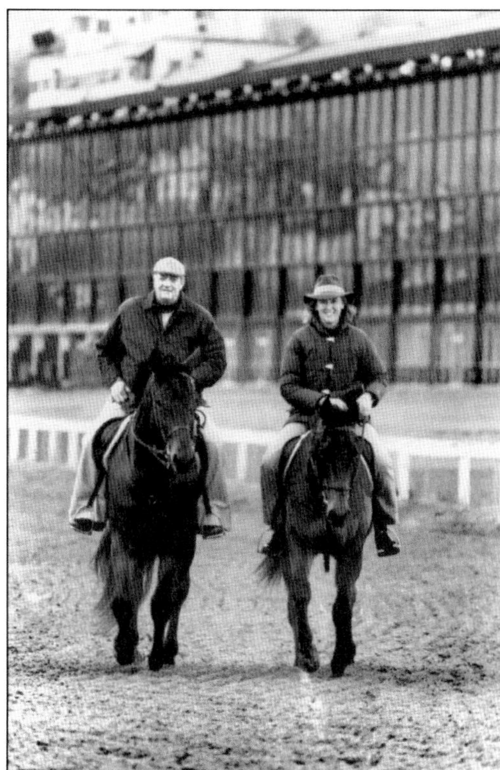

Mr. and Mrs. Moseley. Horses are much more than a business for Jim Moseley and his wife, Patricia, both lifelong equine enthusiasts. Here, they share a leisurely morning on the track. Patricia Moseley became chairwoman of the track when Jim passed away in 1998 at age 66. (Bill Denver/Equi-Photo photograph.)

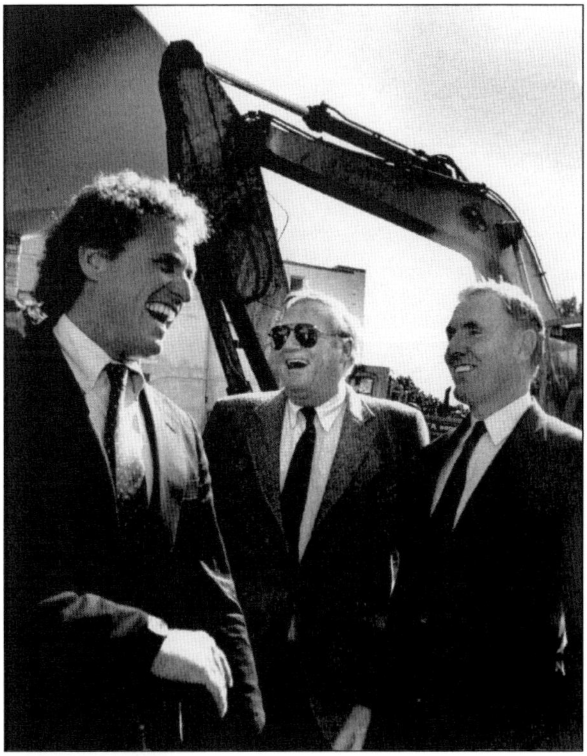

Reopening Plans. Representative Joseph P. Kennedy II, Jim Moseley, and Boston mayor Ray Flynn, seen here from left to right, share a laugh in October 1991 prior to an on-site press conference at which Moseley presented his plans for the track's reopening in 1992. (*Boston Herald* photographs.)

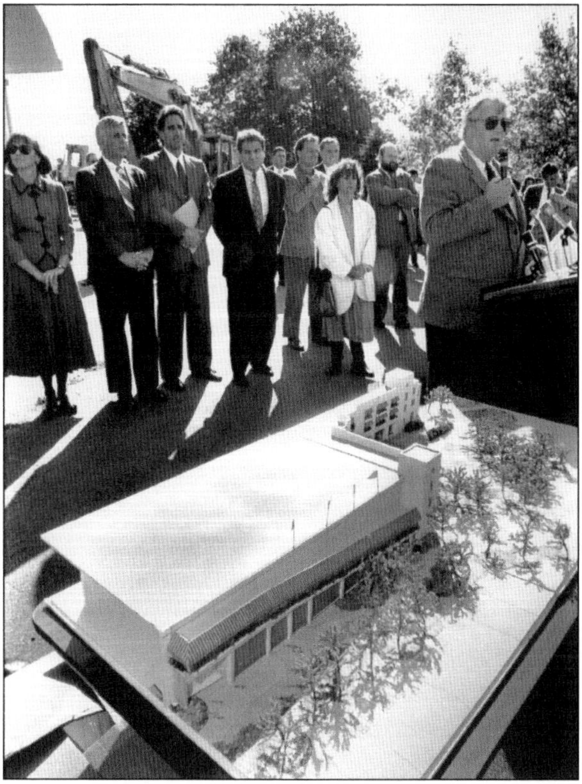

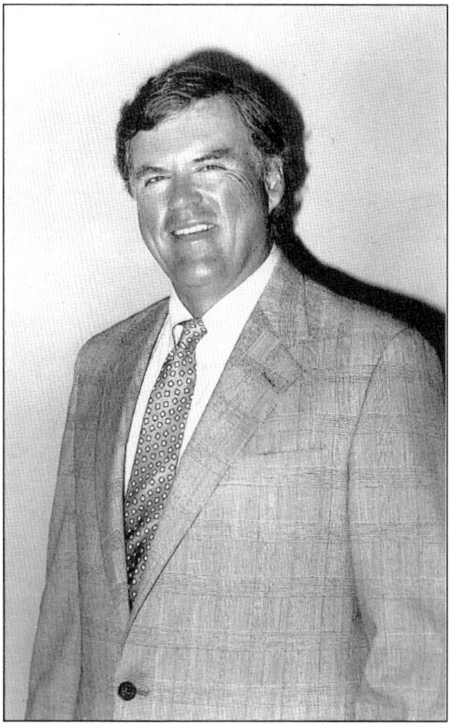

JOHN HALL. As president of Sterling Suffolk Racecourse since its formation in 1991, Boston real estate investor and developer John Hall was a key figure in the reconstruction and reopening of the track in 1992. Hall played a vital role in finalizing the purchase of the track from Buddy LeRoux's Belle Isle Limited Partnership in 1997. (Bill Denver/Equi-Photo photograph.)

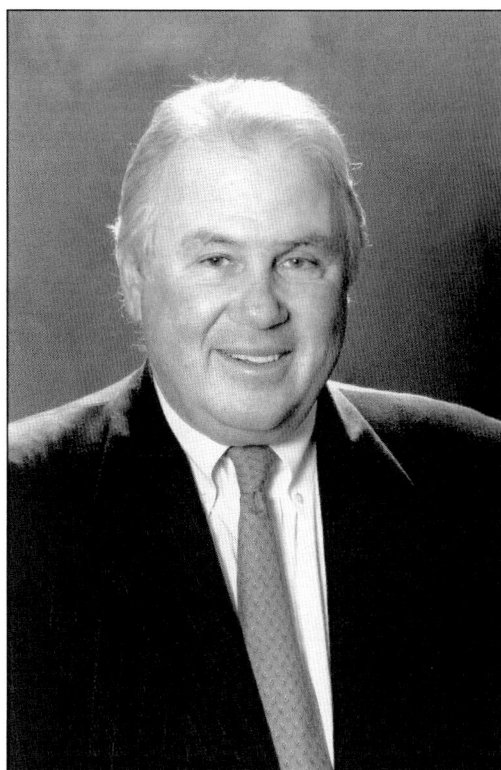

JOE O'DONNELL. Boston concessionaire Joe O'Donnell, a leading investor in Sterling Suffolk Racecourse, joined Moseley and Hall in facilitating the resuscitation of the track and securing ownership from the Belle Isle group. (Courtesy Suffolk Downs.)

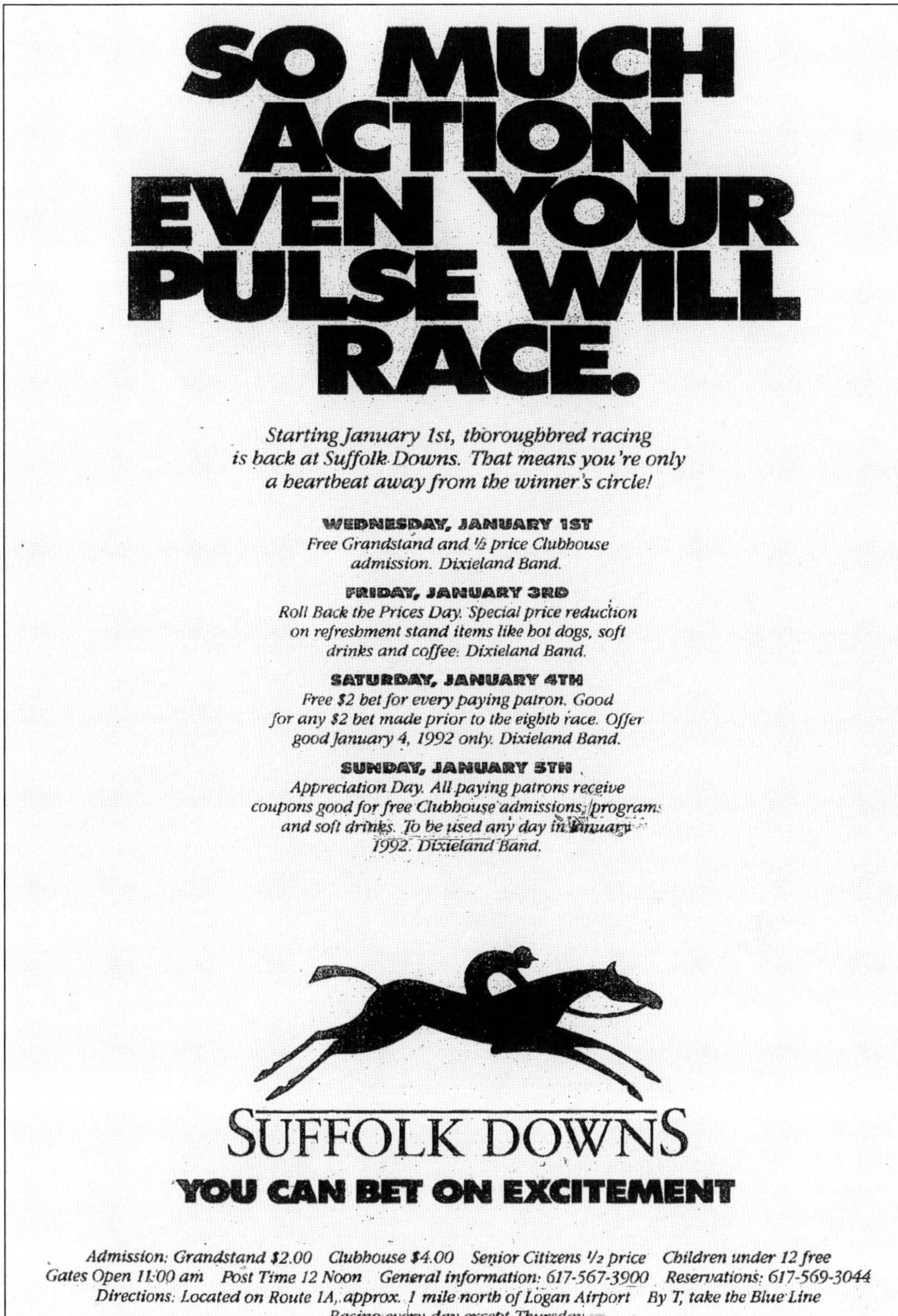

READY FOR ACTION. This print advertisement touts the track's reopening on January 1, 1992. (*Boston Globe* advertisement, courtesy O'Neill Library, Boston College.)

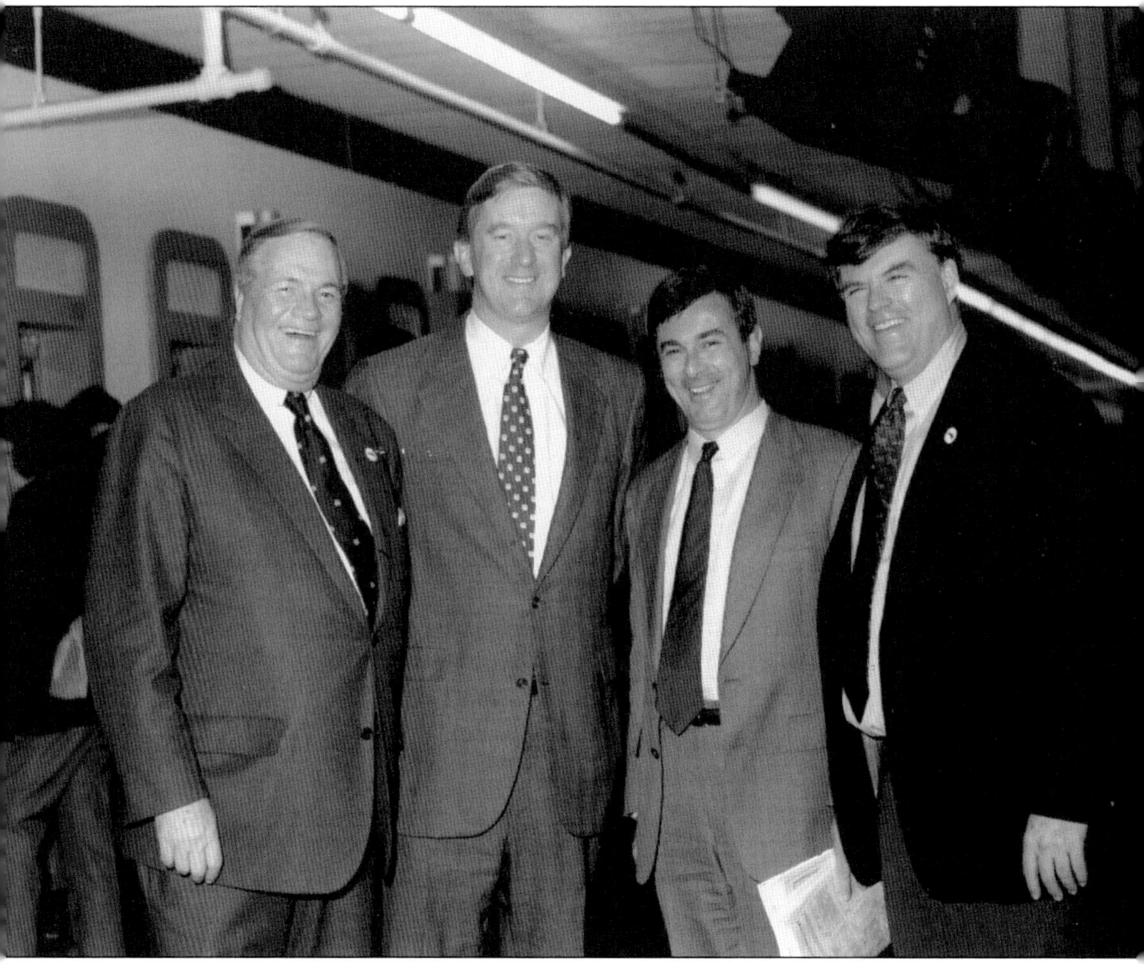

TRACK AND STATE OFFICIALS. Track chairman Jim Moseley (left) and president John Hall (right) welcome Gov. William Weld (second from left) and Lt. Gov. Paul Cellucci (second from right) shortly after the reopening of the track in January 1992. (Bill Denver/Equi-Photo photograph.)

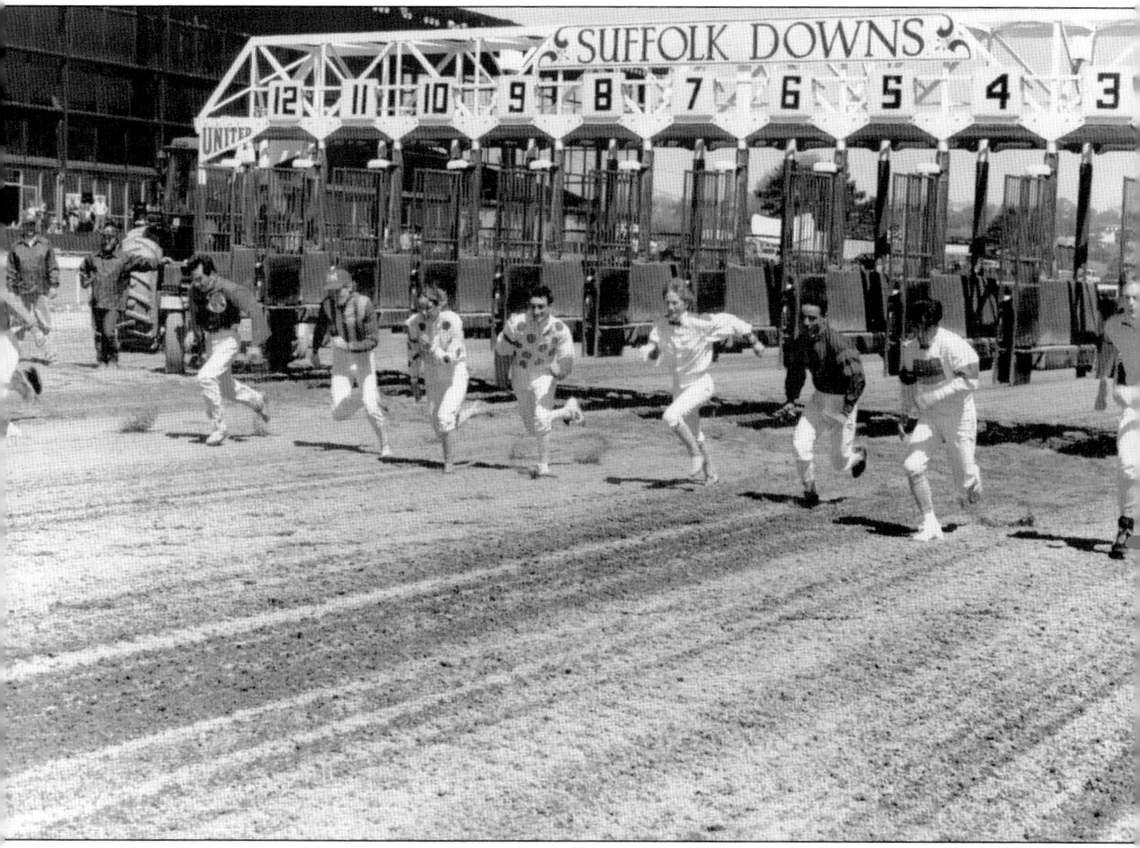

Hoofing It. Jockeys break from the gate without horses in a footrace in 1994. Jose Caraballo (far left, in the lead) won the race for the second straight year. (Bill Denver/Equi-Photo photograph.)

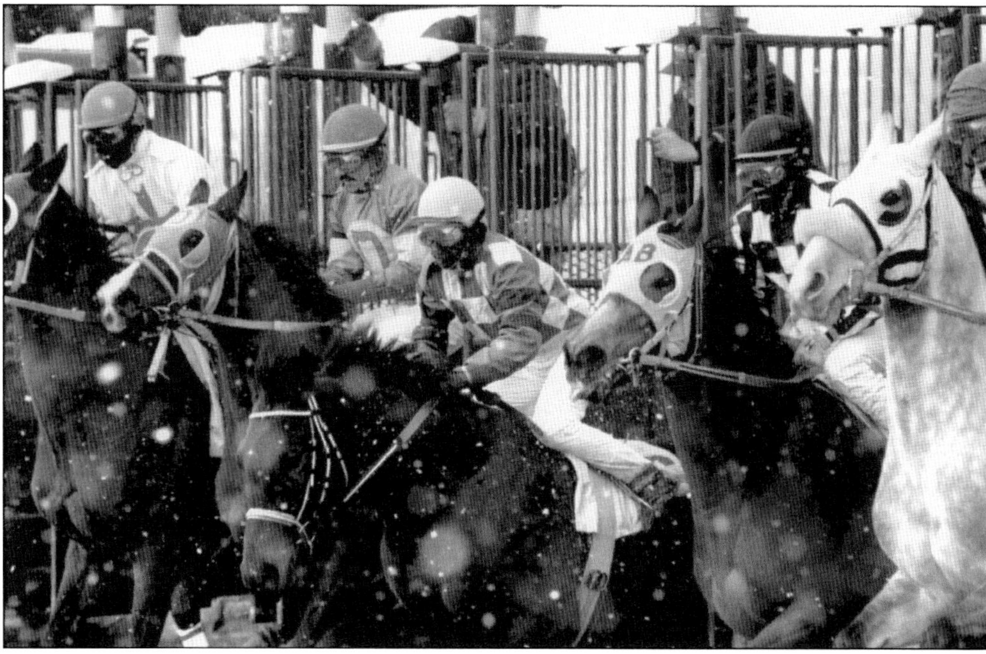

WINTER RACING. Snow falls as horses break from the gate on February 22, 1993. From 1972 to 2003, winter racing was a staple at the track. (Above, Bud Morton photograph; below, Bill Denver/Equi-Photo photograph.)

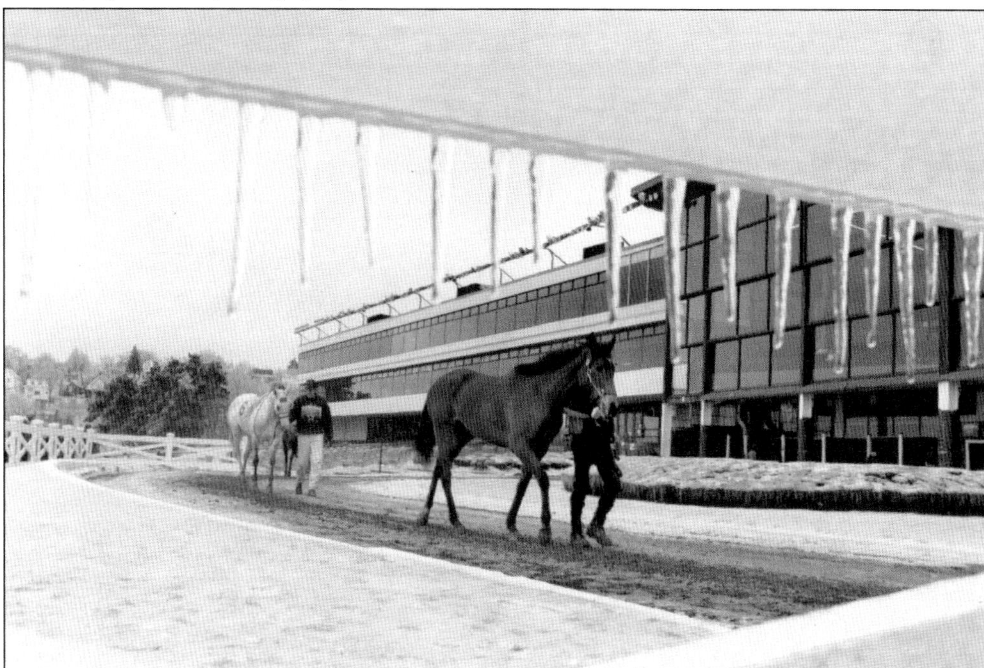

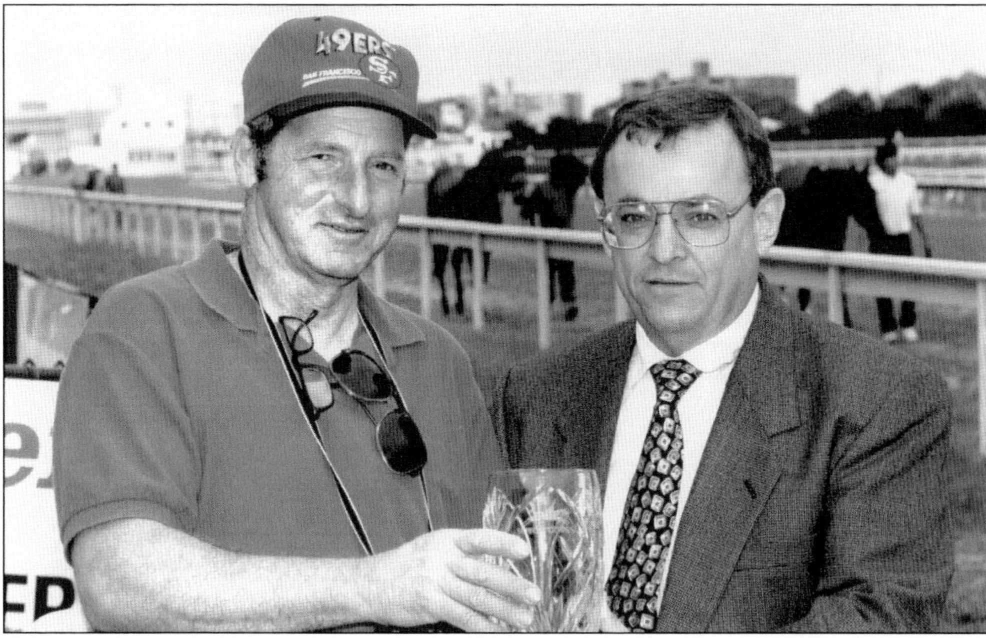

ALLEN BOROSH AND JOHN MORRISSEY. Trainer Allen Borosh receives leading trainer honors in 1995 from racing secretary John Morrissey. Borosh captured the first of his nine meet titles at the track in 1973. Borosh garnered four straight meet titles from 1994 to 1996, equaling the standard set by Bob Klesaris from 1982 to 1983. (Bill Denver/Equi-Photo photograph.)

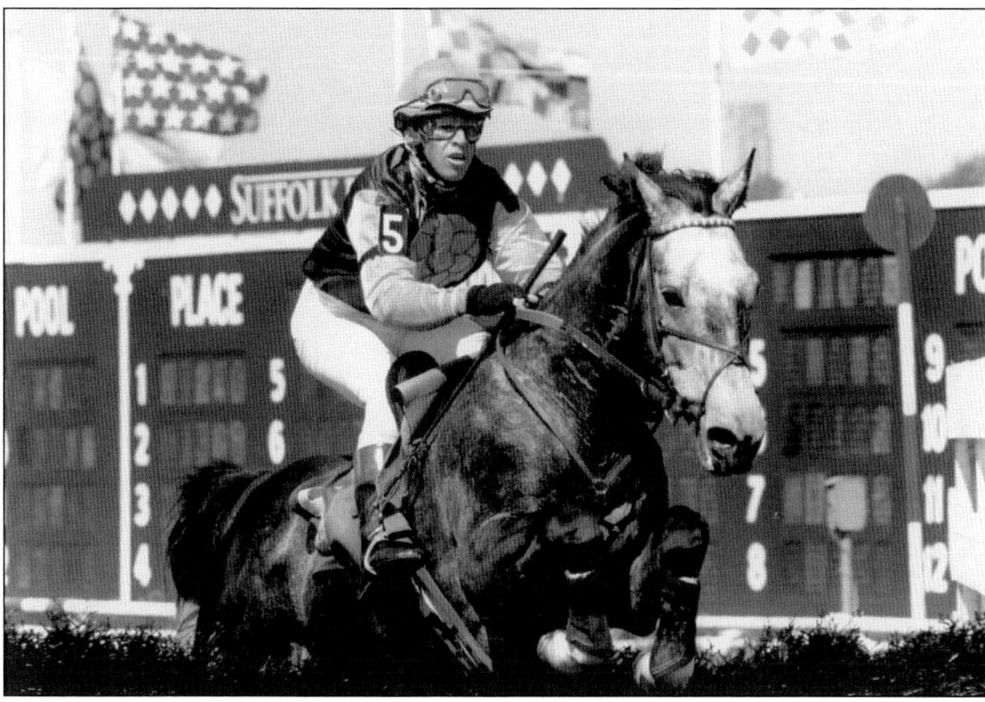

STEEPLECHASE RACING. After a 27-year absence, steeplechase racing returned to the track in 1996. The jumpers came back the following year as part of MassCap week festivities. (Bill Denver/Equi-Photo photograph.)

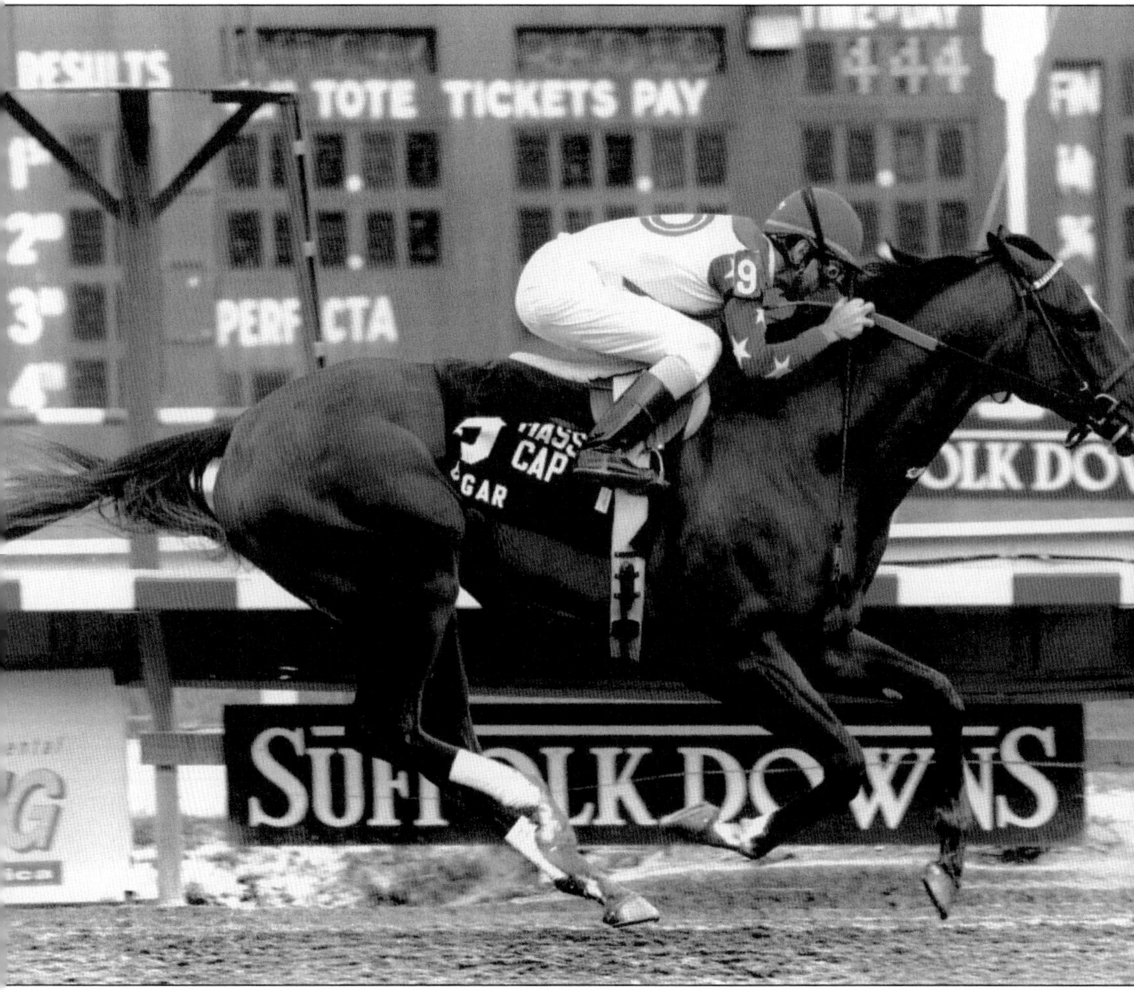

CIGAR WINS THE 1995 MASSCAP. The MassCap returned on June 3, 1995, after a five-year absence, and it immediately regained national merit when eventual Horse of the Year Cigar won it to extend his string of consecutive victories to eight. Cigar was ridden by hall of famer Jerry Bailey. (Bill Denver/Equi-Photo photograph.)

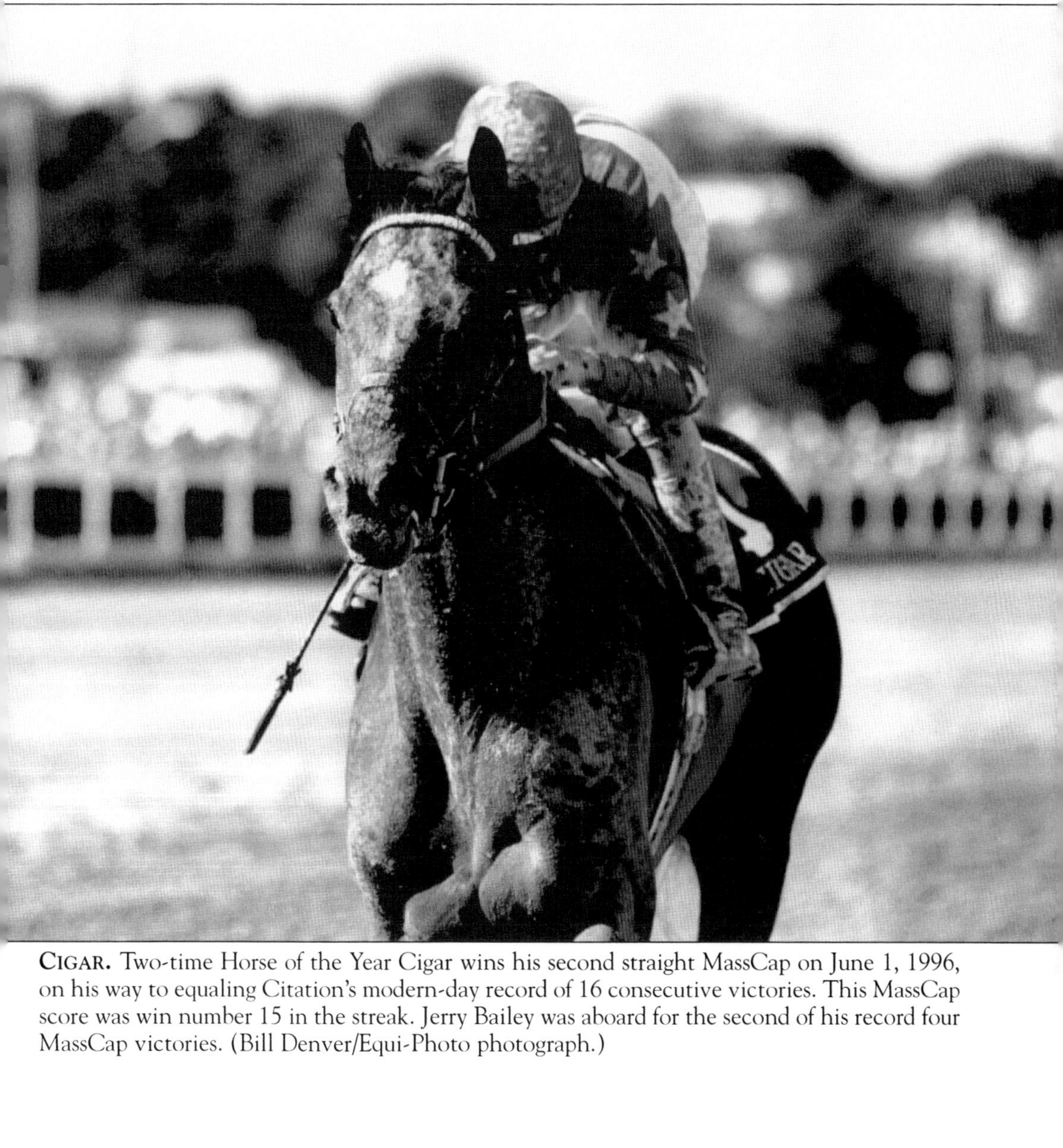

CIGAR. Two-time Horse of the Year Cigar wins his second straight MassCap on June 1, 1996, on his way to equaling Citation's modern-day record of 16 consecutive victories. This MassCap score was win number 15 in the streak. Jerry Bailey was aboard for the second of his record four MassCap victories. (Bill Denver/Equi-Photo photograph.)

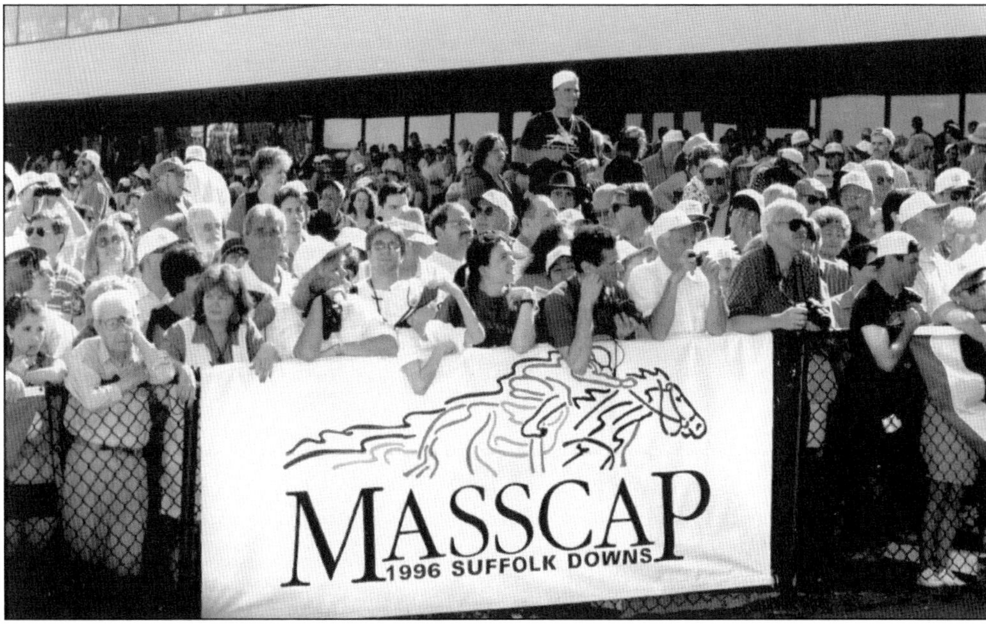

MASSCAP DAY, 1996. An attentive crowd of 22,169 was on hand to witness Cigar's second MassCap victory. (Above, Bill Denver/Equi-Photo photograph; below, Bud Morton photograph.)

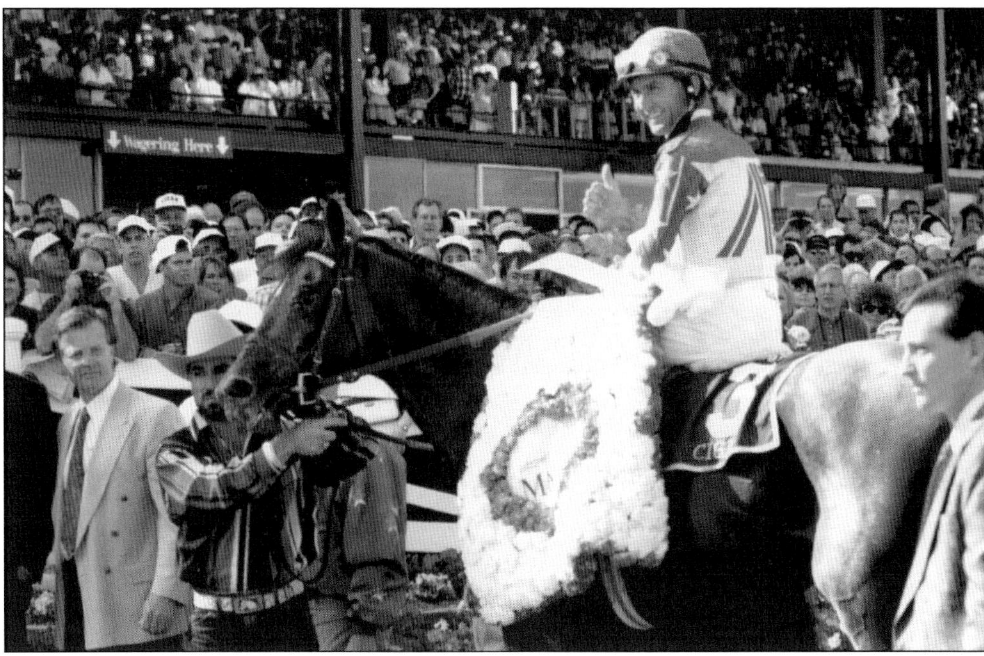

LOU RAFFETTO. As executive vice president of racing from 1991 to 2000, Lou Raffetto helped restore the MassCap to its past greatness. Raffetto traveled as far as Dubai in the United Arab Emirates to help assure Cigar's return in the 1996 MassCap. Cigar and his connections were in Dubai in March 1996 to compete in the $4 million Dubai World Cup, which Cigar won. After a two-month break, Cigar made his next start in the MassCap. (Bill Denver/Equi-Photo photograph.)

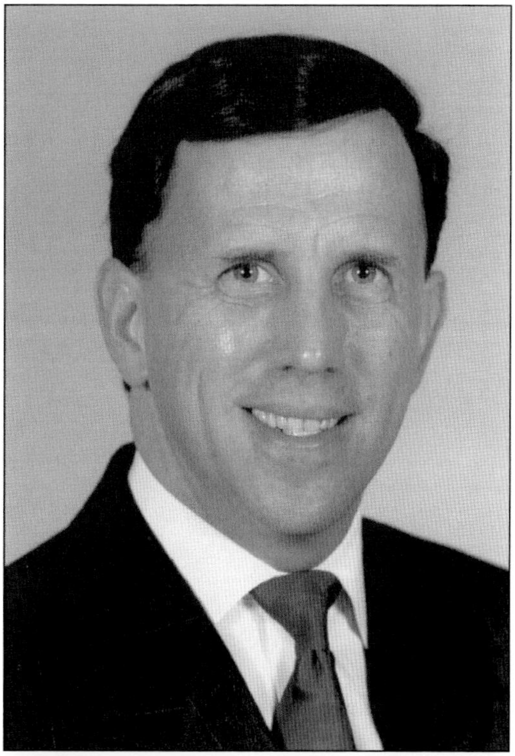

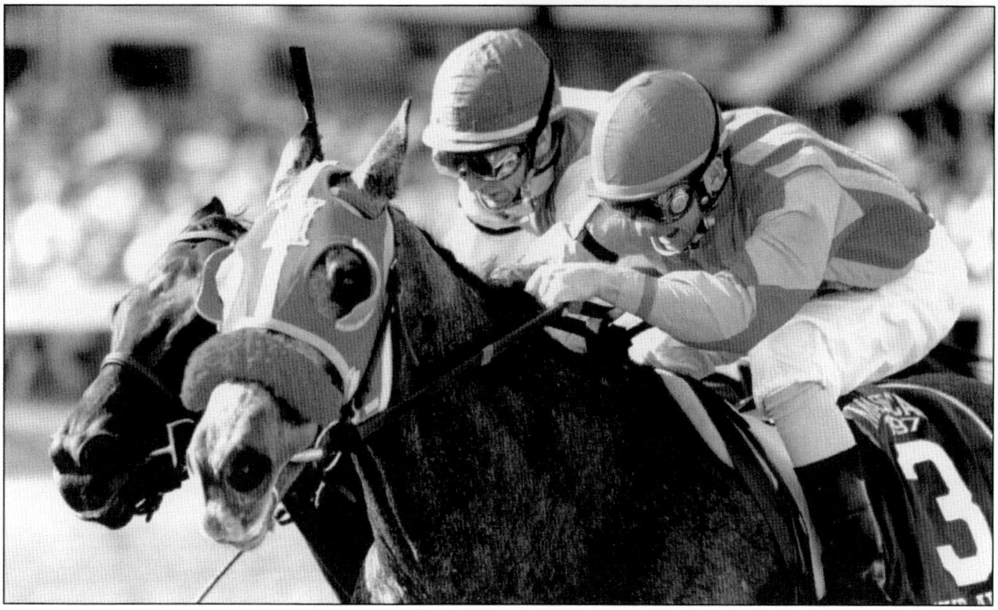

THE 1997 MASSACHUSETTS HANDICAP. Skip Away and jockey Shane Sellers (right) are neck-and-neck with Formal Gold and Jerry Bailey as they near the wire in the 1997 MassCap. Skip Away prevailed by a head in one of the most thrilling finishes in the history of the race. With $5,867,414 wagered on the 13-race program that day, a track record for one-day all-source handle was set. For the first time in New England racing history, over $1 million in purse money was at stake on one day. (Bill Denver/Equi-Photo photograph.)

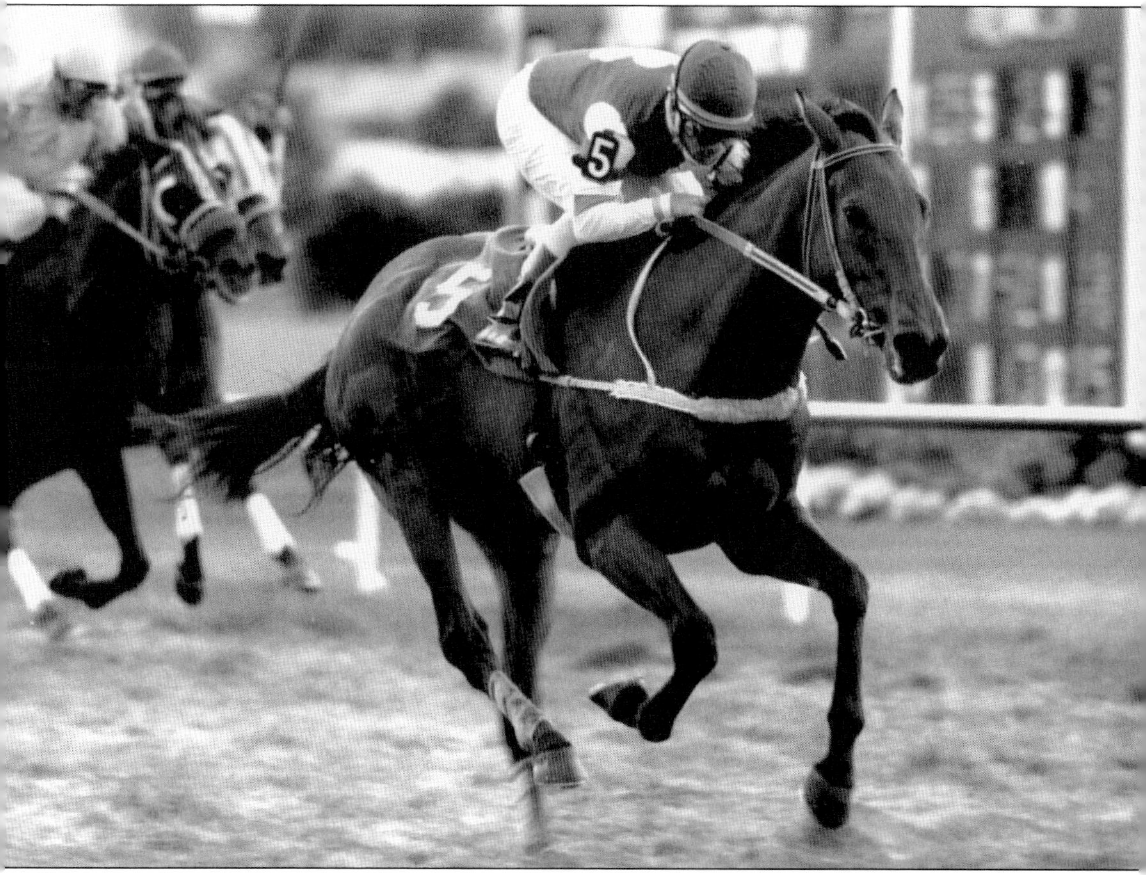

MAYBE JACK. Harry Vega rides Maybe Jack to victory in the 1997 Bruce G. Smith Memorial Stakes on October 4, 1997. Maybe Jack led the nation with 13 wins on the year, the final one coming in a match race against Finger Lakes shipper Pro on Ice, who was tied with Maybe Jack at 12 wins going into the race. (Bill Denver/Equi-Photo photograph.)

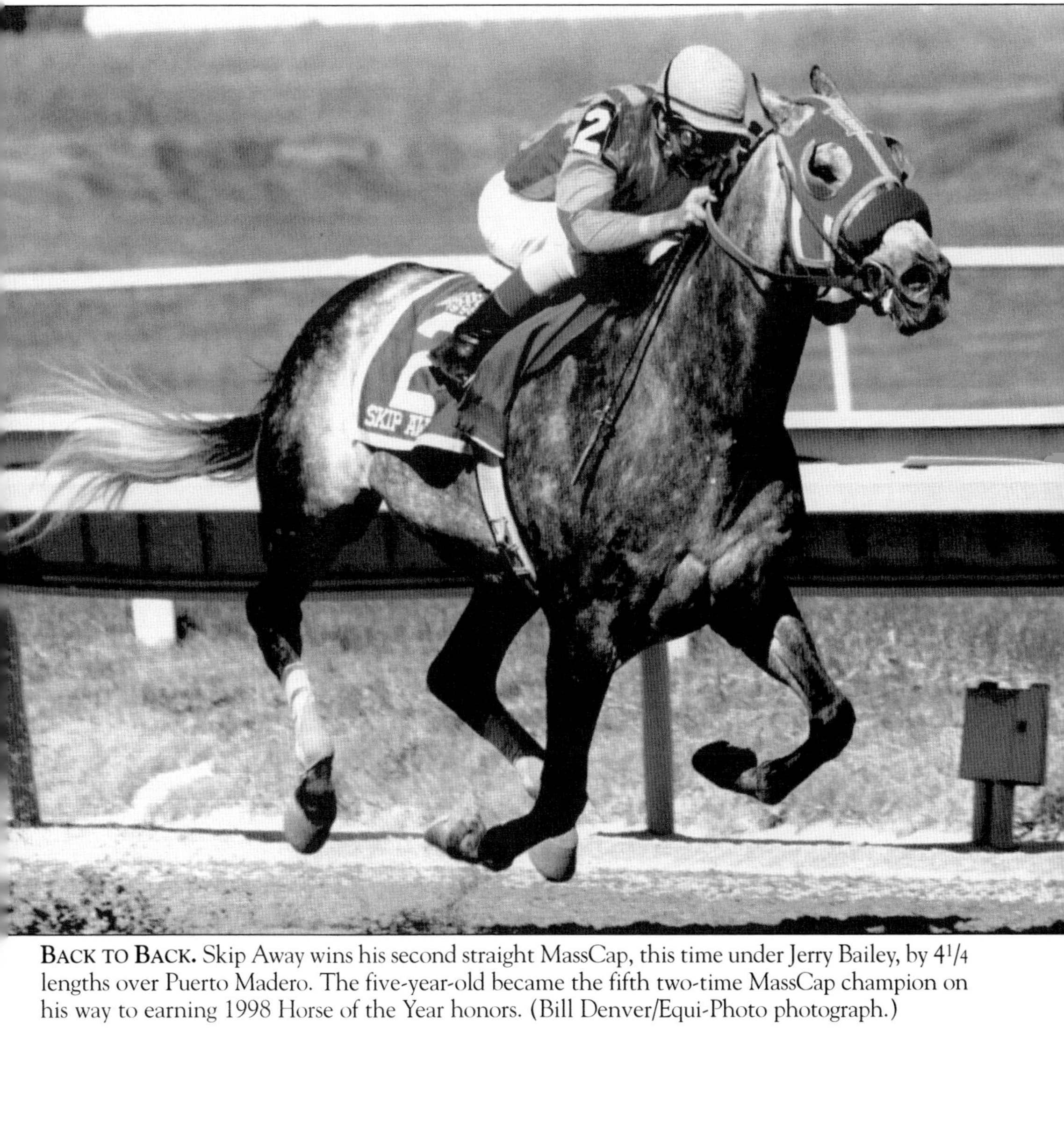

Back to Back. Skip Away wins his second straight MassCap, this time under Jerry Bailey, by $4\frac{1}{4}$ lengths over Puerto Madero. The five-year-old became the fifth two-time MassCap champion on his way to earning 1998 Horse of the Year honors. (Bill Denver/Equi-Photo photograph.)

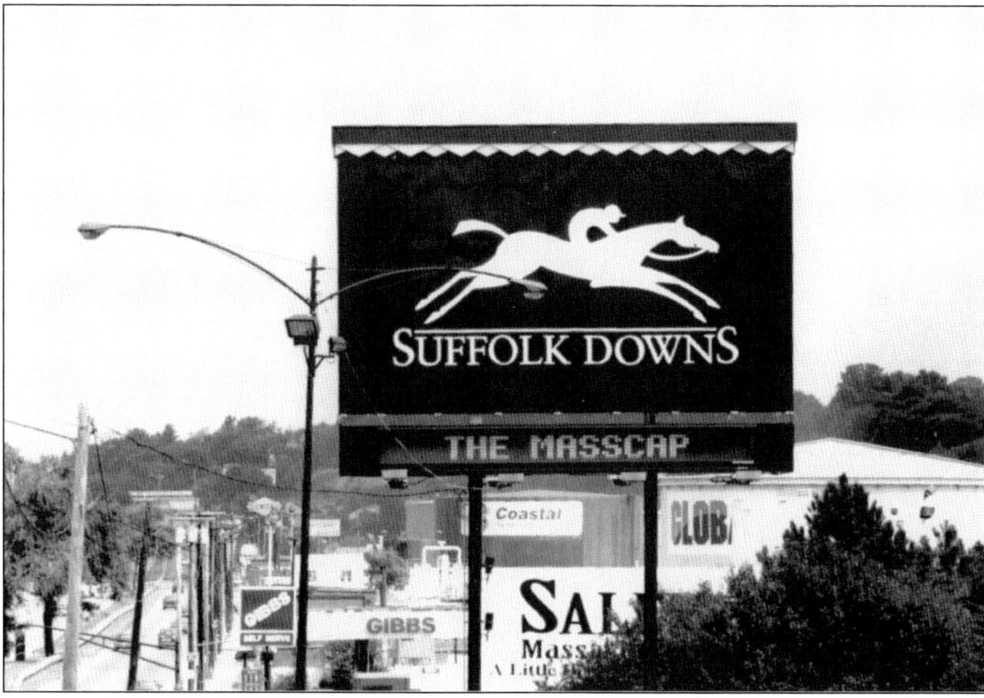

The Route 1A Entrance. The electronic sign informs Route 1A travelers that the MassCap is near. (Bill Denver/Equi-Photo Photograph.)

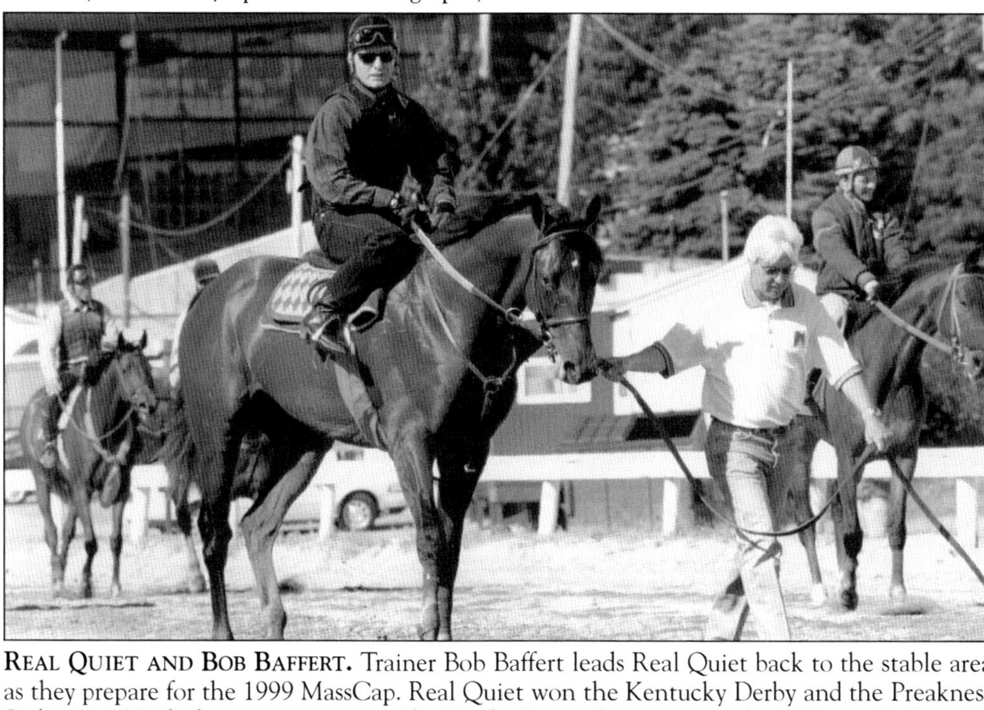

Real Quiet and Bob Baffert. Trainer Bob Baffert leads Real Quiet back to the stable area as they prepare for the 1999 MassCap. Real Quiet won the Kentucky Derby and the Preakness Stakes in 1998 before missing out on the Triple Crown by a nose in the Belmont Stakes. He was the first Derby winner to compete in the MassCap since Riva Ridge in 1973. Real Quiet finished third. (Bill Denver/Equi-Photo photograph.)

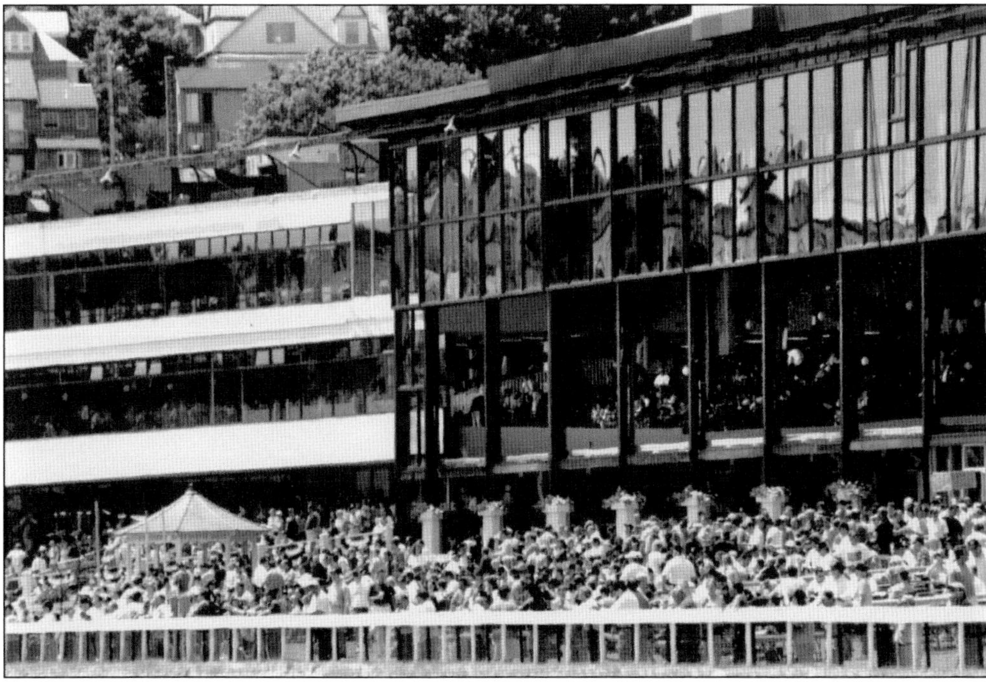

THE 1999 MASSACHUSETTS HANDICAP. The 60th running of the MassCap attracted a big crowd on the track as well as a national television audience. The interest in the race was proven when a track record for the largest single-race mutuel pool was established that day. (Bill Denver/Equi-Photo photographs.)

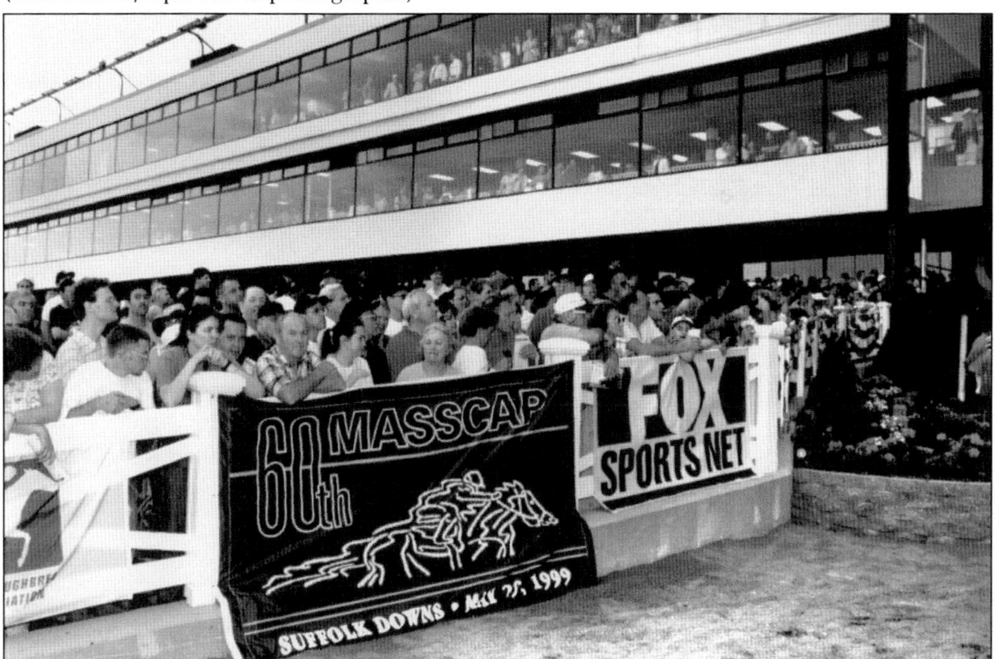

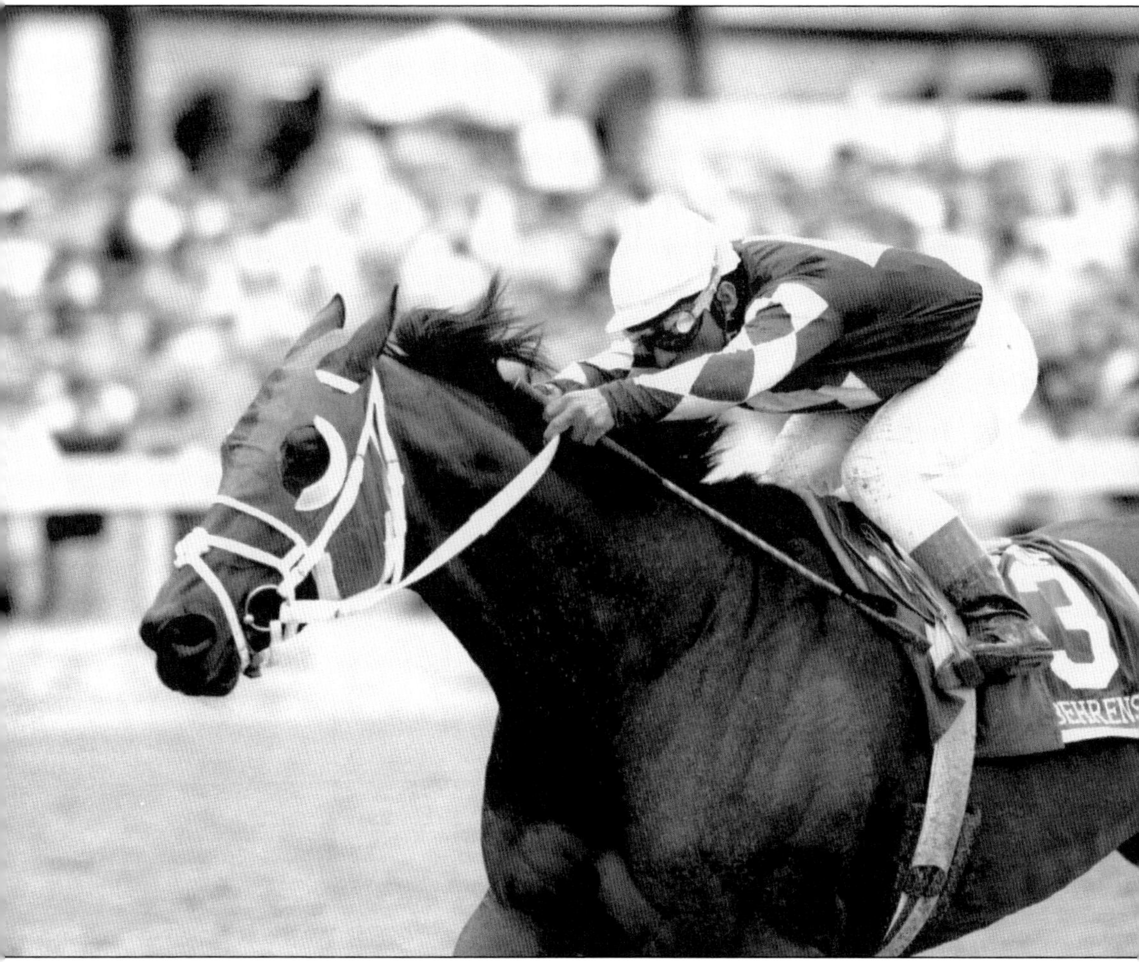

BEHRENS. Jockey Jorge Chavez powers Behrens through the stretch on their way to winning the 1999 MassCap. (Bill Denver/Equi-Photo photograph.)

Eight

PRESENT DAY

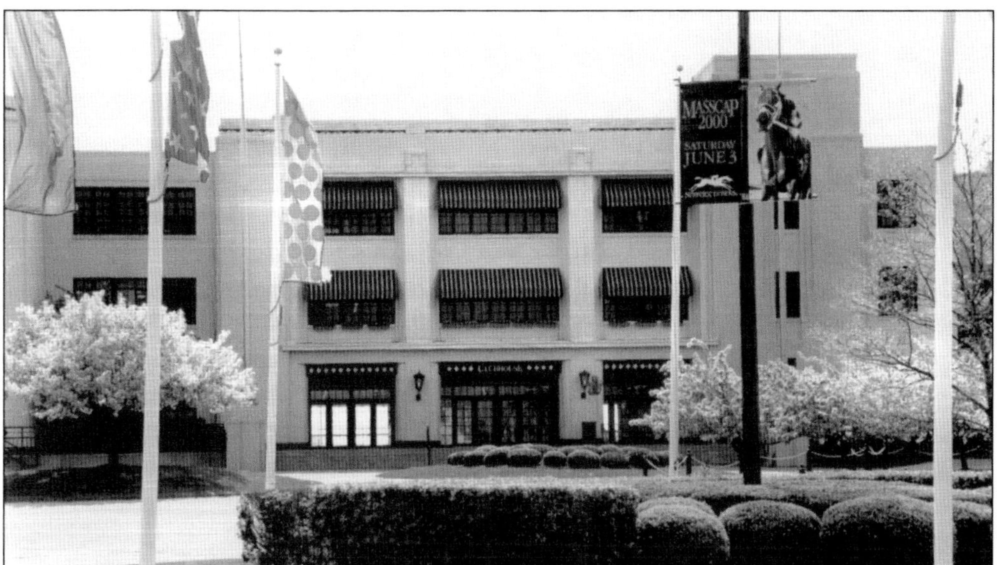

THE CLUBHOUSE ENTRANCE. The grounds are perfectly manicured for MassCap Day 2000. (Bill Denver/Equi-Photo photograph.)

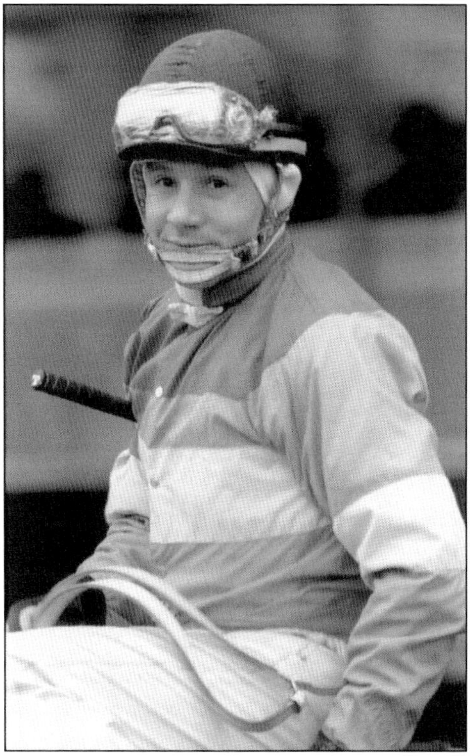

RUDY BAEZ DAY. Jockey Rudy Baez was honored by the track on April 29, 2000 (below). Baez (at left), owner of 14 riding titles at the track, was paralyzed from the waist down after a tragic accident at Rockingham Park in New Hampshire in August 1999. The track renamed a stakes race in Baez's honor, and he was offered a position at the track. Baez won 4,875 races in his illustrious career. (Left, Bill Denver/Equi-Photo photograph; below, Bud Morton photograph.)

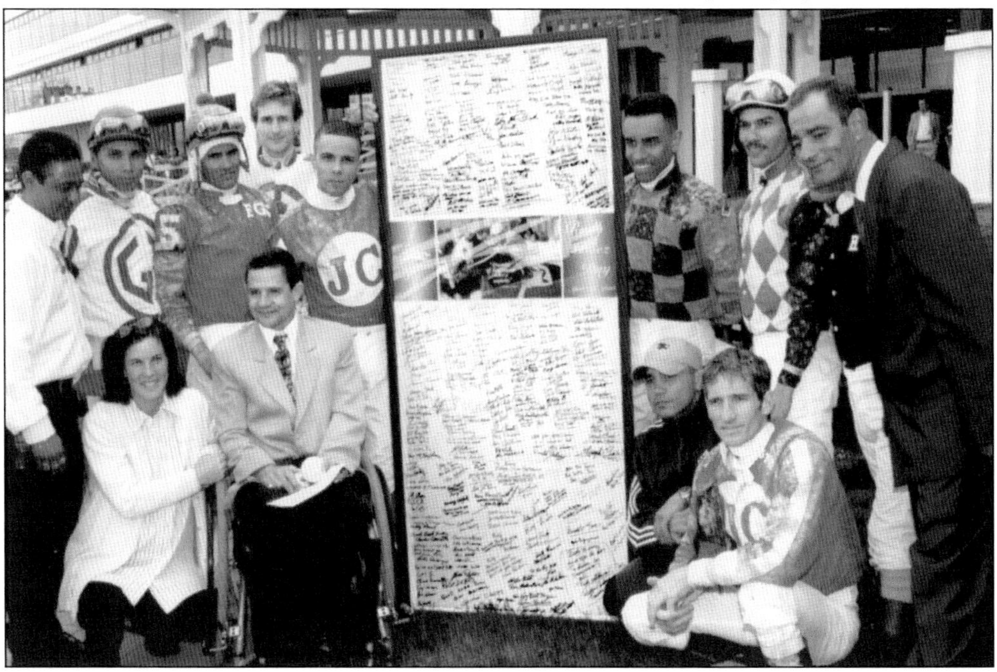

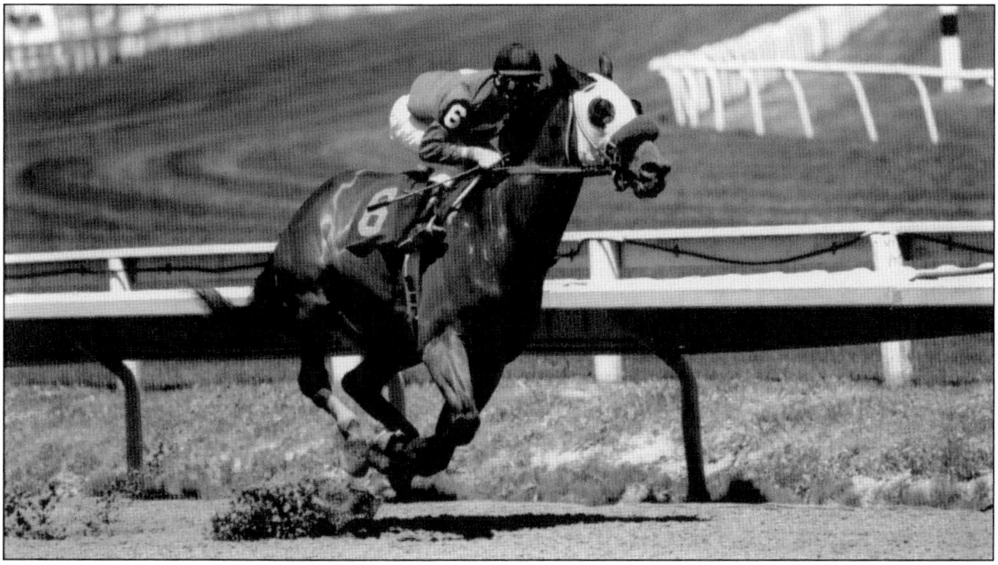

PROLANZIER. Yasou Stable Trust's Prolanzier is on his way to a gate-to-wire win in an allowance race on the MassCap undercard on June 3, 2000. Prolanzier, ridden here by Joe Hampshire, won 32 of his 96 career starts, including several stakes races. The local fan favorite competed in two MassCaps, finishing third in Cigar's second MassCap win in 1996. (Bud Morton photograph.)

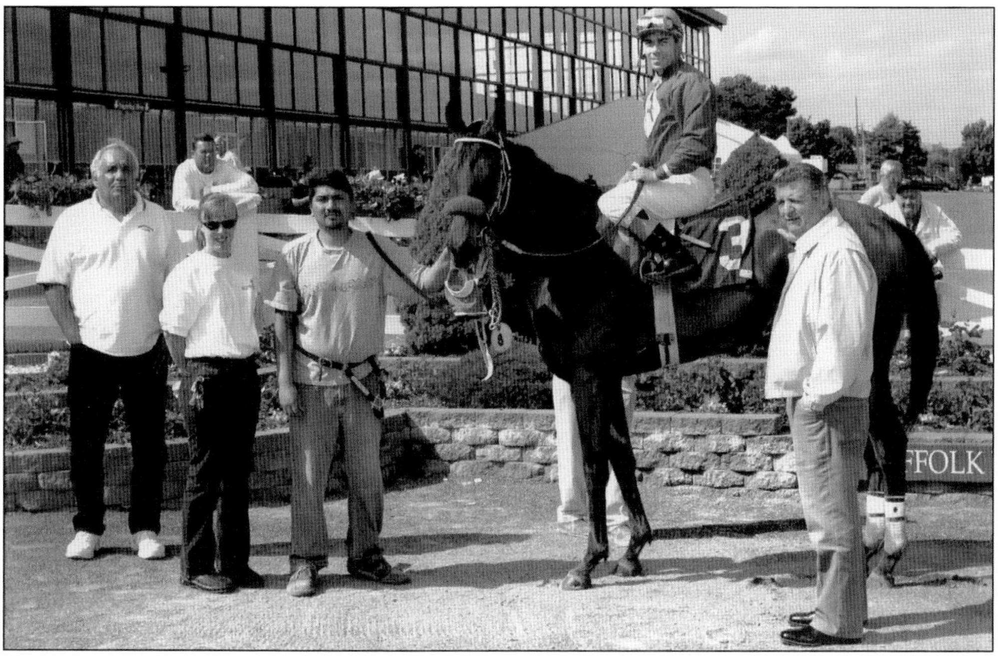

THE YASOU STABLE TRUST. Jockey Jose Bermudez wears the silks of the Yasou Stable Trust in the winner's circle with Special Jule after their victory in a money allowance race on June 2, 2003. Trainer Charlie Assimakopoulos (right) has guided his family's Yasou Stable Trust to numerous leading-owner titles at the track. Over the years, the stable has included stakes winners Kayla's a Gem, Prolanzier, Shadow Caster, and Speedland, among others. (Bill Denver/Equi-Photo photograph.)

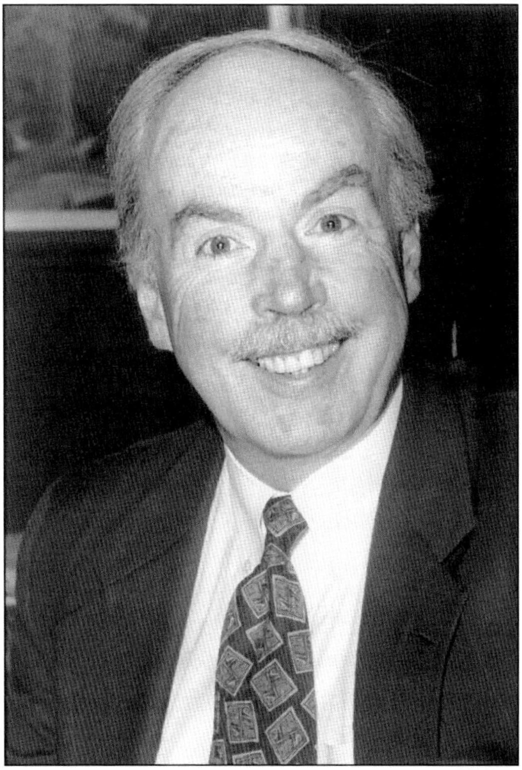

Bob O'Malley. Serving in his fifth decade at the track, chief operating officer Bob O'Malley started out as a part-time employee while a student in 1962. He has been part of the management team since 1974, assuming his current position in 1996. (Bill Denver/Equi-Photo photograph.)

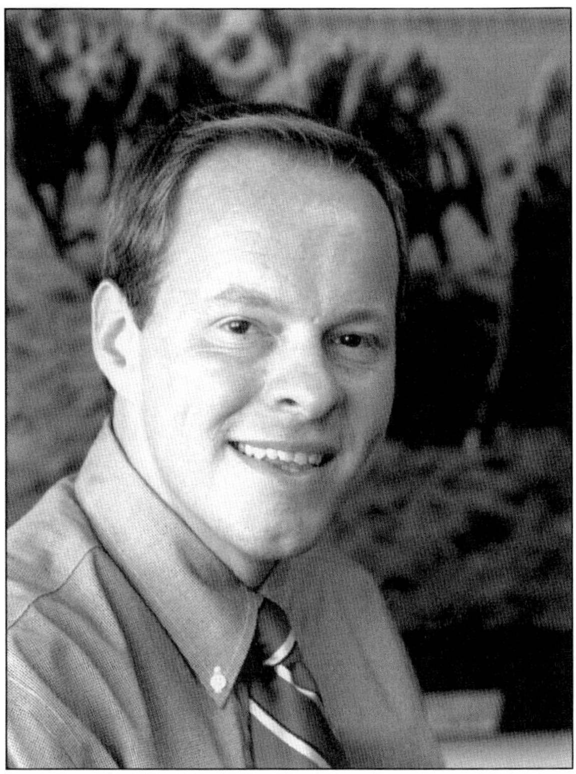

Larry Collmus. Larry Collmus became the track's third full-time announcer when it reopened in 1992 after a two-year hiatus. Collmus was the nation's youngest full-time announcer when he was hired at age 20 by Alabama's Birmingham Race Course in 1987. (Bill Denver/Equi-Photo photograph.)

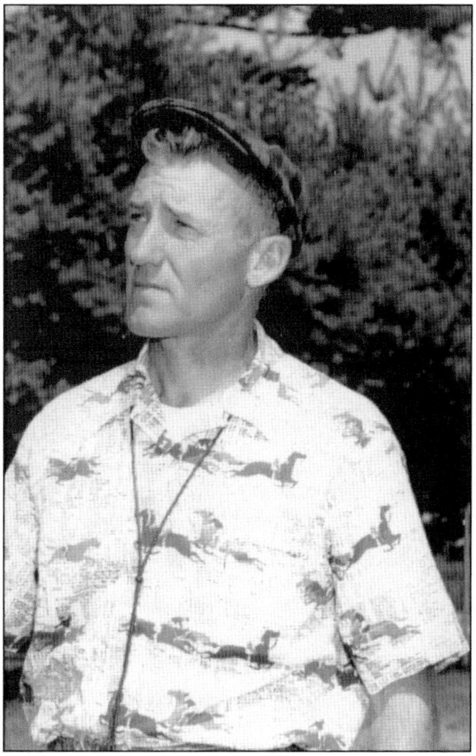

GEORGE HANDY. Trainer George Handy is in his seventh decade of training, having gotten his start in 1946 at Narragansett Park in Rhode Island. Handy has won five training titles at the track. He saddled Paristo to a third-place finish in the 1981 Preakness Stakes. (Right, courtesy Boston Public Library Print Department; below, Bill Denver/Equi-Photo photograph.)

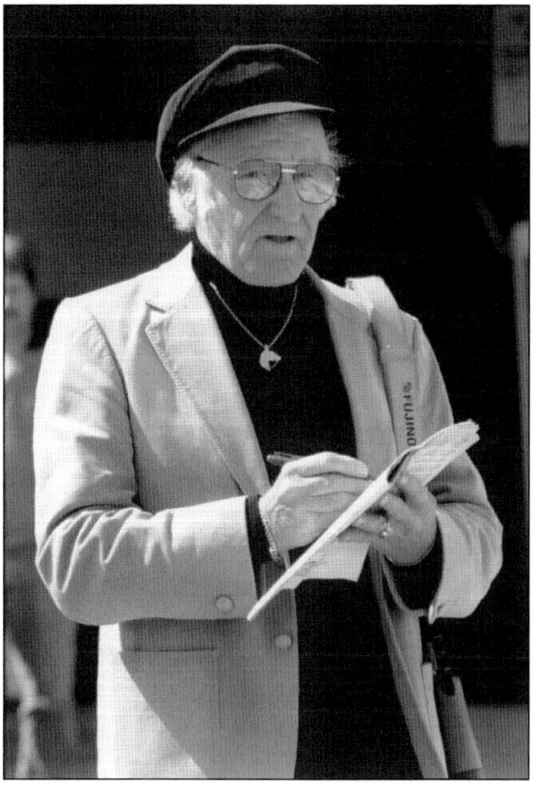

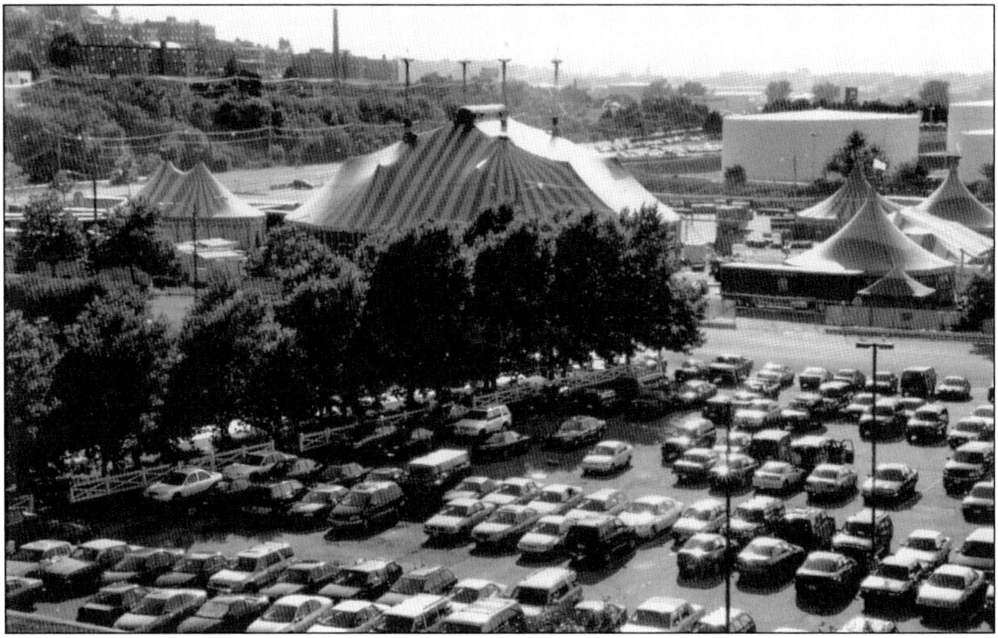

CIRQUE DU SOLEIL. The popular touring entertainment troupe Cirque du Soleil made its third stop at the track in the summer of 2004. Here, its signature blue and yellow "chapiteau" occupies part of the general parking area. Daily shows attracted a diverse following to the track. (Courtesy Suffolk Downs.)

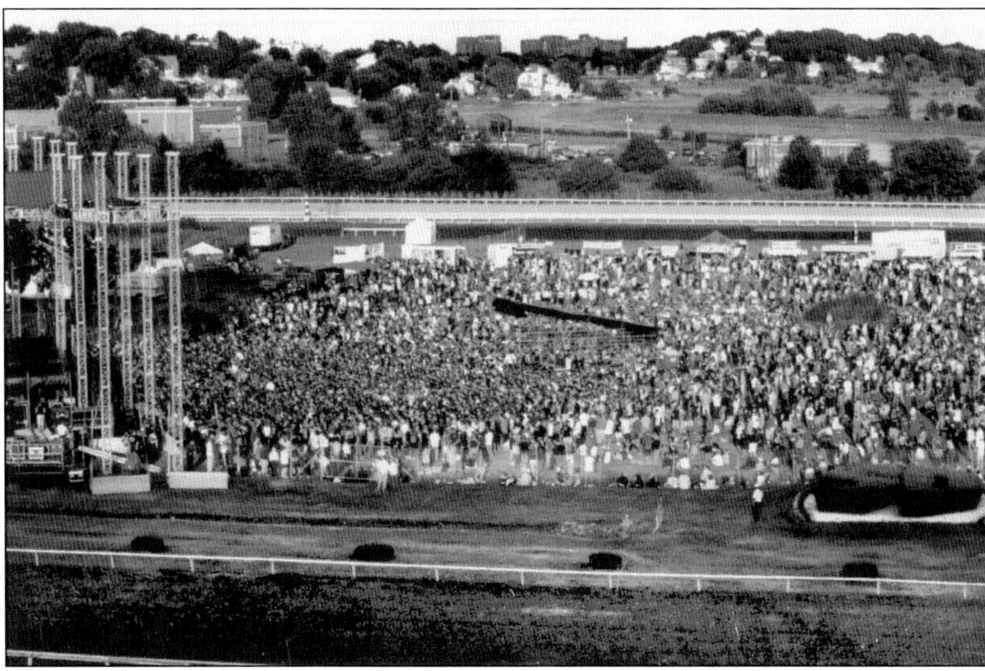

RADIOHEAD. Concert-goers pack the infield to see the band Radiohead on August 14, 2001. Since 1999, the track has hosted a number of concerts, including the Guinness Fleadh, Tattoo the Earth Festival, MixFest 2000, the Rolling Rock Town Fair, the ACME Festival, and the Vans Warped Tour. (Allen Dines photograph.)

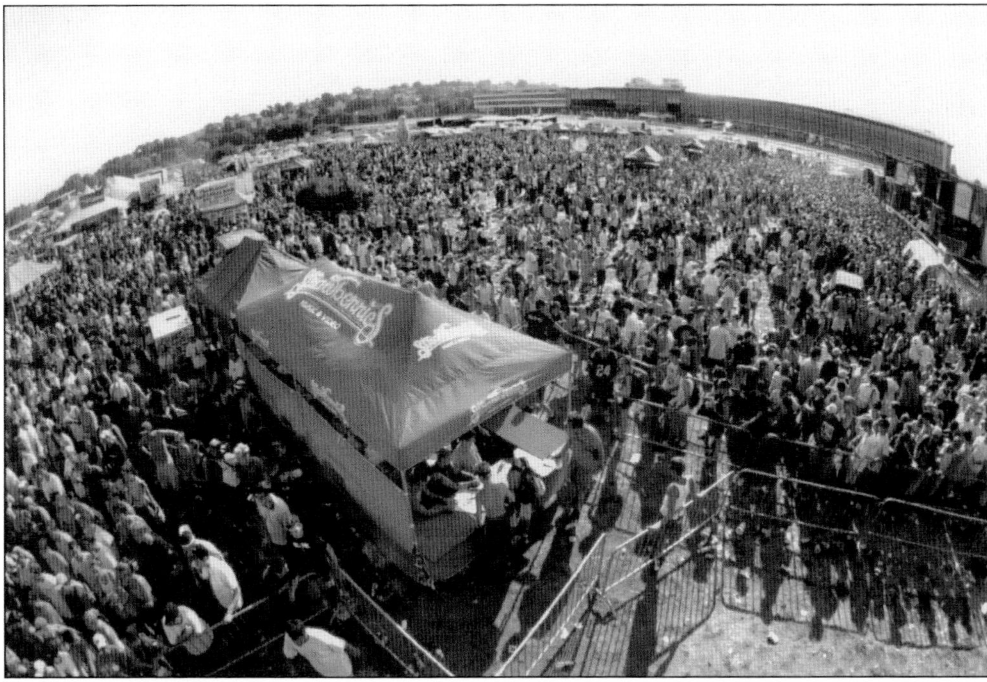

THE VANS WARPED TOUR. Music and extreme sports are united in the Vans Warped Tour concert series, which was held in the track's infield each summer from 2000 to 2002. (Allan Dines photographs.)

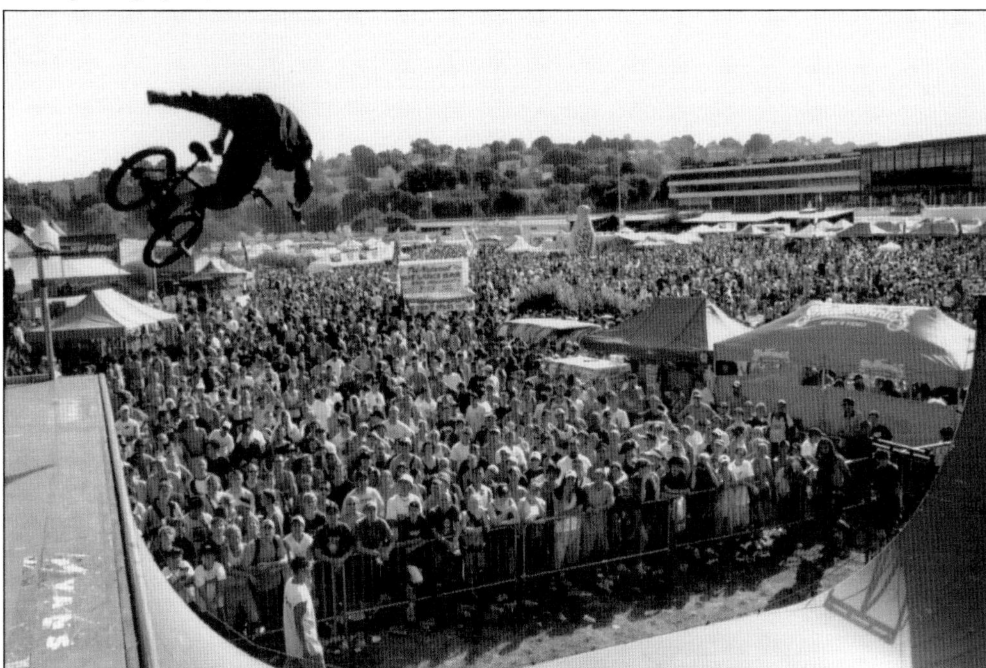

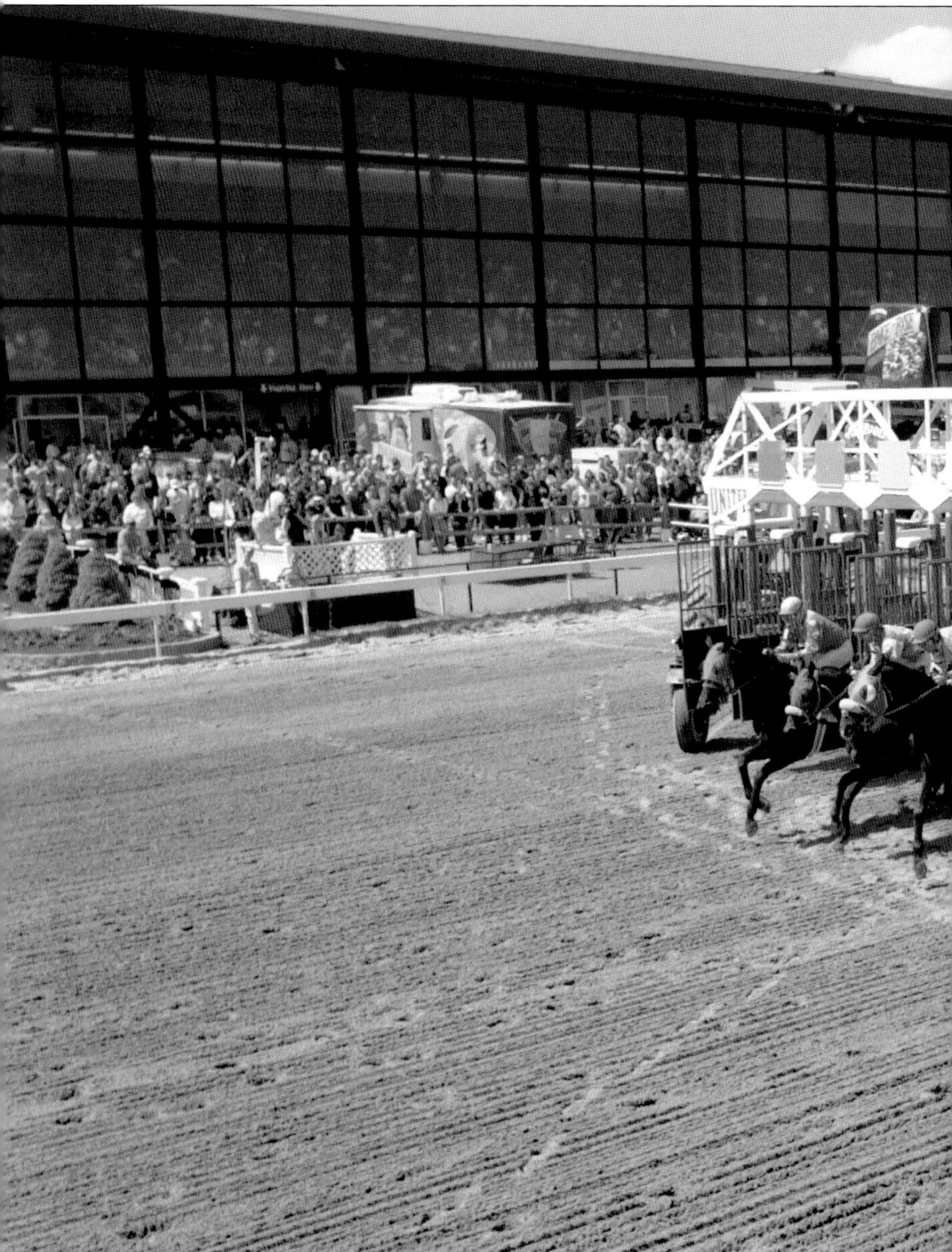

OUT OF THE GATE. Horses break from the gate in front of a festive crowd on a sun-drenched

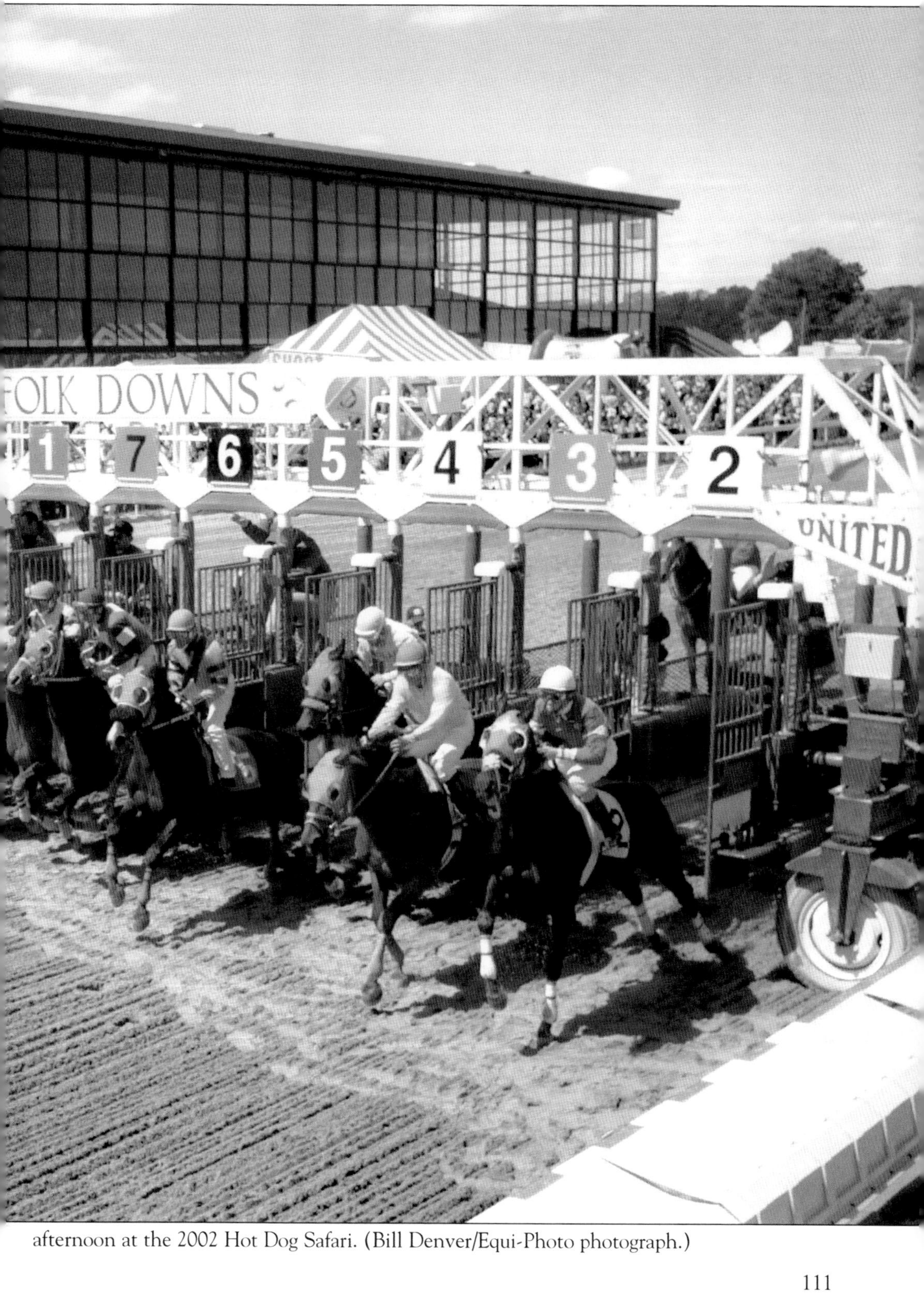

afternoon at the 2002 Hot Dog Safari. (Bill Denver/Equi-Photo photograph.)

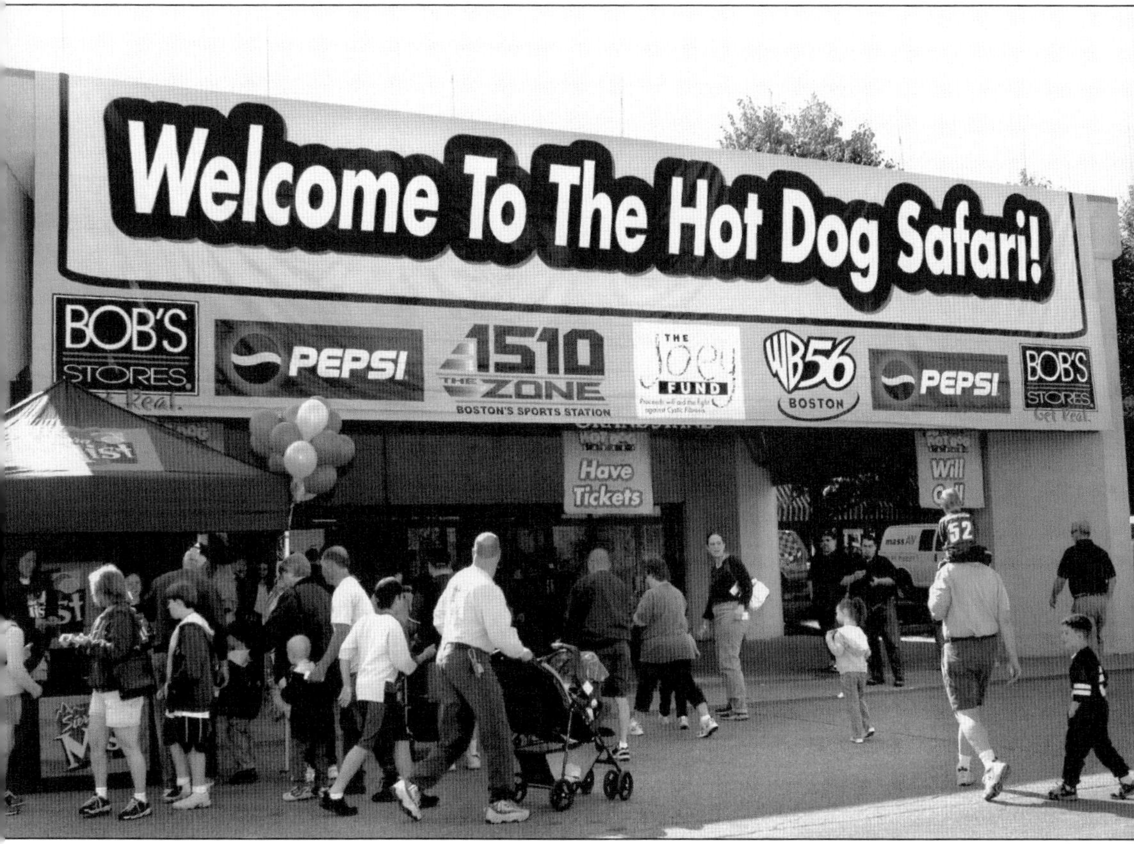

THE HOT DOG SAFARI. Families head for the entrance to Eddie Andelman's Hot Dog Safari, which features live racing, fun and games for children, celebrity appearances, and all the hot dogs and ice cream you can eat. The event raises money for the Joey Fund and the Cystic Fibrosis Foundation. (Chip Bott photograph.)

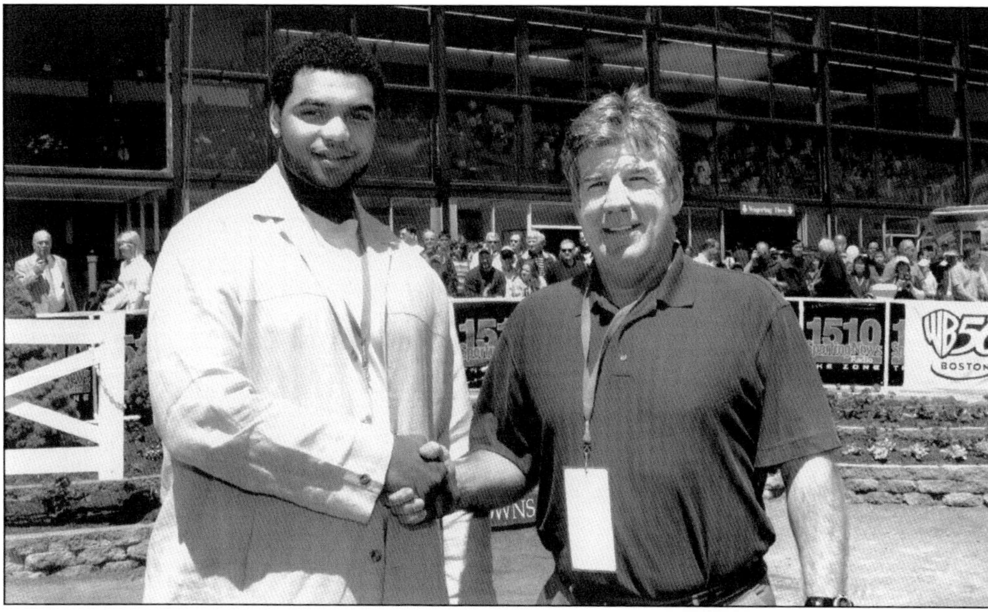

RICHARD SEYMOUR AND TERRY O'REILLY. Pro Bowl player and Super Bowl champion Richard Seymour (left) of the New England Patriots and Boston Bruins legend Terry O'Reilly serve as grand marshals for the 13th annual Hot Dog Safari on May 19, 2002. (Chip Bott photograph.)

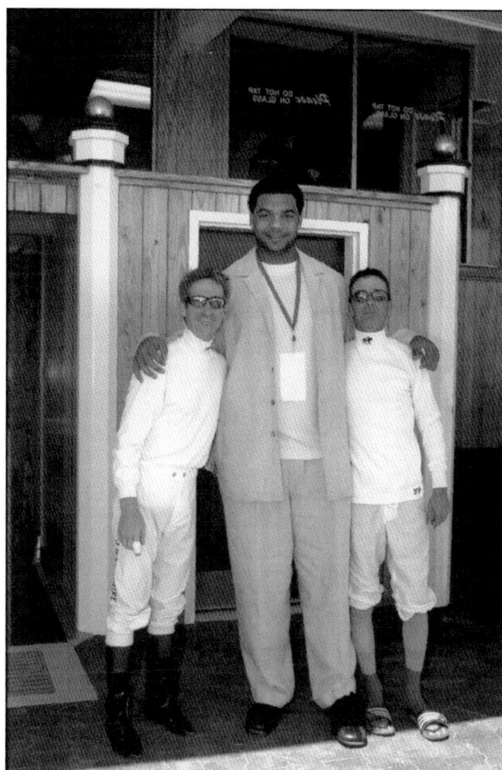

BIG AND SMALL. Richard Seymour of the New England Patriots is flanked by jockeys Joe Hampshire (left) and Jerry Parenti Jr. (right). (Chip Bott photograph.)

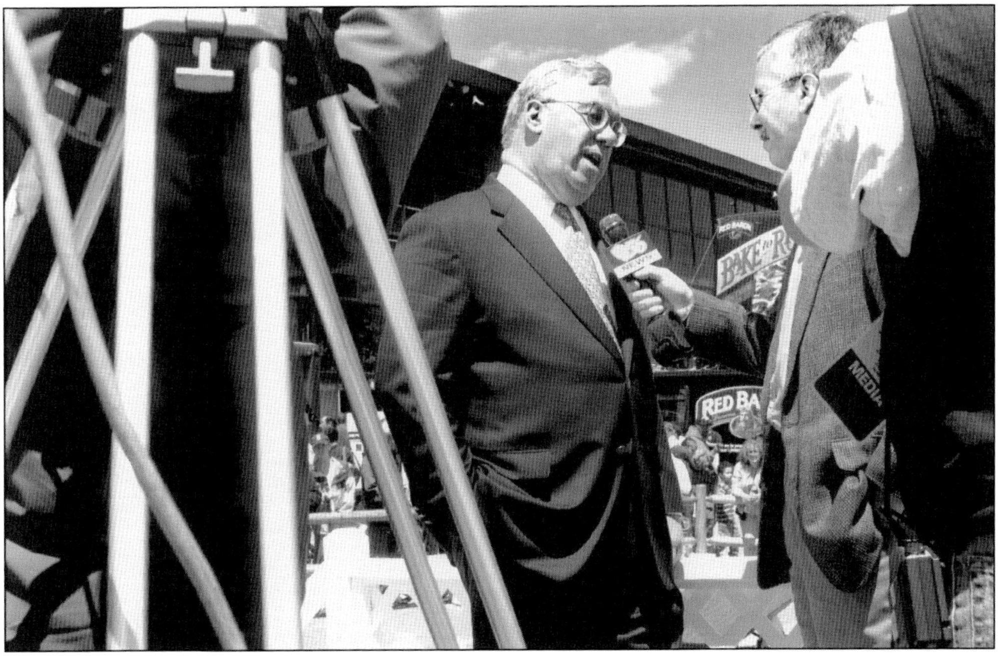

A POLITICAL HORSE RACE. Prominent politicians are interviewed by analyst Jon Keller as part of WB56's television coverage of the 2002 Hot Dog Safari. Above is Mayor Thomas Menino. Below are Gov. Mitt Romney (center) and Lt. Gov. Kerry Healey. (Chip Bott photograph.)

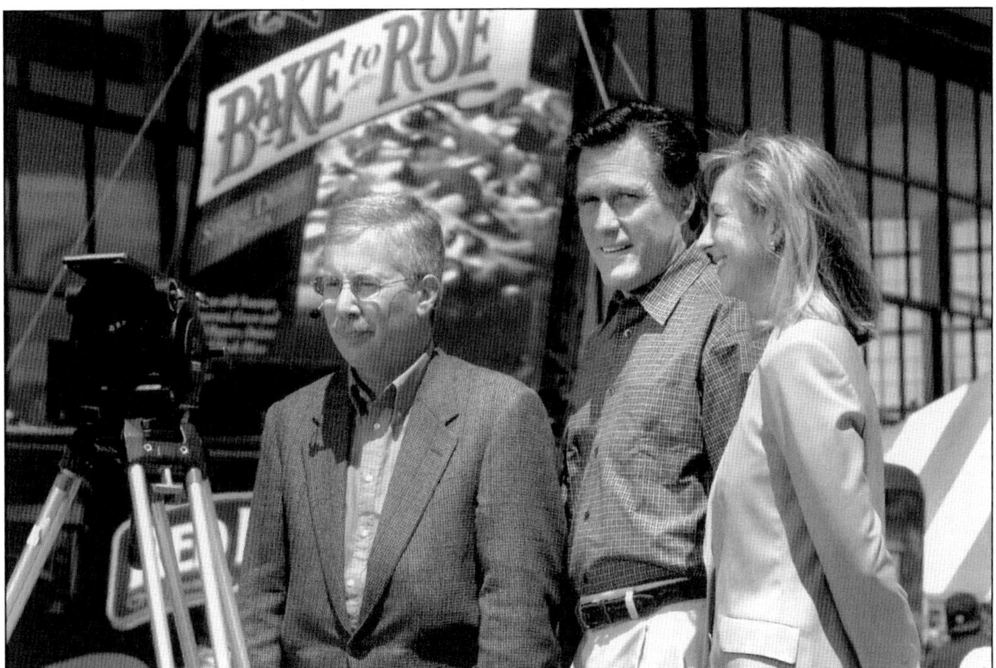

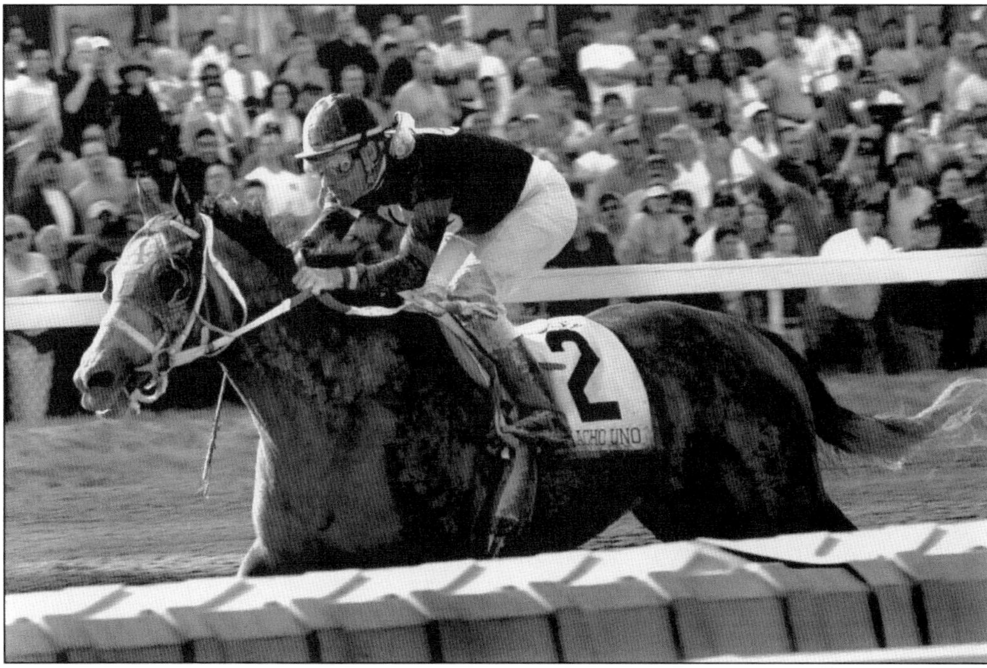

The 2002 Massachusetts Handicap. Stronach Stable's Macho Uno has drawn clear under jockey Gary Stevens on the way to winning the 63rd MassCap on June 1, 2002. The four-year-old colt won the Breeders' Cup Juvenile in 2000. (Bill Denver/Equi-Photo photograph.)

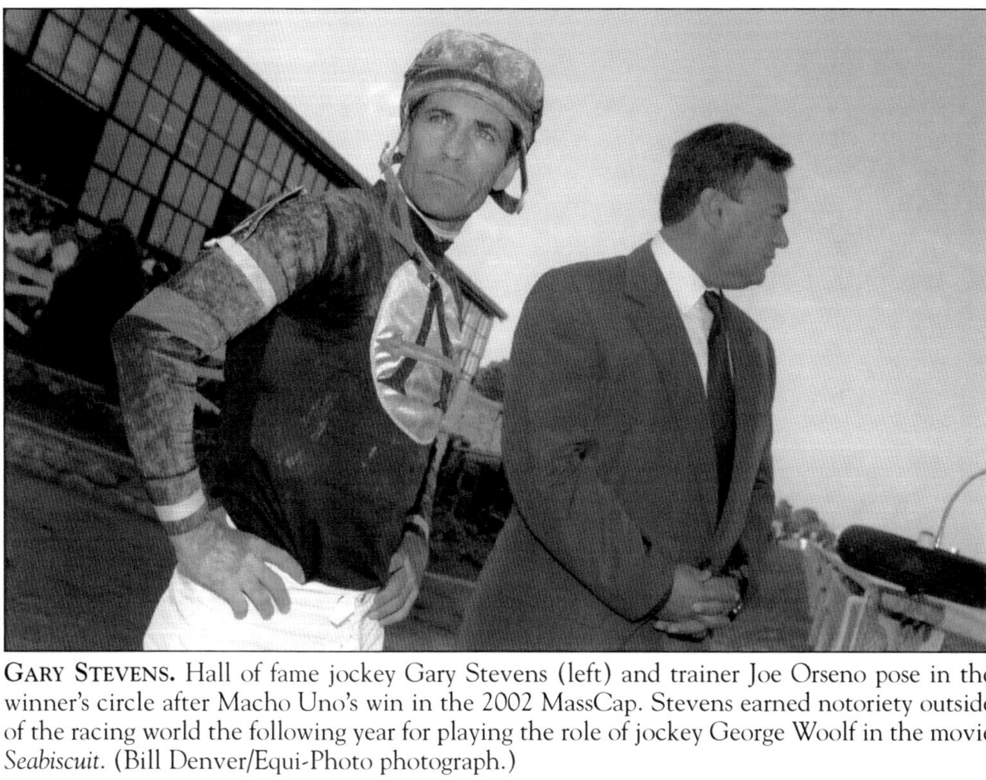

Gary Stevens. Hall of fame jockey Gary Stevens (left) and trainer Joe Orseno pose in the winner's circle after Macho Uno's win in the 2002 MassCap. Stevens earned notoriety outside of the racing world the following year for playing the role of jockey George Woolf in the movie *Seabiscuit*. (Bill Denver/Equi-Photo photograph.)

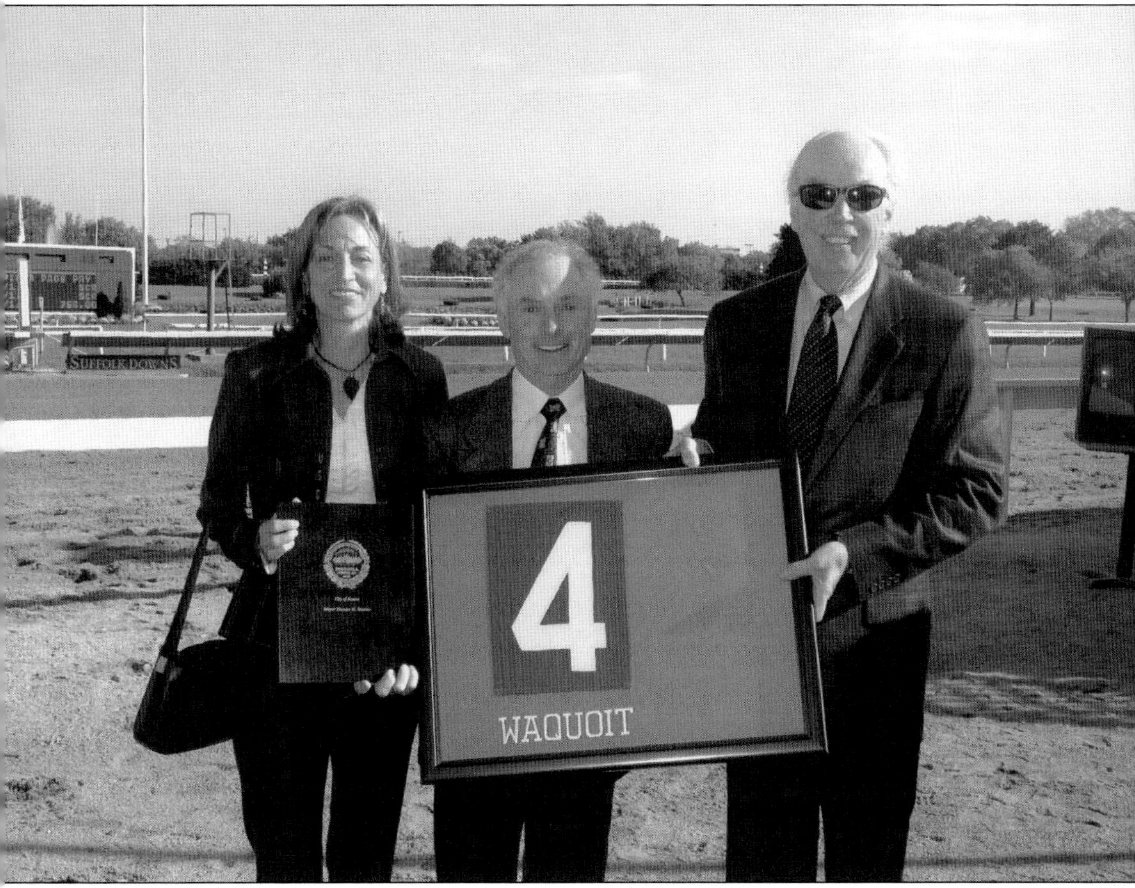

CHRIS MCCARRON DAY. Hall of fame jockey and Dorchester native Chris McCarron (center) is honored in the winner's circle on September 28, 2002. McCarron retired as the all-time career-earnings leader among jockeys in June 2002. Here, the two-time MassCap winner is presented by track chief operating officer Bob O'Malley (right) with a framed saddle towel commemorating his 1987 MassCap triumph aboard local favorite Waquoit. McCarron's wife, Judy (left), holds a proclamation signed by Mayor Thomas Menino declaring the day Chris McCarron Day in the city of Boston. (Bill Denver/Equi-Photo photograph.)

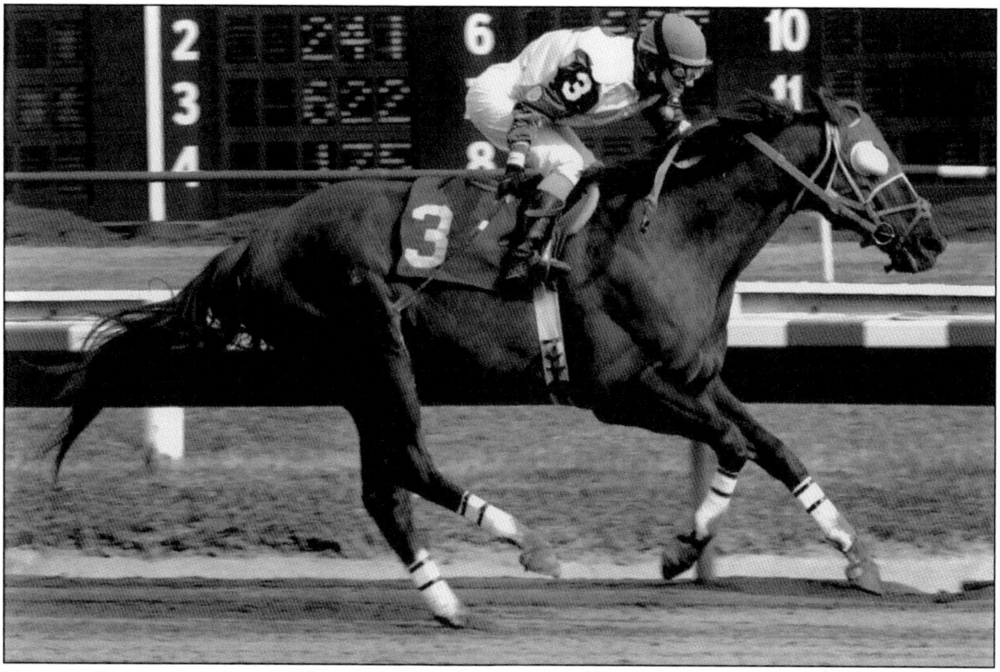

Tejano Couture. Veteran Tejano Couture scores one of his continental-best 11 wins in 2002 on March 25 of that year. He is ridden by Helena Keaveney. (Bill Denver/Equi-Photo photograph.)

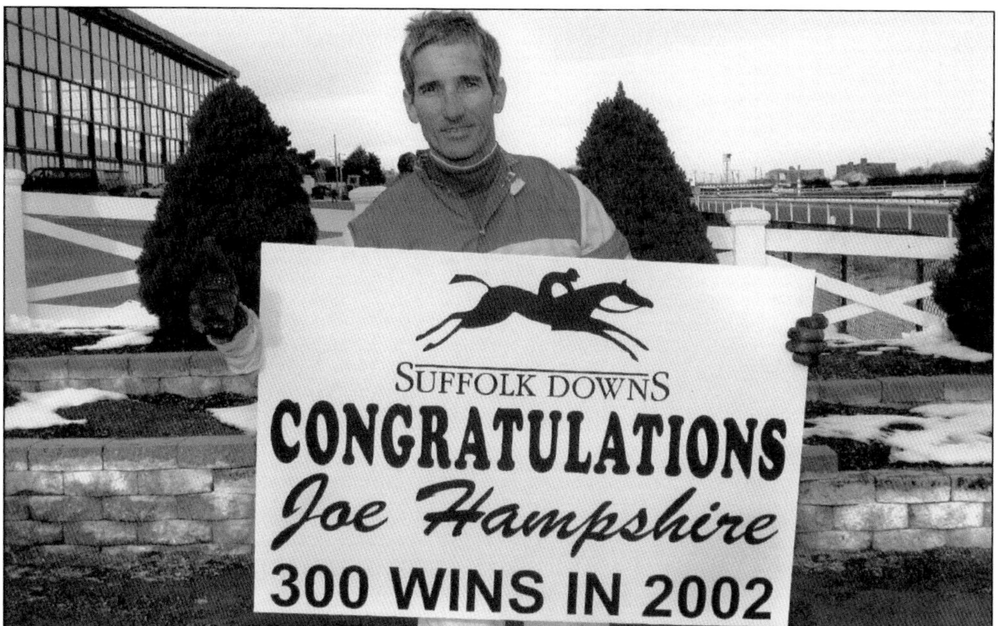

Joe Hampshire. Jockey Joe Hampshire celebrates his 300th win of 2002 on December 30, the final day of the racing season. Hampshire was one of just three riders on the continent to reach that mark for the year. A perennial favorite among local racing fans, Hampshire won eight straight meet riding titles at the track from 2000 to 2003. (Bill Denver/Equi-Photo photograph.)

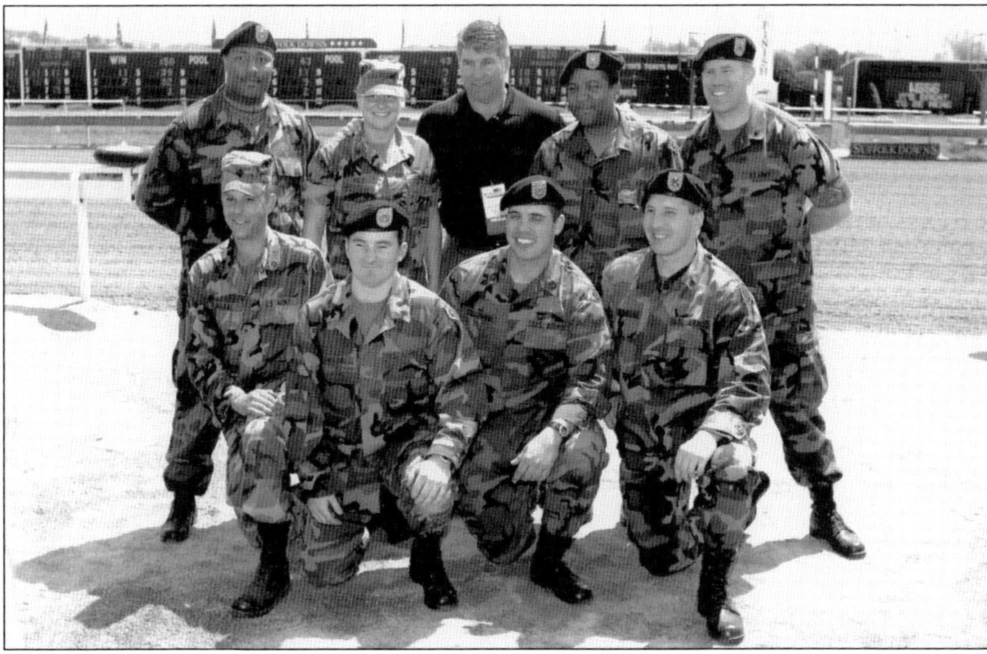

RAY BOURQUE. Hockey hall of famer and Stanley Cup champion Ray Bourque poses with volunteers from the National Guard at the 14th annual Hot Dog Safari on May 18, 2003. Bourque is serving as one of the grand marshals for the event. (Chip Bott photograph.)

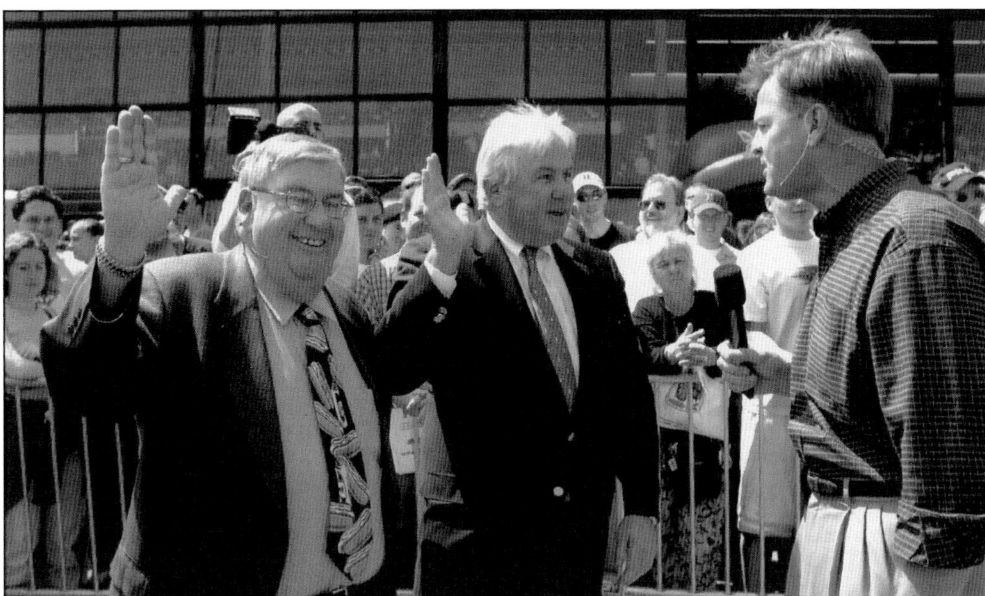

EDDIE ANDELMAN AND JOE O'DONNELL. Hot Dog Safari creator Eddie Andelman (left) and Joey Fund founder Joe O'Donnell (center) are sworn in by WB56 newscaster Frank Mallicoat (right) as the judges for an officially sanctioned hot-dog-eating contest at the Safari. The Joey Fund is named for O'Donnell's son, who died of cystic fibrosis at age 12. A friend of the O'Donnell family, Andelman was inspired to support the Joey Fund after having seen firsthand Joey's courageous fight against the disease. (Chip Bott photograph.)

A HOT-DOG-EATING CONTEST. Contestants have 12 minutes to consume as many hot dogs and buns as possible. The contest is sanctioned by the International Federation of Competitive Eating. (Chip Bott photograph.)

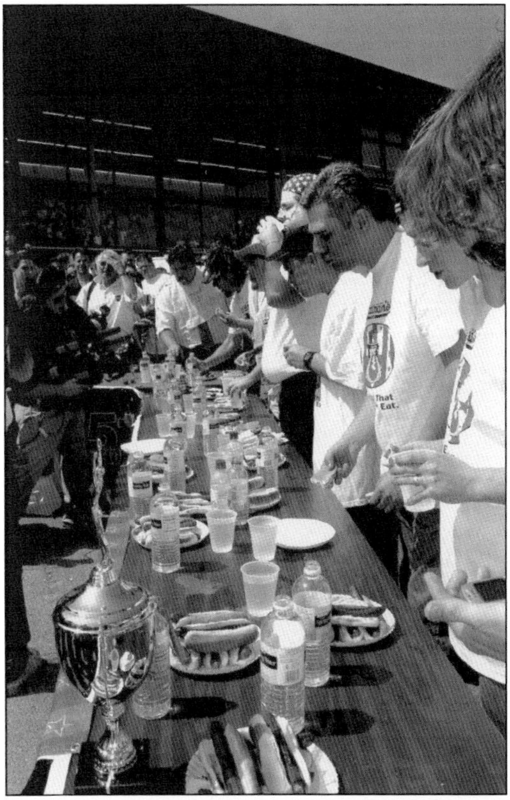

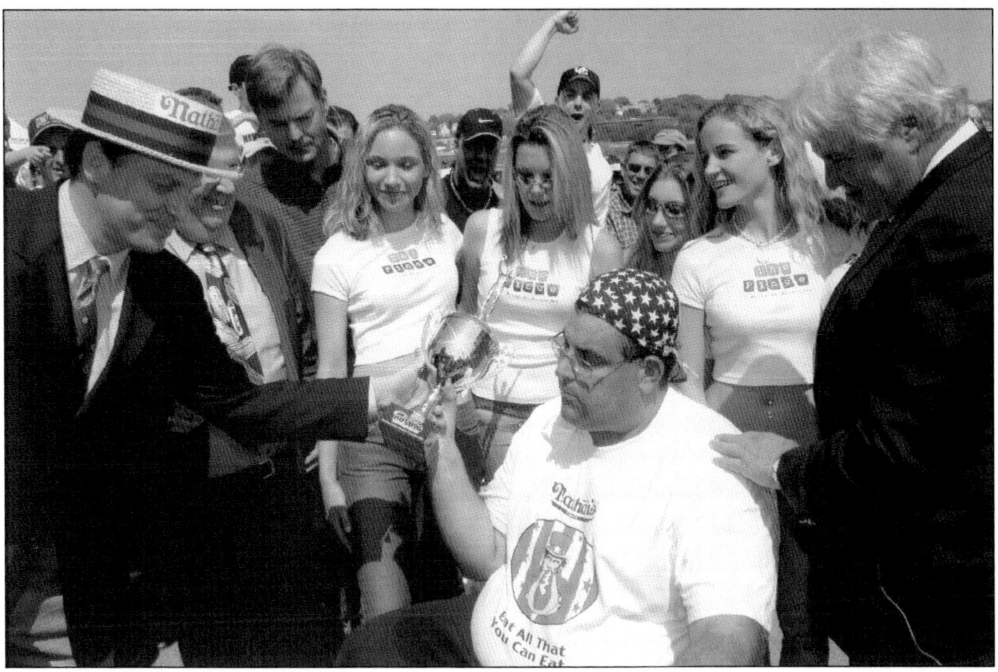

STILL CHAMPION. Ed "Cookie" Jarvis successfully defended his Hot Dog Safari contest title in 2003. (Chip Bott photograph.)

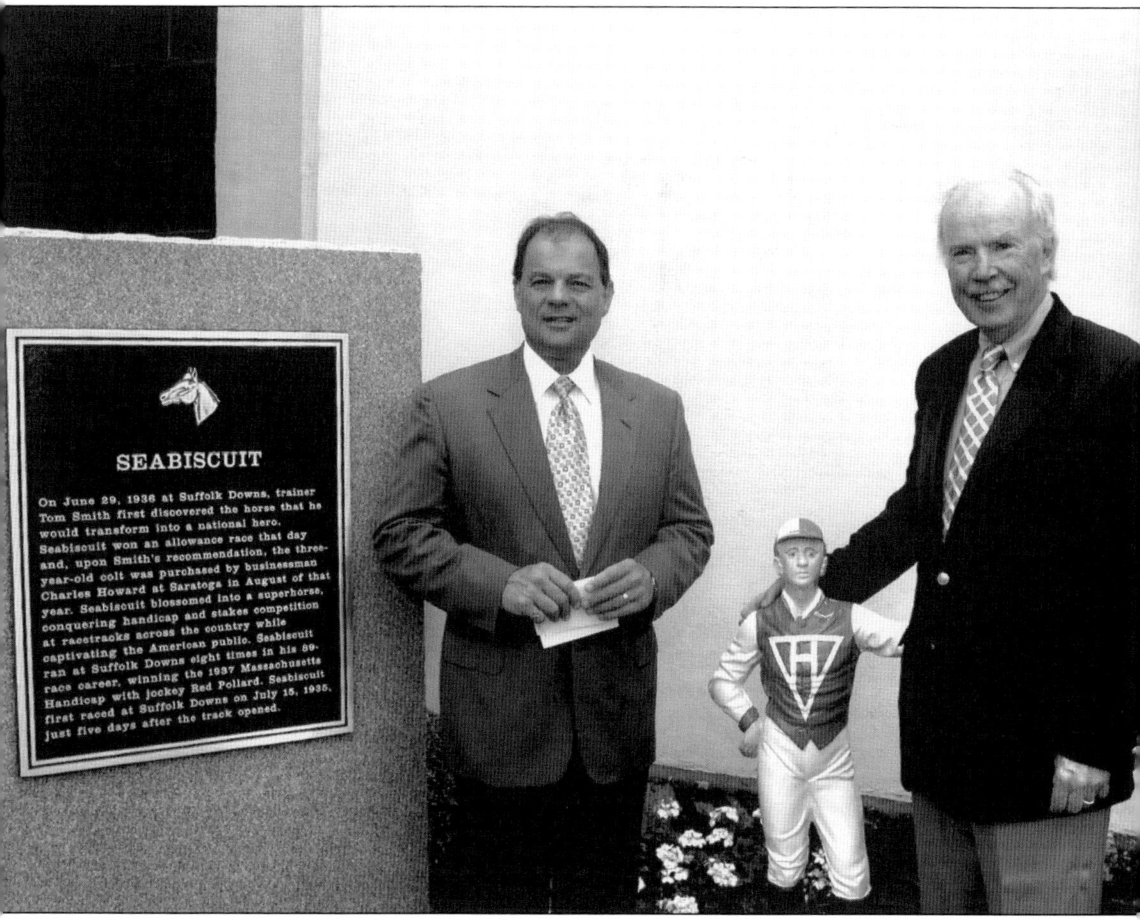

SEABISCUIT DAY. Massachusetts State Senate president Robert Travaglini (left) of East Boston and Suffolk Downs's chief operating officer Bob O'Malley formally dedicate a bronze plaque commemorating Seabiscuit's history at the track on July 22, 2003, three days prior to the release of the movie *Seabiscuit*. The lawn jockey is painted in the silks of Seabiscuit's owner, Charles S. Howard. (Chip Bott photograph.)

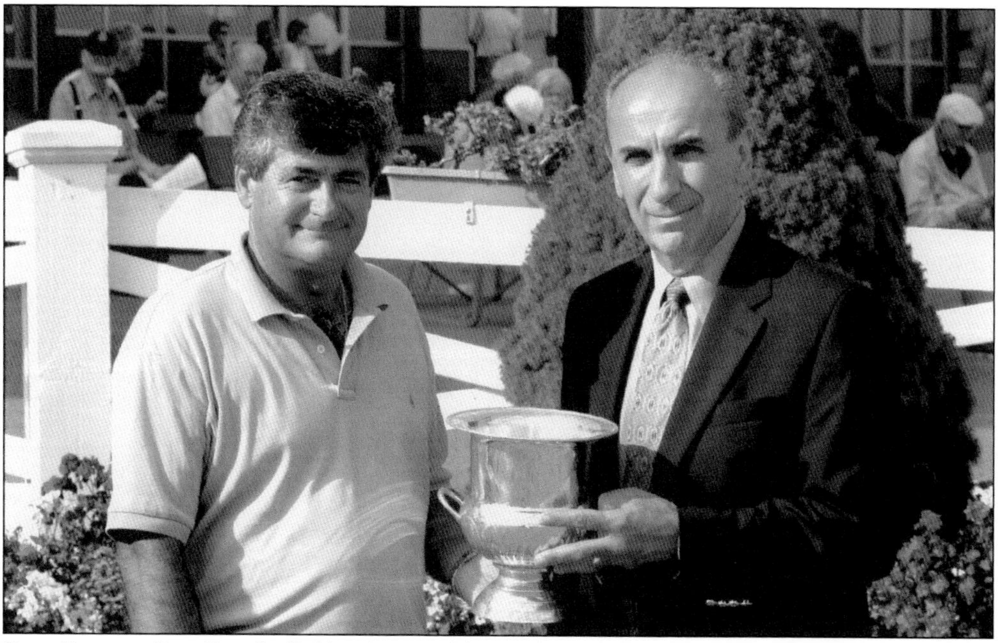

Ron Dandy. Ron Dandy (left) is honored by track general manager Joe Fatalo as the leading trainer for the 2003 winter-spring-summer meet. The feat capped off a track-record string of 10 meet titles for Dandy, giving him 15 career titles at the track, also a record. (Chip Bott photograph.)

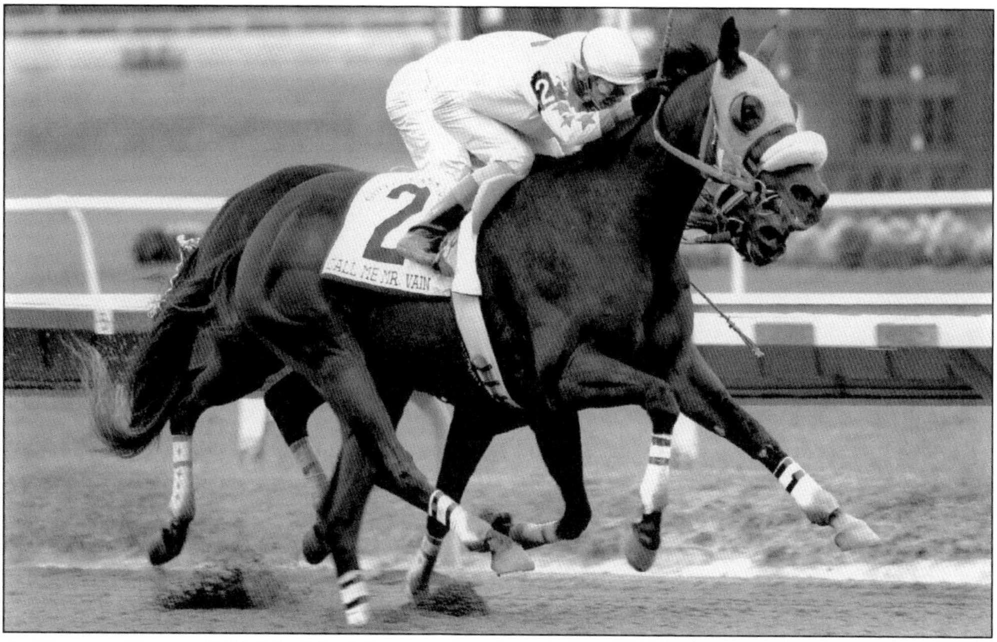

A Match Race. Call Me Mr. Vain, under Angel Stanley, defeats Diplomatical and Peter Sosa Jr. in the $10,000 Suffolk Showdown, a six-furlong match race between the winningest horses in North America at the time. (Each had 10 wins.) The two horses, both locally based, ran virtually inseparably from start to finish, with the final margin just a half-length. Call Me Mr. Vain's 11 wins were not surpassed by year's end. (Chip Bott photograph.)

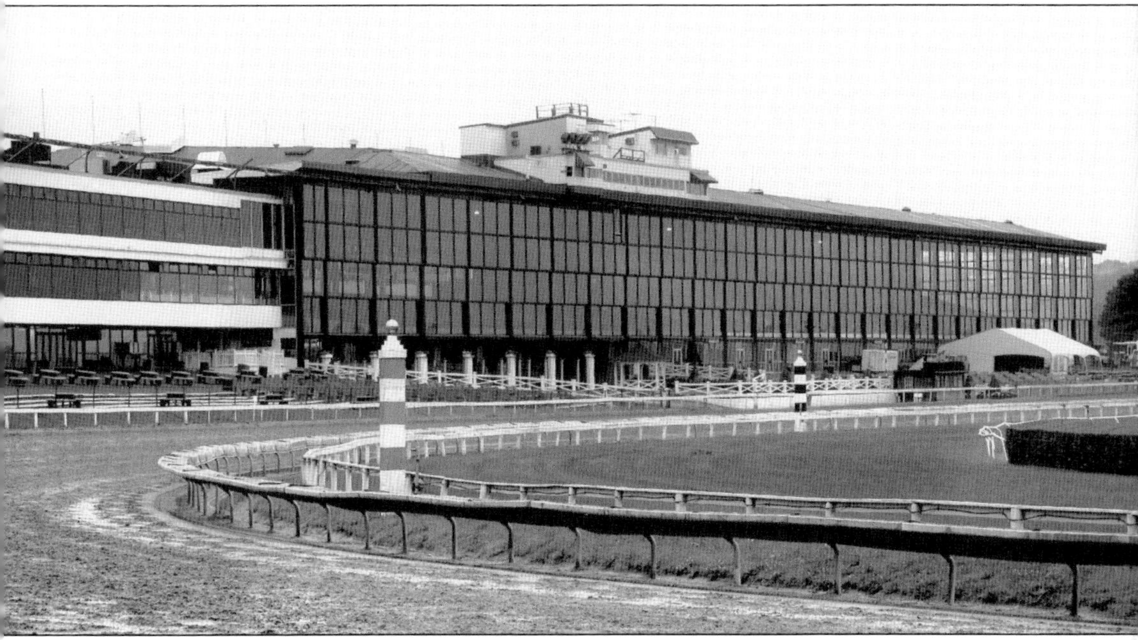

MASSCAP DAY 2004. The track may be quiet in this image, but a crowd of 17,280 soon arrived for New England's richest day of racing. (Chip Bott photograph.)

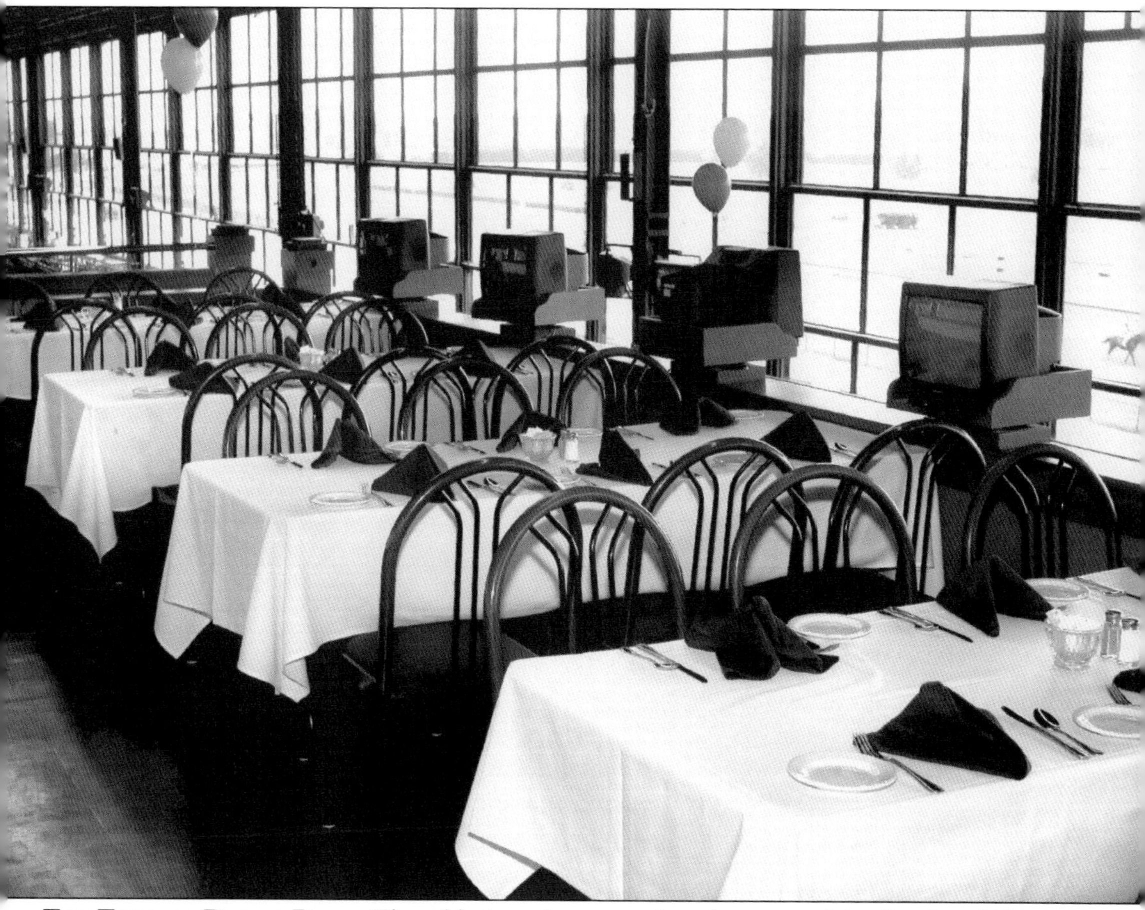

The Terrace Dining Room. The table is set for a great day of racing on MassCap Day 2004. (Chip Bott photograph.)

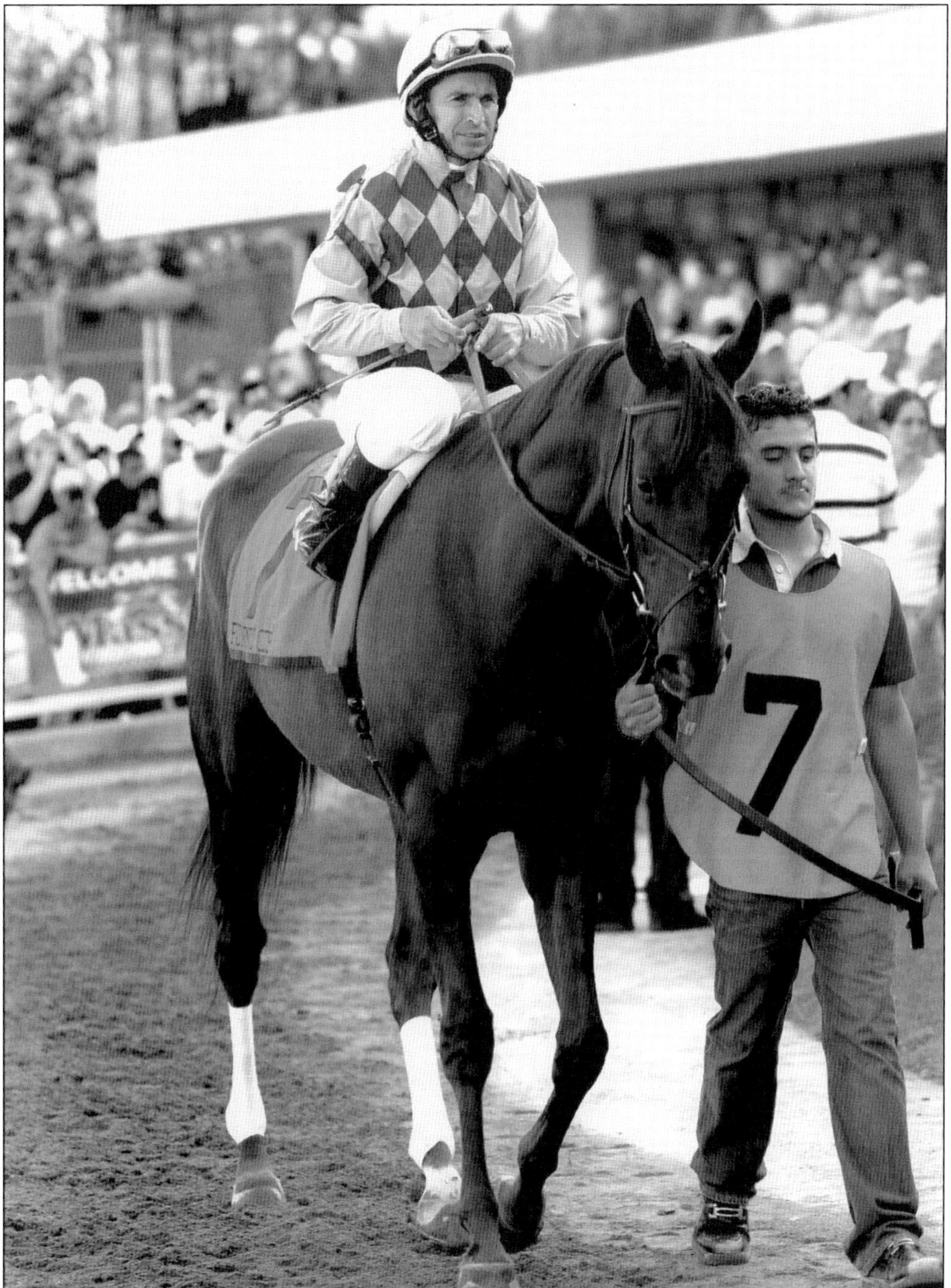

FUNNY CIDE. Sackatoga Stable's Funny Cide, the 2003 Kentucky Derby and Preakness Stakes winner, prepares to run in the 2004 MassCap with jockey Jose Santos aboard. Sackatoga Stable is a group of friends, led by Jack Knowlton, who bought their first racehorse in 1995, when the original six members chipped in $5,000 apiece. They gained national attention during Funny Cide's quest for the Triple Crown. Their travel party was so large that they rode school buses to each race. (Chip Bott photograph.)

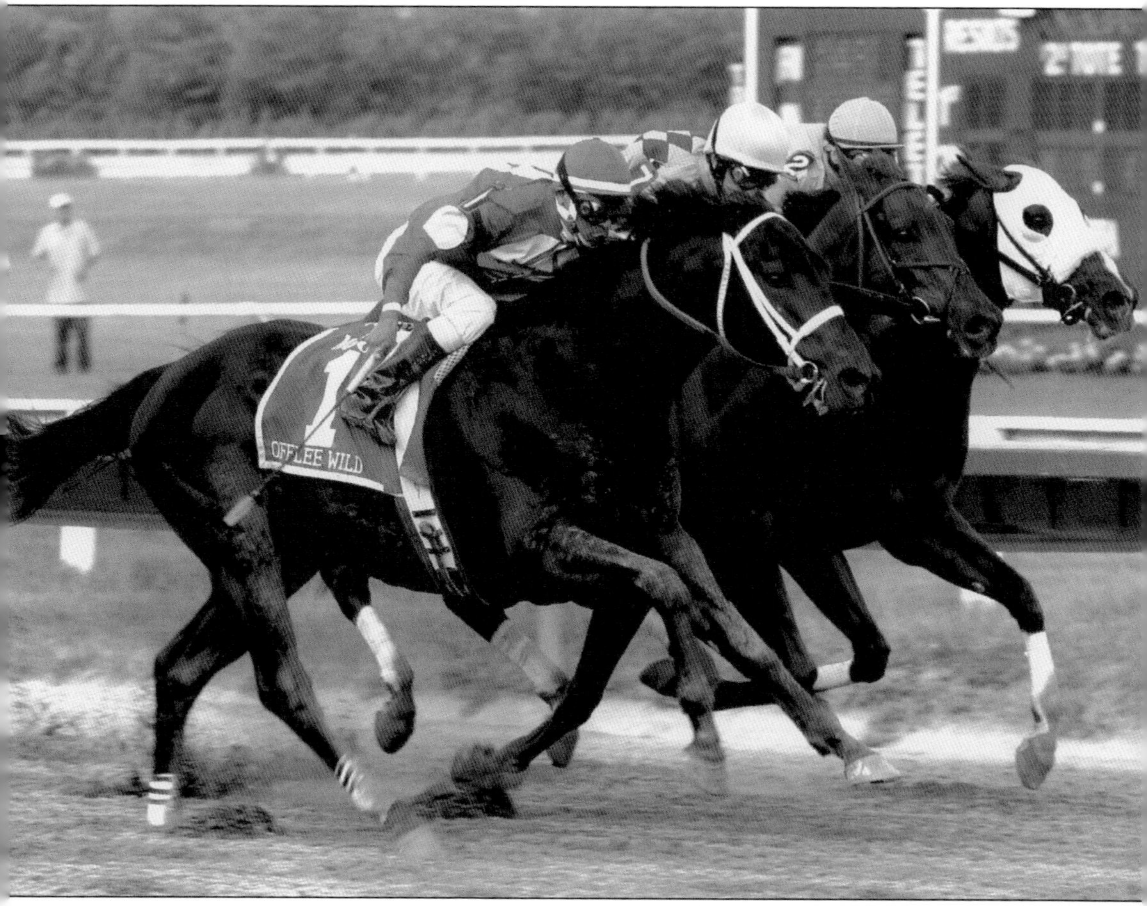

THE 2004 MASSACHUSETTS HANDICAP. Offlee Wild, Funny Cide, and the Lady's Groom, seen here from left to right, are just noses apart near the finish in the 64th running of the MassCap on June 19, 2004. Offlee Wild prevailed under jockey Edgar Prado, narrowly defeating Funny Cide. The Lady's Groom finished third. (Chip Bott photograph.)

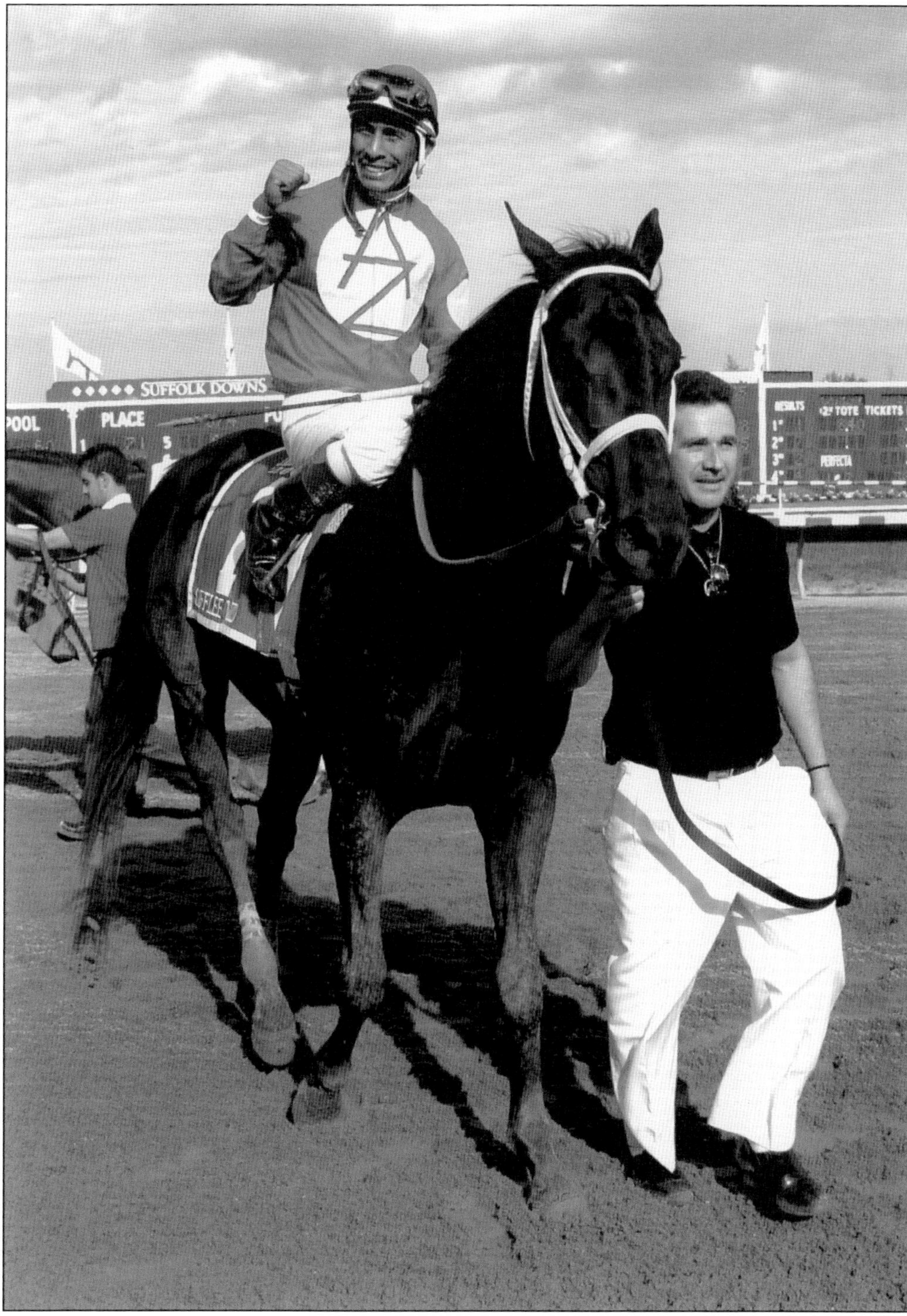

EDGAR PRADO. Jockey Edgar Prado pumps his fist after recording his first MassCap win aboard Offlee Wild in 2004. Prado rode at the track regularly in the late 1980s before gaining national stature on the Maryland circuit in the 1990s. Prado led the nation in wins from 1997 to 1999. (Chip Bott photograph.)

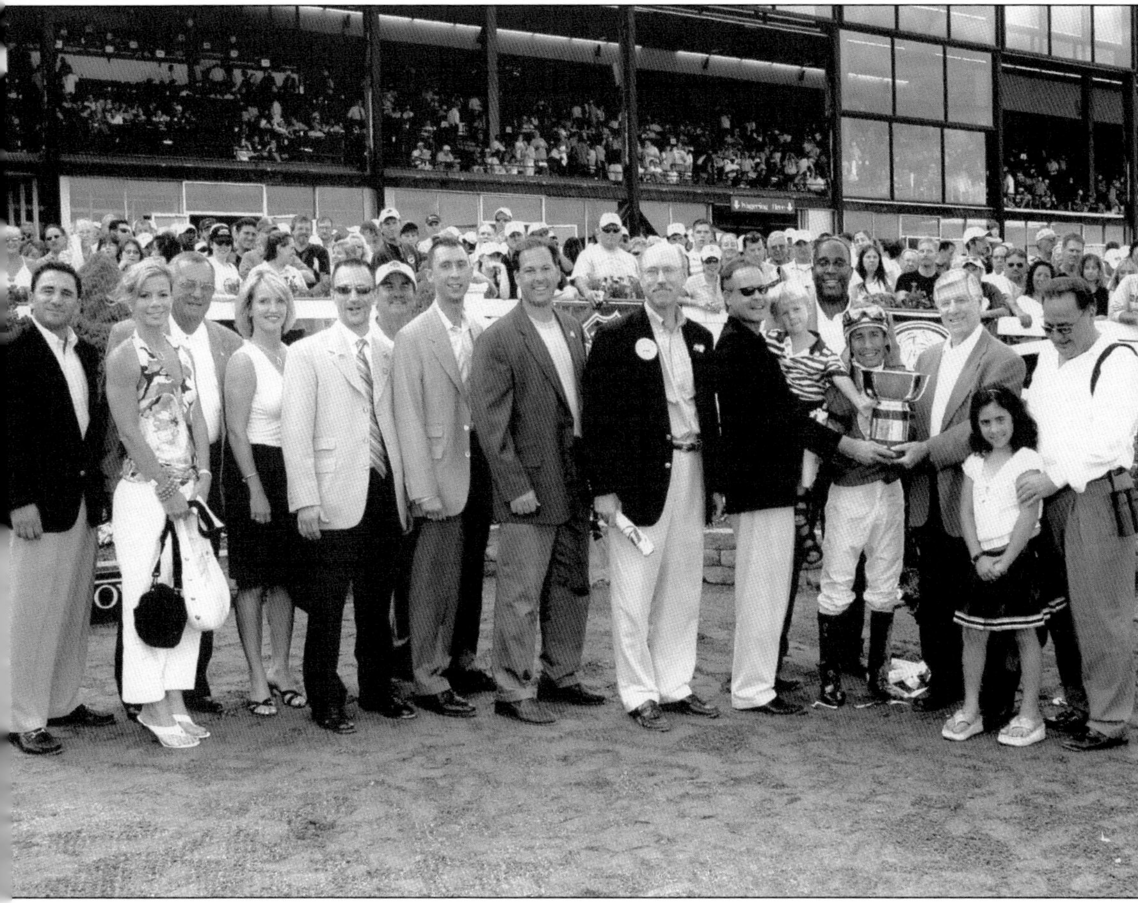

The 2004 MassCap Trophy Presentation. Former Boston Red Sox manager Joe Morgan (third from the right, holding the trophy) presents the MassCap trophy to jockey Edgar Prado and the winning connections of Offlee Wild. Morgan is a longtime fan of New England Thoroughbred racing. (Chip Bott photograph.)

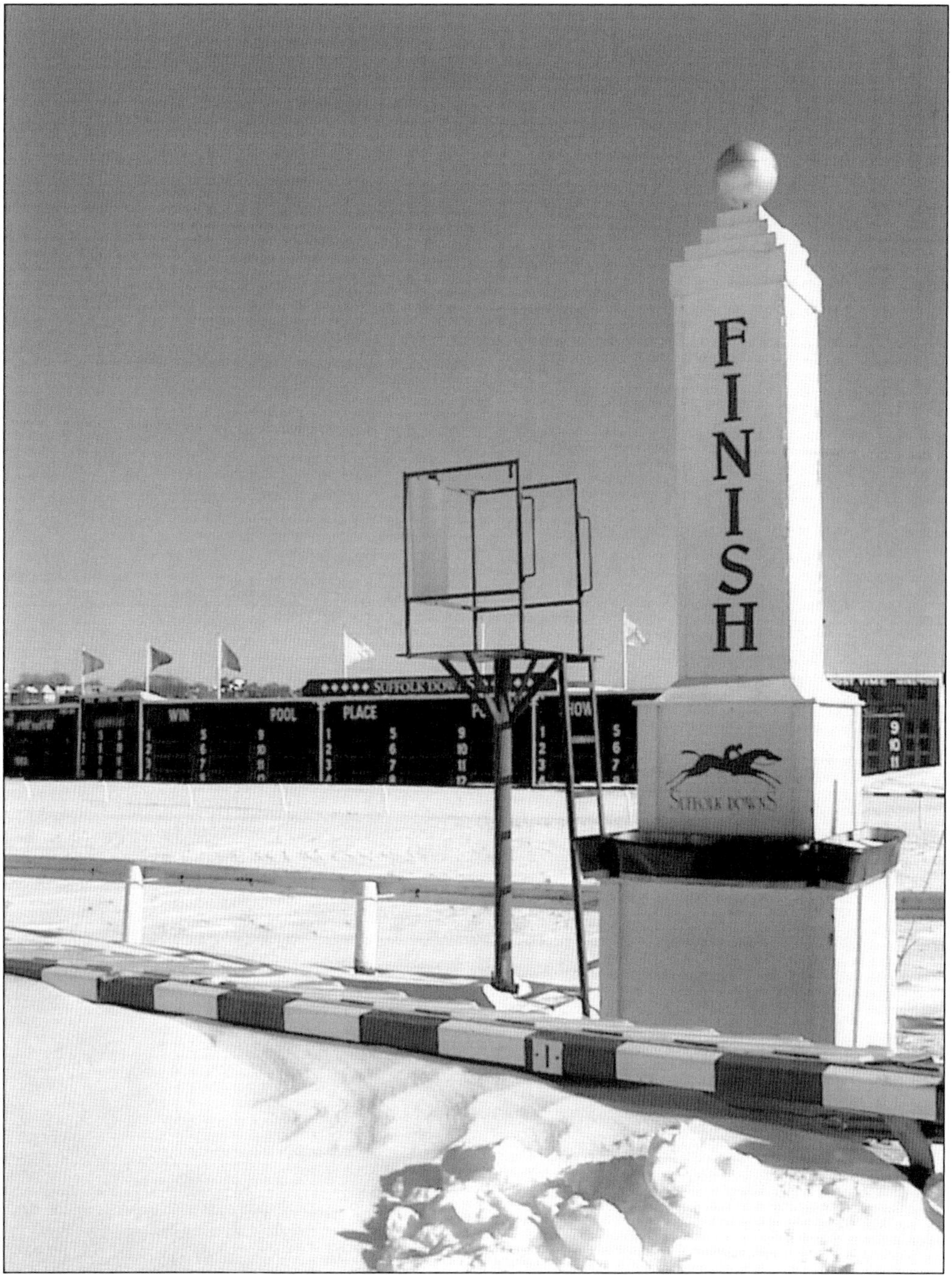

THE BLIZZARD OF 2005. Snowdrifts reach the height of the rail (over three feet) after the blizzard of January 2005. It is just the second winter without racing since the track reopened in 1992. Live racing is more than three months away. (Courtesy Suffolk Downs.)